Communications in Computer and Information Science   1041

Commenced Publication in 2007
Founding and Former Series Editors:
Phoebe Chen, Alfredo Cuzzocrea, Xiaoyong Du, Orhun Kara, Ting Liu,
Krishna M. Sivalingam, Dominik Ślęzak, Takashi Washio, and Xiaokang Yang

Editorial Board Members

More information about this series at http://www.springer.com/series/7899

Karl-Heinz Lüke · Gerald Eichler ·
Christian Erfurth · Günter Fahrnberger (Eds.)

Innovations for
Community Services

19th International Conference, I4CS 2019
Wolfsburg, Germany, June 24–26, 2019
Proceedings

 Springer

Editors
Karl-Heinz Lüke (iD)
Faculty of Business
Ostfalia University of Applied Sciences
Wolfsburg, Niedersachsen, Germany

Gerald Eichler (iD)
Telekom Innovation Laboratories
Deutsche Telekom AG
Darmstadt, Hessen, Germany

Christian Erfurth (iD)
Ernst Abbe University of Applied
Sciences Jena
Jena, Thüringen, Germany

Günter Fahrnberger (iD)
University of Hagen
Hagen, Nordrhein-Westfalen, Germany

ISSN 1865-0929   ISSN 1865-0937   (electronic)
Communications in Computer and Information Science
ISBN 978-3-030-22481-3   ISBN 978-3-030-22482-0   (eBook)
https://doi.org/10.1007/978-3-030-22482-0

This Springer imprint is published by the registered company Springer Nature Switzerland AG
The registered company address is: Gewerbestrasse 11, 6330 Cham, Switzerland

Foreword

The International Conference on Innovations for Community Services (I4CS) returned to Germany for its 19th anniversary in 2019. It emerged in 2011 as the Workshop on Innovative Internet Community Systems (IICS), founded by Herwig Unger and Thomas Boehme, and has continued its success story under its revised name I4CS since 2014. We are proud to say that we received the envisaged number of scientific presentations, have outstanding speaker commitments, and a great social conference program.

The selection of conference locations (alternating foreign and German venues) is part of the conference concept implying that the Program Committee (PC) offers suitable locations. The Steering Committee (SC) had the honor of handing the organizational responsibility over to Karl-Heinz Lüke and selecting a representative venue in the city of Wolfsburg for 2019. The Ostfalia University of Applied Sciences has one of its four campuses in Volkswagen city. This year's focus "Digital Innovations for the Public and Mobility Services" shows the close alliance.

A novelty of I4CS 2019 was the focal day (second conference day) on which participants experienced academic research and industry reality focusing on "Digital Innovations for the Public and Mobility Services."

From 2001 to 2005, IICS/I2CS published its proceedings in Springer's Lecture Notes in Computer Science series (LNCS), followed by publications with the Gesellschaft für Informatik (GI), and the Verein Deutscher Ingenieure (VDI). I4CS had commenced publishing with the Institute of Electrical and Electronics Engineers (IEEE) before going back to Springer's Communications in Computer and Information Science (CCIS) in 2016, creating a permanent partnership in 2018.

Publishing the I4CS proceedings of 2018 at SpringerLink for CCIS Vol. 863, we reached a chapter download of 4.7 k, more than expected. I4CS has maintained its reputation as a class C conference at the CORE Computing Research & Education Conference Portal rating: http://portal.core.edu.au/conf-ranks/?search=I4CS&by=all.

The proceedings of the I4CS 2019 comprise six sessions that cover a selection of 16 of 43 submissions received from authors from 12 countries. Interdisciplinary thinking is a key success factor for any community. Hence, I4CS 2019 covered a plurality of scientific, academic, and industrial topics, bundled into three areas: "Technology," "Applications," and "Socialization."

Technology: Distributed Architectures and Frameworks

- Data architectures and models for community services
- Innovation and social system's management
- Community self-organization in ad hoc environments
- Search, information retrieval and distributed ontology
- Common data models & big data analytics

Applications: Communities on the Move

- Social networks and open collaboration
- User-generated content for business and social life
- Recommender solutions and context awareness
- Augmented reality and location-based gaming
- Intelligent transportation, logistics and connected vehicles

Socialization: Ambient Work and Living

- eHealth challenges and ambient assisted living
- Smart energy and home control
- Business models and municipal infrastructure
- Digitalization, IoT and cyber physical systems
- Security, identity and GDPR privacy protection

Many thanks to the 24 members of the PC representing 14 countries for their worthwhile reviews, especially to the chair, Christian Erfurth, and, secondly, to the publication chair, Günter Fahrnberger, who provides a fruitful cooperation with Springer.

The 20th I4CS will be tentatively organized by the Kalinga Institute of Industrial Technology and will take place in Bhubaneswar/India in January 2020. Please check regularly the permanent conference URL http://www.i4cs-conference.org/ for more details! Applications of prospective PC members and potential conference hosts are welcome at request@i4cs-conference.org.

June 2019   Gerald Eichler

Preface

Wolfsburg (a town of about 125,000 inhabitants in Lower Saxony) is one of the youngest and richest cities in Germany. In 1938, it was founded and given the name Stadt des KdF-Wagens bei Fallersleben (Town of the KdF car at Fallersleben) and then renamed Wolfsburg after the eponymous castle located there, in 1945. In the following years, Wolfsburg grew continuously due to the Volkswagen's car plant attracting many workers. One of the most famous cars (the VW Beetle) was manufactured here and is the icon of the German economic miracle after the Second World War. Today, the heart and the headquarters of the Volkswagen Group are in Wolfsburg. The city is one of the most dynamic industry locations in Germany, and it is indisputably industrial location number one in Lower Saxony. Measuring the economic power, the employees generated an average GDP three times higher than the average of other major cities in Germany (in 2016).

Wolfsburg is also called Autostadt (Automobile City). Consequently, the 19th International Conference on Innovations for Community Services (I4CS 2019) was held in Wolfsburg in June 2019 focusing on "Digital Innovations for the Public and Mobility Services." Wolfsburg features unique locations, such as the Phaeno (interactive science center), the Autostadt (Automobile City), the Kunstmuseum (Museum of Modern Arts), the Planetarium, and not to forget the Volkswagen Arena where VfL Wolfsburg plays their home matches in the 1st Bundesliga. Participants of the conference had the chance to discover these attractions during the conference days.

Many thanks to my colleagues at the Ostfalia University of Applied Sciences (Faculty of Business) for hosting the 19th I4CS in Wolfsburg! The Ostfalia has about 13,000 students and 12 faculties. It is one of the biggest universities of applied sciences in Lower Saxony with its four sites located in Salzgitter, Suderburg, Wolfenbüttel, and Wolfsburg. All four sites are in Ostfalen (Eastphalia) which is a region of Old Saxony bounded by the rivers Elbe and Weser, the Lüneburg Heath, and the Harz mountain range. Since 2009, the University of Applied Sciences has been operating under the name Ostfalia. Today, Ostfalia cooperates with more than 100 universities all over the world.

The Wolfsburg AG (which is a joint venture of the City of Wolfsburg and Volkswagen AG) supports the I4CS 2019. Many thanks for selecting an excellent conference venue at the CongressPark Wolfsburg, the so-called Spiegelsaal (Mirror Auditorium)!

We are proud to continue the successful cooperation with Springer's publication series Communications in Computer and Information Science (CCIS). Many thanks to Gerald Eichler from the Baden-Württemberg University of Mannheim, Christian Erfurth from the University of Applied Sciences Jena, and Günter Fahrnberger from the University of Hagen, who did a great job as steering chair, program chair, and proceedings chair, respectively.

June 2019   Karl-Heinz Lüke

Organization

Program Committee

Marwane Ayaida	University of Reims Champagne-Ardenne, France
Gilbert Babin	HEC Montréal, Canada
Gerald Eichler	Deutsche Telekom Darmstadt, Germany
Christian Erfurth	University of Applied Sciences Jena, Germany
Günter Fahrnberger	University of Hagen, Germany
Hacène Fouchal	University of Reims Champagne-Ardenne, France
Sapna Gopinathan	Coimbatore Institute of Technology, India
Michal Hodoň	University of Žilina, Slovakia
Kathrin Kirchner	Technical University of Denmark Lyngby, Denmark
Peter Kropf	University of Neuchâtel, Switzerland
Ulrike Lechner	Bundeswehr University Munich, Germany
Andreas Lommatzsch	Technical University of Berlin, Germany
Karl-Heinz Lüke	Ostfalia University of Applied Sciences Wolfsburg, Germany
Raja Natarajan	Tata Institute of Fundamental Research Mumbai, India
Dana Petcu	West University of Timisoara, Romania
Frank Phillipson	TNO The Hague, The Netherlands
Srinivan Ramaswamy	Asea Brown Boveri Columbus, USA
Joerg Roth	Nuremberg Institute of Technology, Germany
Denis Royer	Ostfalia University of Applied Sciences Wolfsburg, Germany
Volkmar Schau	Navimatix Jena, Germany
Gerrit Schrödel	Wolfsburg AG, Germany
Maleerat Sodanil	King Mongkut's University of Technology North Bangkok, Thailand
Julian Szymański	Gdansk University of Technology, Poland
Leendert W. M. Wienhofen	City of Trondheim, Norway

Additional Reviewers

Barjis, Joseph
Iyer, Shivkumar
Sudarsan, Sithu

Contents

Communication Systems

Dynamic Connectivity Metric for Routing in VANETs

Frank Phillipson[✉]

TNO, The Hague, The Netherlands
frank.phillipson@tno.nl

Abstract. In vehicular ad-hoc networks a path has to be found to send a message from one vehicle to another vehicle. This path has to have a connectivity rate that is high enough to obtain a high probability of arrival of the message. In other approaches, this path is based on current, static information of the distribution of cars. In this paper we propose a dynamic, probabilistic approach, where we estimate the connection probability assuming Poisson Processes on all roads in the network, based on the current traffic density. The analytic derivation of the connection probability is compared to values derived by simulation.

Keywords: VANET · Location based routing · Metrics · Connection probability

1 Introduction

A Vehicular Ad Hoc Network (VANET) is a specific type of Mobile Ad Hoc Networks (MANET). In a Mobile Ad Hoc Network (MANET) mobile nodes are connected wirelessly. They do not have any central infrastructure and are moving around without any restrictions. A VANET is a special case of a MANET, where the mobility of the nodes is higher and the communication has higher demand regarding delay for security and safety issues. The higher mobility makes it more difficult to capture the topology of the nodes than in the MANET case, where the higher demand asks for a smarter and faster way of discovering the topology. The typical use of VANETs in vehicular systems, however, gives us the possibility to use street patterns as underlying basis for (assumed) topology and use these paths for communication applications.

The special characteristics of VANETs make it hard to use specific topology-based routing protocols for MANETs. However, the possibility to work with GPS systems within the nodes/cars makes it possible to use position based routing protocols like GSR [8], GPSR [7], A-STAR [12], GyTAR [6] and IDTAR [1].

Routing of packets is very important for the success of VANETs, it will make the difference whether network and application requirements will be met. In [9,10] a routing algorithm is proposed based on a simple location system represented by RSUs (Road Side Units). As stated in [3], RSUs are infrastructure communication nodes within vehicular networks, which offer three important features; 1. delivering important information to vehicles, 2. forwarding

© Springer Nature Switzerland AG 2019
K.-H. Lüke et al. (Eds.): I4CS 2019, CCIS 1041, pp. 3–10, 2019.
https://doi.org/10.1007/978-3-030-22482-0_1

received messages to final recipients and 3. providing Internet access to vehicles. They extend vehicle coverage and to improve network performance in vehicular networks.

We will look in this paper specifically to the approach presented in [9,10] and not to other, earlier mentioned approaches, and will do a suggestion to extend this approach. This routing algorithm is able to send a message from a source to the destination by using the most dense path based on a connectivity metric. They assume that at each road junction, a RSU is installed, and each vehicle has a static digital map to get position of all RSUs. Next to this, each vehicle has knowledge of its geographic position by using its GPS, speed and direction of movement. This allows the vehicle to find the closest RSU in order to request it about the (best) path to the destination. In the current implementation, the best path of intersections is determined based on the normalised length of the path and the connectivity of the path. This connectivity is expressed by some connectivity metric. The choice of this connectivity metric is extremely important in this approach. Given this cost function, Dijkstra's shortest path algorithm is used to determine the optimal path. The information is then sent in the direction of the given path, using Improved Greedy Forwarding [5,6]. In [4] an extension is proposed to incorporate congestion control in the planning phase.

In [11] an alternative connectivity metric was proposed that does not only look at the average distance between vehicles, but also takes variation into consideration. This measure is still a static measure, only capturing the traffic situation of a specific point in time. Changes in the (near) future are not incorporated nor any dynamic behaviour of the system. In this paper we propose an alternative method for calculating the metric, now expressing the connection probability assuming a dynamic system.

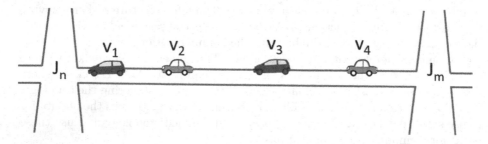

Fig. 1. Example road with junctions and cars.

2   Current Approach

In the implementation of the Location Service of [9] the Link Connectivity (LC) is based on the average distance between two consecutive vehicles on a road. A road is defined as the a piece of street between two junctions J_n and J_m, containing a number of vehicles, see for example Fig. 1. For this, a link between two vehicles is defined by [9] as:

$$Link(v_i, v_j) = \begin{cases} R_{tr} - dist(v_i, v_j) & \text{if } dist(v_i, v_j) \leq R_{tr}, \\ 0 & \text{otherwise.} \end{cases} \tag{1}$$

Here R_{tr} denotes the transmission radius and $dist(v_i, v_j)$ the distance between vehicles i and j. Note that $Link()$ represents the remaining communication distance between two vehicles. The Mean Link (ML) for all N vehicles on a specific road, which has two endpoints, junctions J_n and J_m, is expressed as:

$$ML_{road} = \frac{Link(J_n, v_1) + \sum_{i=1}^{N-1} Link(v_i, v_{i+1}) + Link(v_N, J_m)}{(N+1)}. \tag{2}$$

From this connectivity metric can be defined as

$$LC_{road} = \frac{ML_{road}}{R_{tr}}, \tag{3}$$

which is a function on $[0, 1]$.

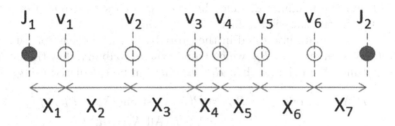

Fig. 2. Example for definition of X.

In [11] we showed some shortcomings of the proposed metric and proposed to use the sum of the average and standard deviation of the distances between the cars and the junctions. Say we have two junctions J_1 and J_2, now define $X_1 = dist(J_1, v_1)$, $X_{N+1} = dist(v_N, J_2)$ and $X_i = dist(v_{i-1}, v_i)$ for $i = 2, ...N$. In Fig. 2 this is shown for 6 cars and 2 junctions, leading to $N = 6$ and X_1 unil X_7. Using

$$\overline{X} = \frac{\sum_{i=1}^{N+1} X_i}{N+1}, \tag{4}$$

now the new metric can be defined as

$$LC_{road}^{ASD} = \overline{X} + \sqrt{\frac{\sum_{i=1}^{N+1} (X_i - \overline{X})^2}{N+2}}. \tag{5}$$

To make this a metric that scores between zero and one, giving the best value at one, we proposed to use

$$LC_{road}^* = \frac{\max(0, 2R_{tr} - LC_{road}^{ASD})}{2R_{tr}}. \tag{6}$$

3 Connection Probability

In this paper we propose a metric that expresses the connectivity of the path as the connection probability of a dynamic system. The original metric and our earlier improvement are still static metrics that only consider the current traffic situation, not that within the coming time interval. For this we will need to model the dynamic behaviour of the traffic movements within the next (small) time interval and use that to estimate the connection probability.

Again, we look at a road between two junctions. From both sides cars enter this road, where we have λ_1 and λ_2 as the arrival rates from the two sides of the road. We assume that the arrivals occur with interarrival times that are independent and exponential distributed. Each of the arrival processes are then Poisson Processes [13]. If a road i has more than one lane, each lane j can have its own arrival rate $\lambda_{i,j}$. These arrival processes together are again a Poisson Process with rate $\lambda_i = \sum_j \lambda_{i,j}$ [13]. Now, due to the time-reversibility of the Poisson Process, also the overall process is a Poisson Process with rate $\lambda = \lambda_1 + \lambda_2$. This λ represents the traffic intensity in the near future.

The speed of the cars are assumed equal, v (m/s). Length of the road equals L $(meter)$ and the maximal distance between two cars for connection equals R_{tr} $(meter)$, the transmission radius.

Given n cars we are interested in the probability that at least one inter-car distance (X_i) is larger than R_{tr} which equals the probability that the inter-car distance in time (X_i^t) is larger than R_{tr}/v. This can be calculated using:

$$P(\text{At least one } X_i > R_{tr}) = P(\text{At least one } X_i^t > R_{tr}/v) \tag{7}$$
$$= 1 - P(\text{All } X_i^t \leq R_{tr}/v)$$
$$= 1 - \prod_{i=1}^{n} P(X_i^t \leq R_{tr}/v)$$
$$= 1 - \prod_{i=1}^{n} (1 - e^{-\lambda R_{tr}/v})$$
$$= 1 - (1 - e^{-\lambda R_{tr}/v})^n. \tag{8}$$

The probability to observe these n cars in the process can be derived from the number of arrivals within the time span of $t = L/v$, which is the time it takes a car to drive the total distance of the road:

$$P(N(t) = n) = \frac{(\lambda t)^n}{n!} e^{-\lambda t}. \tag{9}$$

The total (system) probability having at least one inter-car distance larger than R_{tr} comes from:

$$P_{\text{no connection}} = \sum_{n=1}^{\inf} \frac{(\lambda t)^n}{n!} e^{-\lambda t} \left(1 - (1 - e^{-\lambda R_{tr}/v})^n \right). \tag{10}$$

Leading to the connection probability

$$P_C = 1 - \left(\sum_{n=1}^{\inf} \frac{(\lambda t)^n}{n!} e^{-\lambda t} \left(1 - (1 - e^{-\lambda R_{tr}/v})^n \right) \right). \tag{11}$$

4   Numerical Results

To give some insight in the working of this connection probability and to show that the combination of entering the system from two ways gives indeed a compound Poisson Process we give some numerical results from simulation to compare it with the outcome of the formula of the previous section. Note that the main purpose of the metric is the use in the optimal path finding. However, having the relation gives us also the possibility to do some sensitivity and what-if analysis.

We simulated the system (road) both as a (close to) continuous and as a discrete event system. In the continuous system we calculate the state of the system every τ seconds, where τ is small compared to the inter arrival times, here we used $\tau = 0.02$ s. In the discrete event simulation we calculate the state of the system at the event of a new entrance to the system. If the entrances follow a Poisson Process, these snapshots should observe the average state of the system, using the 'PASTA' property (Poisson Arrivals See Time Averages) [14].

For the simulation 20,000 arrivals are used, 10,000 from each side of the road. For the first analysis we take a speed (v) of 5 m/s (18 km/h) and a transmission radius (R_{tr}) of 50 m. Then we varied the (system) arrival rate λ from 0.1 to

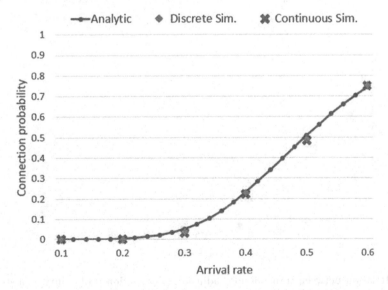

Fig. 3. Relation between arrival rate and connection probability at a speed of 5 m/s. Comparison between the Analytic derivation and the simulation results.

0.6. The results are depicted in Fig. 3. There is shown that the results of both simulations and of the analytic formula are the same. Both the realisations of the discrete simulation, and the analytic results compared with the continuous simulation show that the total process behaves like a Poisson Process. In the

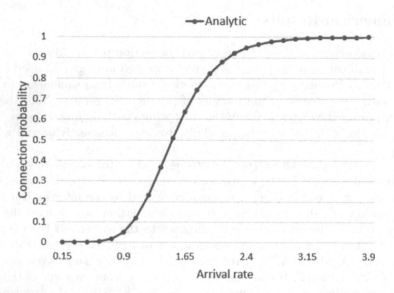

Fig. 4. Relation between arrival rate and connection probability at a speed of 15 m/s.

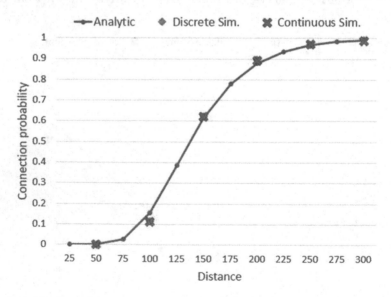

Fig. 5. Relation between transmission radius and connection probability at a speed of 15 m/s.

figure is also shown that the connection probability increases as the arrival rate increases.

In Fig. 4 we see the same relation but now for a speed of $15\,\mathrm{m/s}$ ($54\,\mathrm{km/h}$). We now can derive what the arrival rate should be to obtain a certain connection probability. To get a probability higher than 0.9 there should be an arrival rate of at least 2.17.

In Fig. 5 the relation between the transmission radius (R_{tr}) and the connection probability is shown. Now $v = 15\,\mathrm{m/s}$ and $\lambda = 0.4$. From Fig. 4 we learned that a transmission radius of $50\,\mathrm{m}$ at this speed gives a connection probability of around 0. To get a connection probability of 0.9 we then need a radius of at least $208\,\mathrm{m}$. Again, the correctness of the analytic approach is shown by the simulations.

5   Conclusion and Further Research

In this paper we proposed an approach to determine the connection probability to be used as metric for a VANET system. In contrast to earlier approaches, this approach is not static, but gives a view on the dynamic properties of a road network. We gave an analytic expression for this probability and, using simulation, we showed that the system, under assumption of Poisson Processes for all individual streams of cars, behaves in total as a Poisson Process.

Using this analytic approach it is much easier to determine, using sensitivity analysis, in which environments, concerning (average) speed and arrival rates, the transmission radius gives a proper connection probability.

In future research, this connection probability can be tested in a realistic simulation of traffic in cities to see how this approach influences the overall VANET performance. Also, more sophisticated (or realistic) headway models can be used [2].

References

1. Ahmed, A.I.A., Gani, A., Ab Hamid, S.H., Khan, S., Guizani, N., Ko, K.: Intersection-based distance and traffic-aware routing (IDTAR) protocol for smart vehicular communication. In: 2017 13th International Wireless Communications and Mobile Computing Conference (IWCMC), pp. 489–493. IEEE (2017)
2. Chen, X., Li, L., Shi, Q., et al.: Stochastic Evolutions of Dynamic Traffic Flow. Springer, Heidelberg (2015). https://doi.org/10.1007/978-3-662-44572-3
3. Fogue, M., Sanguesa, J., Martinez, F., Marquez-Barja, J.: Improving roadside unit deployment in vehicular networks by exploiting genetic algorithms. Appl. Sci. 8(1), 86 (2018)
4. van Gulik, K., Phillipson, F., Fouchal, H.: Congestion control in a location service for VANETs. In: Renault, É., Boumerdassi, S., Bouzefrane, S. (eds.) International Conference on Mobile, Secure, and Programmable Networking, vol. 11005, pp. 289–293. Springer, Cham (2018). https://doi.org/10.1007/978-3-030-03101-5
5. Jerbi, M., Senouci, S.M., Meraihi, R., Ghamri-Doudane, Y.: An improved vehicular ad hoc routing protocol for city environments. In: IEEE International Conference on Communications, ICC 2007, pp. 3972–3979. IEEE (2007)

6. Jerbi, M., Senouci, S.M., Rasheed, T., Ghamri-Doudane, Y.: Towards efficient geographic routing in urban vehicular networks. IEEE Trans. Veh. Technol. **58**(9), 5048–5059 (2009)
7. Karp, B., Kung, H.T.: GPSR: Greedy perimeter stateless routing for wireless networks. In: Proceedings of the 6th Annual International Conference on Mobile Computing and Networking, pp. 243–254. ACM (2000)
8. Lochert, C., Hartenstein, H., Tian, J., Fussler, H., Hermann, D., Mauve, M.: A routing strategy for vehicular ad hoc networks in city environments. In: Proceedings of Intelligent Vehicles Symposium, pp. 156–161. IEEE (2003)
9. Nebbou, T., Fouchal, H., Lehsaini, M., Ayaida, M.: A cooperative location service for VANETs. In: 2017 IEEE Symposium on Computers and Communications (ISCC), pp. 54–58. IEEE (2017)
10. Nebbou, T., Fouchal, H., Lehsaini, M., Ayaida, M.: A realistic location service for VANETs. In: Eichler, G., Erfurth, C., Fahrnberger, G. (eds.) I4CS 2017. CCIS, vol. 717, pp. 191–196. Springer, Cham (2017). https://doi.org/10.1007/978-3-319-60447-3_14
11. Phillipson, F., Fouchal, H., Gulik, K.V.: Alternative connectivity metric for routing in VANETs. In: Renault, E., Boumerdassi, S., Bouzefrane, S. (eds.) MSPN 2018, vol. 11005. Springer, Cham (2018). https://doi.org/10.1007/978-3-030-03101-5
12. Seet, B.-C., Liu, G., Lee, B.-S., Foh, C.-H., Wong, K.-J., Lee, K.-K.: A-STAR: a mobile ad hoc routing strategy for metropolis vehicular communications. In: Mitrou, N., Kontovasilis, K., Rouskas, G.N., Iliadis, I., Merakos, L. (eds.) NETWORKING 2004. LNCS, vol. 3042, pp. 989–999. Springer, Heidelberg (2004). https://doi.org/10.1007/978-3-540-24693-0_81
13. Tijms, H.C.: A First Course in Stochastic Models. Wiley, Hoboken (2003)
14. Wolff, R.W.: Poisson arrivals see time averages. Oper. Res. **30**(2), 223–231 (1982)

A Holistic Communication Network for Efficient Transport and Enhanced Driving via Connected Cars

Dirk von Hugo[✉], Gerald Eichler[ID], and Thomas Rosowski

Deutsche Telekom AG, 64295 Darmstadt, Germany
{Dirk.von-Hugo,Gerald.Eichler,
Thomas.Rosowski}@telekom.de

Abstract. Growing markets and novel technologies for cooperative and integrated vehicular communication are offering excellent opportunities for innovative business and coordinated research and standardization worldwide. Network operators as well as manufacturers of cars and devices for automotive connectivity are heading towards a next generation ecosystem in framework of 5G permitting to provide a bunch of new applications. These shall contribute to improved traffic safety by reduction of number of accidents or even their avoidance, to a higher level of traffic efficiency by enabling better road utilization and reduced traffic congestion, to a significant reduction in energy consumption and CO_2-emission, and to increased comfort for both drivers and passengers in cars. Such a vision can only be achieved by 5G-enabled connectivity and cooperation between vehicles and infrastructure on basis of a convergent, reliable, secure, and robust communications network that will enable real-time traffic control support.

This paper reports on the approach selected by project 5G NetMobil to enable a reliable, secure, and robust connectivity between vehicles, other road users, and infrastructure for real-time applications of a cooperative intelligent transport system, forming a new kind of traffic and transport-related community.

Keywords: 5G · Automotive · Connected car · Intelligent transport system · Integrated communication network

1 Challenges of Automotive and Transport Communication

To address increasing challenges with road traffic and transport services connectivity between cars and infrastructure allowing for reliable communication are under broad investigation. In addition to direct message exchange between vehicles and towards road infrastructure entities a concept of fully and heterogeneously networked cars would provide comprehensive solutions to provide driver assistance and allow for advanced levels of automation to face current automotive problems related to e.g. traffic congestion, accidents, and pollution of daily commutation towards Cooperative Connected and Automated Mobility (CCAM).

K.-H. Lüke et al. (Eds.): I4CS 2019, CCIS 1041, pp. 11–24, 2019.
https://doi.org/10.1007/978-3-030-22482-0_2

1.1 Network View

The success of Next Generation Mobile Networks (NGMN)[1] of 5th Generation (5G) will depend not only on the availability of novel technologies, but also on the fruitful cooperation between multiple stakeholders from the respective business areas, i.e.

- Network and device manufacturers,
- Network operators,
- Service providers,
- Tenants e.g.,
  - Mobile Virtual Network Operators (MVNO),
  - Vertical market players,
  - Over-The-Top (OTT) players.

5G will comprise numerous diverse network technologies and types of end user terminals and a universal infrastructure enabling flexible configuration of different logical network slices serving specific tenants' needs much more efficiently than today. A dedicated network slice will serve various vehicular usage scenarios like

- Connectivity for broadcasted infotainment,
- Exchange of messages within the Intelligent Transport System (ITS),
- Cooperative driving enabled within fleets,

all guided by a dedicated operator infrastructure and heading towards the final goal of autonomous driving.

This is one precondition for the secure autonomous driving, resembling one of multiple network slices provided by a 5G operator as shown in Fig. 2.

1.2 Architectural View

Architectural concepts and design of components as well as new technological models are investigated for selected use cases within multiple projects. One of these is the public funded research project 5G NetMobil (5G solutions for future conNEcTed MOBILity) [1] that is investigating approaches for future vehicular connectivity provided by upcoming so-called integrated holistic 5G systems. This activity is executed within the framework of tactile (i.e. extremely real-time) communication by a consortium of network operators, car and telco manufacturers, academia, and Small and Medium Enterprises (SME). According to ETSI [2] technical innovations in sectors such as medicine, agriculture, manufacturing, etc., are largely driven by availability of computational power and digital tool advancements. It will give rise to innovative categories of application ecosystems. For example, industrial and infrastructure automation will generate a diverse set of sensors and IoT devices of massive scale that must be interconnected, while other scenarios such as transportation tracking systems will have high mobility requirements but less variation in sensors. Even more challenging is autonomous driving that requires dynamic connections across a high number of vehicles and multiple sensors with satisfactory mobility functions. Already by looking at these few

---

[1] URL: https://www.ngmn.org/.

use cases, different kinds of communication patterns can be recognized, each with a specific demand for latency, mobility, data rate, and energy efficiency.

Smartphone-based telematics is an emerging application [3]. Communication between vehicles and smartphones can be realized without relying on any other hardware devices. Community-aware vehicular information can help to enhance the convenience and security of traveling [4]. In case of emergencies related to travel safety such as traffic accidents and natural disasters, vehicles need to send the information collected from sensors to emergency response vehicles, especially those of police, fire, and ambulance services. In the framework of 'Internet of Vehicles' this community-based approach has been recently reported [5]. [6] details the need for a V2X architecture deriving requirements both from market and from technology point of view. It extends existing concepts for an in-car Controller Area Network (CAN) with new interfaces to the CAN bus[2] and the Local Interconnect Network[3] (LIN) subsystems, especially for sensors and actors. Additionally, Media Oriented System Transport[4] (MOST) for infotainment is introduced, enabling innovative automotive services.

1.3   Communication View

Future 5G systems will – contrary to quite monolithically designed cellular networks of today on the one hand side and to infrastructure-less Mobile Ad-hoc Networks (MANET) on the other – be planned and deployed largely in a flexible service specific way, tailored according to customers' needs. Logical network slices shall efficiently provide the required system performance. A Vehicle to Anything (V2X) slice would work across the whole range of expected vehicular speeds as well as density and type of users e.g., private and emergency vehicles and public transport, other road users as cyclists and pedestrians – aka Vulnerable Road Users (VRUs). The ITS service specific infrastructure as resembled by ('smart') traffic lights, traffic signs, entities supporting parking or fueling (charging) has also to be served as well as car manufacturer systems and those for other specific services as fleet control or infotainment. Architecture enhancements for pre-5G systems to enable automotive communications for all kind of Vehicle-to-Everything (V2X) services have been already specified by 3GPP (e.g. [7–9]), ETSI [10], and ISO [11]. This includes connectivity between multiple vehicles and to other (in general more vulnerable) road users either directly or via a specific ITS related infrastructure (the entities of which typically denoted as Road Side Units, RSUs) or the wide area cellular networks. Therefore, the generic "X" in V2X is replaced by a dedicated letter:

- Vehicle to Vehicle (V2V),
- Vehicle to Pedestrians, (V2P), including also multiple variants of 'bikers'
- Vehicle to Infrastructure (V2I),
- Vehicle to Network (V2N),
- Vehicle to Driver (V2D).

---

[2] URL: http://esd.cs.usr.edu/webres/can20.pdf.

[3] URL: https://www.cs-group.de/:LIN_Specification_Package_2.2A.pdf.

[4] URL: https://www.mostcooperation.com/.

Additionally, the communication between the vehicle and its driver is improved by smart assistants e.g., to control navigation, as well as recommendation and infotainment systems [6] which are typically connected to the infrastructure outside the car. Multiple Standards Defining Organizations (SDO) as 5GAA (5G Automotive Association)[5], 3GPP (3rd Generation Partnership Project)[6], ETSI (European Telecommunications Standards Institute)[7], IETF (Internet Engineering Task Force)[8], and ITU (International Telecommunication Union)[9] have described a wide range of corresponding use cases and thereof derived service requirements. See e.g. [12] and [13] for current work in progress at 3GPP and IETF, respectively.

2 5G NetMobil Approach

The primary goal of 5G NetMobil is to develop an overall communication infrastructure for connected tactile driving by extending existing and future access technologies: 3GPP's LTE/NR (Long Term Evolution/New Radio) in both network based and direct link mode, and IEEE 802.11p[10] towards architectures supporting tactile connected driving with the aim of enabling increased traffic safety and efficiency. Since the ultimate goal of autonomous driving cannot be achieved based on local sensors and inter-vehicular communication only but requires support by corresponding features of a future mobile communication system, the project addresses especially network technologies providing ubiquitous coverage to enable high availability for car-to-infrastructure communication based on heterogeneous access technologies.

Such a hybrid access approach has already been considered in early 5G network concepts (see e.g. [14]) while multiple network based features as inclusion of cloud computing within the core or even at the edge of the network [15] have been proposed by technology driving organizations. An overview on the potential and challenges as well as main design aspects of hybrid V2X communications is provided in [16] considering the latest technological developments. Measures to counteract multipath inefficiencies have been proposed and implemented, e.g. by use of Network Coding to improve utilization of available resources and cope with packet losses [17]. A comprehensive overview on currently broadly discussed scenarios, requirements and technologies in a heterogeneous network environment are described and detailed in a recently published tutorial [18]. Focusing on research and standardization questions the authors emphasize once more the need for co-operation and coordination between the multiple stakeholders in this area of vehicular communication.

Different sets of use cases are considered to derive the underlying requirements and to allow for scenario definitions to achieve system validation and proof of concepts in

---

[5] URL: http://5gaa.org/.

[6] URL: https://www.3gpp.org/.

[7] URL: https://www.etsi.org/.

[8] URL: http://www.ietf.org.

[9] URL: https://www.itu.int/.

[10] URL: https://standards.ieee.org/standard/802_11p-2010.html.

terms of simulations, system modeling, and demonstrational trials. The use cases deal on one hand with "Tactile Cooperative & Strategic Driving" (platooning) with a focus on improving efficiency of traffic and transport as well as energy consumption and drivers working load. "Connected Driving" on the other hand aims at improving safety and comfort for all road users, especially in urban areas (smart traffic light and coexistence of critical and non-critical data exchange).

For those use cases, the resulting communication connections are identified and Key Performance Indicators (KPIs) are derived for selected applications. Metrics for performance and evaluation measures for the KPIs are designed to be examined for a final assessment of the technical components within the context of the proposed architecture enhancements.

A market analysis within the competitive environment of actors and stakeholders with their respective roles in the future automotive value chain has helped to assess business opportunities in comparison of existing business models with proposed alternatives. Opportunities and chances as well as risks and drawbacks for network operators in relation to other players are considered. Based on the project use cases, further topics as data for connected cars, infotainment, hybrid communication

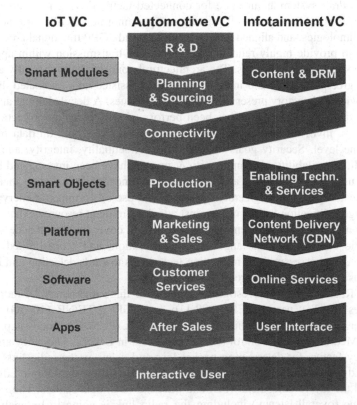

Fig. 1. Evolution of the value chain (VC) in the connected car ecosystem.

provision, smart automotive 5G networks, any type of machine communication, and software development and licensing have been analyzed.

The value chains (VC) of different industries or players in the new 'Connected Car Eco-System' differ from the previous ones, separated for traditional automotive business, Internet of Things (IoT) or Machine Type Communication (MTC) scenarios, and Internet 3rd party OTT content and service provisioning. Where possible the same modules may apply such as joint Research & Development (R&D), concepts for providing connectivity, and of course, the same end user and customer addressed. As shown in Fig. 1, the aspects of providing smart modules and objects or Apps will remain with the IoT business (left) while production and marketing & sales remain topics for traditional automotive tenants (middle). Content and rights management as well as online services are under responsibility of Internet companies (right).

More details on recent research, current economic situation and future perspective of European automotive industry can be found in [19].

3   5G NetMobil Concepts and Technical Approaches

Currently, a draft system architecture for connected tactile driving is described based on both, IEEE 802.11p and as well existing as upcoming new 3GPP radio access and network technologies, and aligned with existing ITS and 3GPP functional architectures. The aim is to provide highly reliable end-to-end data transmission within application and service specific delay bounds. The architectural concept shall inherently allow for the high degree of security and integrity needed in assisted and automated driving as well as provide satisfactory preservation of privacy issues. A detailed threat analysis of the proposed CCAM architecture has been performed with focus on protection goals, trust relations, involved entities (stakeholders), and attacks - both on data plane and control plane level. Security goals in terms of confidentiality, integrity, authenticity, accountability, availability, and anonymity & privacy have been investigated based on the project use cases resulting in a provisional recommendation including measures as an authenticated group key agreement protocol and use of asymmetric encryption for key exchange. Mitigation techniques against attacks aiming at resource exhaustion and manipulation of new functional entities in the network cover traditional access control, offline traffic control, firewalls and network separation, and scope-limited resource allocation. A final assessment of mitigation techniques towards detection and blocking of malicious traffic is work in progress.

Tactile Radio Access is investigated in terms of three different V2X radio access technologies (RATs), namely IEEE 802.11p and 3GPP LTE/NR (4G/5G) for both cellular (Uu interface) and side-link/ad-hoc/direct link (PC5). The focus is put on the respective Medium Access Control (MAC) protocols in Layer 2 since they are judged as being key factors for determining packet loss and delay on the radio link.

Agile Edge Computing is studied in terms of service shift to the Mobile Edge Cloud (MEC) and the layers of frontend (FE) and backend (BE) data centers. The impact on reaction time (overall latency) including the radio link is going to be analyzed and measured as a function of various network parameters like bandwidth, delay, jitter, etc. Therefrom strategies for decision on optimum location of service execution shall be derived.

Usage of context information for efficient service execution in the (A)gile MEC is seen as essential to improve network performance such as mobility and QoS (Quality of Service) support, e.g. in terms of demand prediction and subsequent decision on service instantiation and removal, respectively, at different distributed cloud sites. Mobility mechanisms for seamless inter-MEC transfer of functionalities are investigated and established for subsequent assessment.

Development of a highly flexible software-based control plane solution considering the demand for cross-domain multipath connectivity shall enable ambitious KPIs of 5G automotive services such as secure and highly reliable data transmission, low end-to-end delay, and global availability and interoperability. The solution builds on 5G concepts as a SBA (Service Based Architecture) as well as Software Defined Networking (SDN) and Network Function Virtualization (NFV) for mobile networks as outlined e.g. in [20]. Flexible and service-tailored network slice configurability gains from fine-granularly assembled functional modules as well as network programmability and a split in shared and dedicated control of corresponding functions and resources.

Following the NGNM paradigms, network slicing is a concept for running multiple logical networks configured and operating based on virtually independent business and service requirements on a common physical infrastructure in core network domain and/or on a common physical infrastructure and shared radio resources in access network domain (see Fig. 2). Low latency requirements will be provided by mobile edge computing as depicted in Fig. 4.

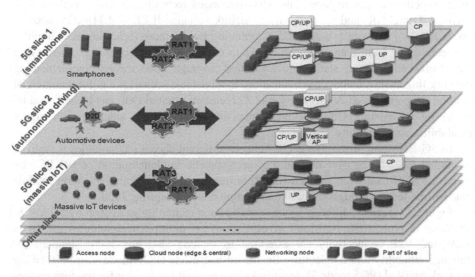

Fig. 2. Dedicated 5G network slicing with flexible assignment of User Plane (UP) and Control Plane (CP) (source: [14]).

The definition of network functionalities in automotive communications for application specific QoS/QoE (Quality of Experience[11]) providing concepts for vehicular radio access may have to respect resource aspects in the AMEC and in the Centralized or Cloud Radio Access Network (C-RAN). Further investigations, an implementation and integration of context aware control, and various QoS/QoE monitoring and control approaches are planned.

An important feature for reliable provision of an automotive service is the improved predictability of QoS along the route. As long as possible the communication network with comprehensive knowledge of network load and expected performance with high resolution will keep the QoS at the agreed level utilizing all available mechanisms. In case this is no longer possible (e.g. due to resource shortage) it will inform the application in advance of impending changes of the provided QoS parameters (e.g. in terms of delay, reliability). The in-car system will be able to subsequently adapt an application (e.g. slow down or increase distance to the car ahead) to ensure safety and/or driving efficiency.

The final evaluation and validation of selected concepts and solutions for exemplary use cases and applications will be deployed and integrated as far as possible in testbeds and laboratory setups, in order to allow measurements and demonstrations.

4 5G NetMobil Performance Considerations

As already mentioned above the aim of a hybrid multi-technology access approach is to increase reliability, coverage, and capacity of connectivity between road users and road infrastructure. This is achieved by selection of appropriate available technology to fulfill specific service requirements. Heterogeneous technologies cover cellular link (3GPP LTE/5G NR) and multiple direct sidelink variants: IEEE 802.11p (G5) and ad-hoc sidelink or network assisted PC5. Combining two or more technologies in a multi-connectivity or multi-path approach allows to exploit diversity gains e.g., by relaying data from cellular base stations to an out-of-coverage node means complementing network links with sidelink communication. In a business scenario (e.g. for commercial platoon support), the SLA (Service Level Agreement) granted QoE can be achieved by switching an existing G5 V2V interconnection to a cellular sidelink with higher availability and reliability.

In 5G NetMobil, the convergence between different access technologies is realized on higher layer (at or near IP) and a project specific implementation of NR PC5 by means of SDR (Software Defined Radio) is integrated into a communication module that will be tested throughout 2019 and demonstrated in spring 2020.

Figure 3 visualizes different usage scenarios and technologies as seen by 5GAA. In addition, in project 5G NetMobil investigations on multiple technologies for direct V2V and V2P connectivity are extended to include also non-3GPP standards to enhance reliability and availability. Beside ad-hoc mode (PC5 mode 4 or G5/11p) or network-assisted (PC5 mode 3) direct links, connectivity to local infrastructure entities

---

[11] QoE refers to the service quality experienced by the end user or application.

as traffic lights or beacons (V2I) also access to more complex and/or centralized services relying on 3GPP cellular (LTE/5G) are examined. Cooperative driving in terms of longitudinal or parallel platooning for efficiency improvement as well as connected road users in terms of city crossing scenario for safety and security as depicted will contribute to a holistic CAAM system. Also neighboring application scenarios in a stationary MTC environment (e.g. parking) which can be deployed with LTE variant Narrowband IoT (NB-IoT) shall cooperate with V2X connectivity optimally based on standard interfaces.

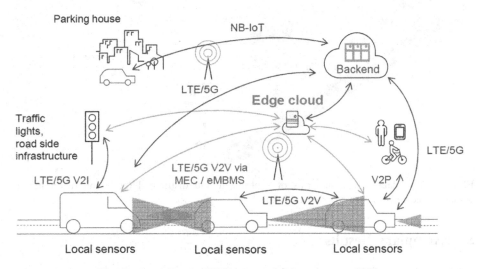

Fig. 3. Overview on V2X communications (source: [21]).

Different cloud instantiations are shown in Fig. 4 (e.g. decentral MECs at the edge, regional data centers, and central operator cloud - or 3rd party provided ones) as well as mobility support for services in terms of APP(lication) movement between these instances demanding for a tightly coordinated and efficiently controlled inter-operation between logical network entities.

These edge cloud entities may comprise beside the distributed data centers (multiple) radio access network(s) (e.g. when operated in a C-RAN manner) and SDN based Wide Area Networks (WAN) for interconnection, and a comprehensive management system for them needs to be supported by intelligent data analytics. Such a support is provided e.g. by 3GPPs Network Data Analytics (NWDA) functionality (for more details on V2X related solutions to gather and apply network data for performance improvement, see e.g. [12]) to enable a proper – context-aware - decision on the optimum location of APP execution. Investigation on specifics of different data analytics measures and technologies as Machine Learning (ML) or Artificial Intelligence (AI), however, are out of scope in the project.

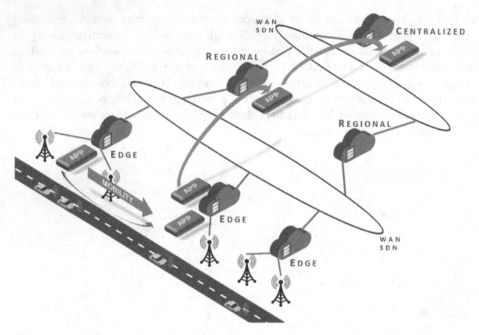

Fig. 4. Cloud data centers in terms of centralized and distributed (edge) provision in the vehicular scenario as seen by 5G NetMobil.

5 Exemplary Results

As mentioned before, a major aim of the project is to support specific network slices for applications and industries based on a common physical infrastructure. New features and network services for a 5G control plane approach shall facilitate implementation and integration of QoS/QoE enforcement concepts within the framework of a flexible network platform. The aim is to provide a 5G-ready methodology to enable a SBA-compatible control plane service set for vehicular network slices. Focus is to ensure a dynamically configurable E2E QoS performance for cross-domain multipath connectivity including QoS/QoE negotiation, monitoring, and control compatible with concepts currently discussed in 3GPP (see [22]).

Different approaches have been proposed in European 5G projects 5GEx, Virtuwind, and 5G-MoNArch all coordinated within the 5G Infrastructure Public Private Partnership (5GPPP) (see e.g. [23] for more details). The results are based on centralized API-based orchestration and management ('5GEx'), federated credential exchange for QoS orchestration in both a central ('Virt centr') and decentral hop-by-hop fashion ('Virt dec'), and a cross-slice congestion controller within a Network Slice Management Function (NSMF) ('Monarch'), respectively, and have been analyzed in the project in detail and compared against each other.

The signaling volume M for QoS orchestration is shown in Fig. 5, and the set-up time T required for the QoS negotiation for the four approaches is shown in Fig. 6. The overall estimated time remains only marginally affected by the amount of parties involved (with increasing amount and size assumed the delay will slightly increase) since the different signaling can happen in parallel, with exception of the hop-by-hop approach ('Virt dec') where the overall time needed increases with the amount of domains involved. The set-up time is identical for approaches 'Virt centr' and 'Monarch'. A minimum round trip time of 40 ms between domains and entities has been assumed as well as a (control plane signaling) message volume exchange of 15 kB per negotiation (request/reply).

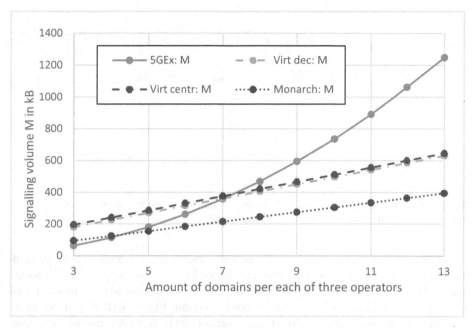

Fig. 5. Effort for QoS slice set-up in terms of signaling traffic volume for message exchange M for orchestration as a function of operator domains involved.

Based on the outcome of the results mentioned above the cross-domain QoS negotiation will follow the approach of 5G MoNArch allowing for minimum service provisioning time and effort. In addition applying their concept of an elastic NSMF offering a cross-domain Management and Orchestration (MANO) layer causing an improved exploitation of the network resources, less of scarce network resources need to be employed to guarantee the same QoS while more service requests can be accepted and treated at the same time [24]. Being able to configure and re-configure a vehicular network slice in a flexible and dynamic way, improving the network efficiency and reducing redundancy in resource exploitation this approach can contribute to the overall goal to provision essential CCAM services via cost-efficiently deployed future 5G infrastructure.

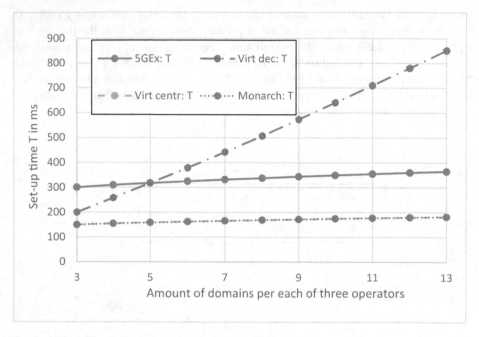

Fig. 6. Effort for QoS slice set-up in terms of required message exchange time T for orchestration as a function of operator domains involved.

Another important aspect is how to efficiently and effectively provide management and orchestration of logical vehicular sub-networks including edge cloud aspects. Approaches are discussed as well at 3GPP (e.g. SA5 on Telecom Management), ETSI (ISGs NFV and MEC), as in Open Standards gremia like ONAP (Open Network Automation Platform) and OSM (OpenSourceMANO) focusing on an optimum management system for a new communication system growing in size and complexity. Related aspects range from requirements and a (service-oriented) architecture of the future 5G network management system to well-known aspects as Life Cycle Management (LCM) (of entities as e.g., physical and virtual network service functions), Configuration, Performance, and Fault handling. Implementation and testing of an OAI (Open Air Interface) based ONAP tool is currently ongoing within a laboratory environment examining ONAP as platform for management, orchestration and automation for NFV/SDN networks meeting the requirements of ETSI MANO (Management and Orchestration) framework. The platform shall provide the capabilities for design, creation and LCM of vehicular network services and large-scale workloads as expected with future traffic growth enabling delivery of an efficient E2E network slicing on the 5G ecosystem. An assessment of final results of the open source testbed will be available at time of project completion.

As automotive communication has a global dimension, multi-vendor interoperability and standardization of inter-operator communication aspects are of high importance. Corresponding activities are currently monitored and taken into account in the underlying concepts, and the results will be checked for potential exploitation in terms of SDO contributions. Further aspects to be covered during project lifetime are evaluation of the design in simulations and laboratory set-up as well as prototypical implementations for real-life trials and public demonstrations. More details on already available outcome and planned future events will be provided on [1].

6 Conclusion

The targeted goal of autonomous driving cannot be achieved with local sensors and inter-vehicular communication only but requires in addition a continuous mobile network coverage to enable high availability for car-to-infrastructure communication. High-performance mobile edge computing and network slicing are essential concepts to facilitate low latency and high quality of service requirements. Among numerous architectural and functional components both of these concepts are investigated in 5G NetMobil in respect of the provisioning of automotive services in the framework of 5G systems. Future challenges – amongst others – which can be only partially addressed in the framework of this project are:

- Access and allocation of radio spectrum to cellular and non-cellular technologies (e.g. co-existence of 3GPPs 'Cellular V2X' variants and IEEE 802.11p),
- Elaboration of multi-operator solutions and required interfaces together with corresponding security add-ons,
- Further development of NGMN standards to cover new use cases of the connected car ecosystem,
- Pro-active status supervision of network performance in terms of KPIs by advanced big data analytics.

Acknowledgement. The authors would like to thank all members/partners of 5G NetMobil project for the productive cooperation.

References

1. 5G NetMobil project web site. (in German only) www.5G-NETMOBIL.de/en/, see also https://www.forschung-it-sicherheit-kommunikationssysteme.de/projekte/5g-netmobil. Accessed 24 Apr 2019
2. ETSI White Paper No. 17: Next Generation Protocols – Market Drivers and Key Scenarios. Sophia Antipolis, France (2016). https://www.etsi.org/media-library/white-papers/. Accessed 24 Apr 2019
3. Webb, C., Spina, S.P., Young, S.: Integrating smartphone communication strategy and technology into clinical practice: a mixed methods research study. Health Policy Technol. 5(4), 370–375 (2016)
4. Khan, J.A., Ghamri-Doudane, Y.: Saving: socially aware vehicular information-centric networking. IEEE Commun. Mag. 54(8), 100–107 (2016)
5. Qiu, T., Liu, X., Li, K., Hu, Q., Sangaiah, A.K., Chen, N.: Community-aware data propagation with small world feature for internet of vehicles. IEEE Commun. Mag. 56(1), 86–91 (2018)

6. Lüke, K.-H., Eichler, G., Erfurth, C.: Potentials and requirements of an integrated solution for a connected car. In: Fahrnberger, G., Eichler, G., Erfurth, C.(eds.) I4CS 2016. CCIS, vol. 648, pp. 211–216. Springer, Cham (2016). https://doi.org/10.1007/978-3-319-49466-1_14
7. 3GPP TR 22.861: Feasibility Study on New Services and Markets Technology Enablers for Massive Internet of Things; Stage 1 (Release 14) (2016)
8. 3GPP TR 22.862: Feasibility Study on New Services and Markets Technology Enablers for Critical Communications; Stage 1 (Release 14) (2016)
9. 3GPP TS 22.185: Service requirements for V2X services; Stage 1 (Release 14) (2017)
10. ETSI TR 102 638 V1.1.1: Intelligent Transport Systems (ITS); Vehicular Communications; Basic Set of Applications; Definitions. Sophia Antipolis, France (2014)
11. ISO/TS 17423: Intelligent transport systems—Cooperative systems—ITS application requirements and objectives for selection of communication profiles (2014). https://www.iso.org/obp/ui/#iso:std:iso:ts:17423:ed-1:v1:en
12. 3GPP TR 23.786: Study on architecture enhancements for EPS and 5G System to support advanced V2X services (Release 16), (draft) January 2019. work in progress
13. Jeong, J. (Ed.): IP Wireless Access in Vehicular Environments (IPWAVE): Problem Statement and Use Cases. draft-ietf-ipwave-vehicular-networking, November 2018. work in progress
14. Next Generation Mobile Network Alliance: NGMN 5G White Paper, NGMN, Frankfurt, Germany (2015)
15. ETSI ISG MEC: MEC in 5G networks, ETSI White Paper No. 28, Sophia Antipolis, France (2018)
16. Jacob, R., Franchi, N., Fettweis, G.: Hybrid V2X communications: multi-RAT as enabler for connected autonomous driving. In: 2018 IEEE 29th Annual International Symposium on Personal, Indoor and Mobile Radio Communications (PIMRC), Bologna, Italy (2018)
17. Gabriel, F., Rischke, J., Fitzek, F., Mühleisen, M., Lohmar, Th.: No plan survives contact with the enemy: on gains of coded multipath over MPTCP in dynamic settings. In: 2019 IEEE Wireless Communications and Networking Conference (IEEE WCNC 2019), Marrakech, Morocco (2019)
18. MacHardy, Z., Khan, A., Obana, K., Iwashina, S.: V2X access technologies: regulation, research, and remaining challenges. IEEE Commun. Surv. Tutorials 20(3), 1858–1877 (2018)
19. Konrad, K., Stagl, S. (eds.): Competitiveness of the European automotive manufacturing industry. Institute for Innovation and Technology (iit), Berlin, August 2018. https://www.iit-berlin.de/en/publications/competitiveness-of-the-european-automotive-manufacturing-industry/at_download/download. Accessed 24 Apr 2019
20. An, X., et al.: Architecture modularisation for next generation mobile networks. In: European Conference on Networks and Communications (EuCNC), Oulu, Finland (2017)
21. 5GAA White paper: Toward fully connected vehicles: Edge computing for advanced automotive communications, December 2017. http://5gaa.org/wp-content/uploads/2017/12/5GAA_T-170219-whitepaper-EdgeComputing_5GAA.pdf. Accessed 24 Apr 2019
22. 3GPP TR 23.742: Study on Enhancements to the Service-Based Architecture (Release 16) (2018)
23. 5GPPP project overview. https://5g-ppp.eu/. Accessed 24 Apr 2019
24. 5G MoNArch project Deliverable D4.2: Final design and evaluation of resource elasticity framework, March 2019. https://5g-monarch.eu/deliverables/. Accessed 24 Apr 2019

Efficient Event Dissemination Using Bluetooth Protocol

Kévin Thomas, Geoffrey Wilhelm, Hacène Fouchal$^{(\boxtimes)}$, Stephane Cormier, and Francis Rousseaux

CReSTIC, Université de Reims Champagne-Ardenne, Reims, France
{Kevin.Thomas,Geoffrey.Wilhelm,Hacene.Fouchal,
Stephane.Cormier,Francis.Rousseaux}@univ-reims.fr

Abstract. A C-ITS is a system where mobile stations OBU (On-Board Units) exchange messages with other ITSS-V or RSU (Road Side Units). Messages are sent through a specific WIFI (IEEE 802.11p) denoted also ETSI ITS-G5. The efficiency of this technology has been proven in terms of latency. However, RSU are common everywhere, for this reason we look for another mean to guarantee this communication. Cellular networks are widely deployed and ma support these communications.

In this paper, we present an architecture which ensures communication between RSUs and mobile stations using Bluetooth protocol.

We have measured some indicators as latency (notification delay), packet delivery ratio (number of messages arrived after a threshold). These indicators confirmed that our proposed architecture has a interesting performances and could be deployed widely.

Keywords: C-ITS · VANETs · Cellular networks ·
Hybrid communications · BLE

1 Introduction

The deployment of connected vehicles is an interesting challenge since a decade. The connectivity is one of the most important issue to solve. Indeed, a dedicated WIFI has been designed for connected vehicles: IEEE 802.11p (denoted also ETSI ITS-G5). However, the deployment of ITS-G5 hotspots (denoted Road Side Units) s not generalized. This deployment of such technology takes a lot of time and is an expensive task. Indeed, the penetration rate of the connected vehicles is increasing slowly. Therefore, the coverage of such technology remains limited. However, it is very important to receive the events to avoid accidents and save lives. To deal with this, the coverage could be enhanced using the cellular communication. In this paper, we intend to use the cellular network (3G/4G) in order to ensure the collection and the delivery of warning messages to and from vehicles. Every vehicles send continuously it Cooperative Awareness Messages (CAM) to the Central ITS Station (ITSS-C). The latter maintains the location of the vehicles up-to-date. If an event is triggered in a zone, the event is then

© Springer Nature Switzerland AG 2019
K.-H. Lüke et al. (Eds.): I4CS 2019, CCIS 1041, pp. 25–36, 2019.
https://doi.org/10.1007/978-3-030-22482-0_3

automatically forwarded using cellular communication to the nodes that are in the relevance area.

The remainder of this paper is organized as follows: Sect. 2 describes the related works. Section 3 details the architecture of the proposed system. Section 4 presents some performance indicators of our solution and Sect. 5 concludes the paper and gives some hints about future works.

2   Related Works

[13] proposes an evaluation of vehicular communications networks through car sharing scenarios. The authors have investigated three parameters. They adopted a specific mobility model which has been imported to a simulator. They have worked on a grid Manhattan network and they observed some performance parameters such as delay, packet loss, etc. The most important objective of the study is to show that vehicular communication is feasible and realistic under some conditions.

[12] studies throughput over VANETs system along an unidirectional traffic for different conditions and transmission ranges of wireless equipments. All studied vehicles are randomly connected. The paper gives few results of simulation studies achieved on NS-2 toolbox. They have measured performances indicators in case of congestion. A comparison of the obtained results with the expected connectivity has been done and have shown that the throughput over simulation is lower due to packet losses caused by collisions.

Authors of [19] presents an alternative to WAVE/DSRC using an hybrid system, which uses Wi-Fi Direct and Cellular Network. They show that such a system could work for C-ITS. However, this paper does not take into account the hybridation between ITS-G5 and Cellular Network.

[20] presents another alternative to WAVE/DSRC solution using here Wi-Fi Direct, ZigBee and Cellular Network. Wi-Fi Direct is used as a direct link between nodes. ZigBee is used to connect roadside sensors and Cellular Network for long distance communication. In this study, the ITS-G5 is also ignored.

In [7], the authors provide their network architecture which has been deployed in Spain, where communicating vehicles are switching between 802.11p and 3G, depending on RSU's availability.

[15] presents a detailed study on performance evaluation of IEEE 80211.p networks versus LTE vehicular networks. The authors analyzed some performance indicators like the end-to-end delay for both networks in different scenarios (high density, urban environments, etc.). Many important issues have been measured as network availability and reliability. The authors have proved through simulations that LTE solution meets most of the application requirements in terms of reliability, scalability, and mobility. However, IEEE 802.11p provides acceptable performance for sparse network topologies with limited mobility support.

[17] gives an efficient solution for routing messages over VANETs by using the vehicle's heading.

[6] gives an overview of how research on vehicular communication evolved in Europe and, especially, in Germany. They describe the German field operational test sim TD. The project sim TD is the first field operational test that evaluated the effectiveness and benefits of applications based on vehicular communication in a setup that is representative for a realistic deployment environment. It is, therefore, the next necessary step to prepare for an informed deployment decision of cooperative systems.

[16] is dedicated to routing over VANETs in an urban environments. [14] is a study about movement prediction of vehicles. Indeed, an adapted routing algorithms are proposed in [10] and in [11]. [9] gives an overview of strategies to use for routing on VANETs. [18] reviews much more actual strategies on vehicular networks. The ETSI has proposed a set of relevant standards about messages and processes to use with C-ITS oiver G5 [1–5,8].

All the works presented below handle the communications between vehicles using Wifi networks. In this study we show how to handle the bluetooth protocol to send messages to vehicles.

3   Event Dissemination

In order to propose an alternative solution to cellular, we provide the possibility to send information, thanks to the Bluetooth Low Energy (BLE). So, the following architecture is proposed to allow this kind of event dissemination.

Some Bluetooth Low Energy Senders (BLETransmitter) are installed on roadside. They transmit information which comes from the Road Operator like an event on the road (DENM), parking information, etc...

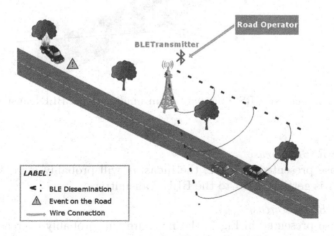

Fig. 1. BLETransmitter on the road. (Color figure online)

As we can see in Fig. 1, the Road Operator can send some information to the BLETransmitter which forward them to adjacent vehicles. For this purpose, the BLE antenna will broadcast information thanks to the advertise data, with Standard BLE Beacon.

But it is necessary to identify if a vehicle is concerned by the message or not. Indeed in Fig. 1 the black car has to receive the DENM because the event is on its lane, but, the red car must not receive the message, it is on the opposite lane.

We experimented 3 solutions to identify Traffic Direction:

3.1   Solution 1: Measure the RSSI

The first solution is based on measure of the BLE signal power. Indeed, we can deploy unidirectional BLETransmitter and just save some received messages when we pass near an antenna. With some message, thus some RSSI measure, we can establish a trend: increasing or decreasing.

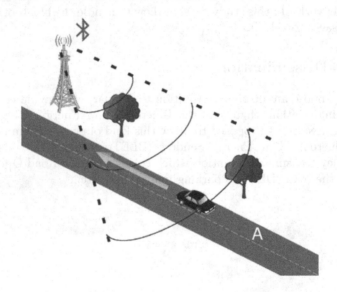

Fig. 2. An increasing RSSI measure of an unidirectional BLETransmitter.

Case 1: The RSSI increase
    In the case presented in Fig. 2, the measure will probably increase because the black car is getting closer to the BLETransmitter.

Case 2: The RSSI decrease
    In the case presented in Fig. 3, the measure will probably decrease because the black car goes away from the BLETransmitter.

The Road Operator knows how their BLETransmitter are oriented, what is the lane A or B, and identifies the lane concerned by the event. With all of this information, the Road Operator can indicate, in the BLE message, if the message concerns decreasing signals or increasing signals.

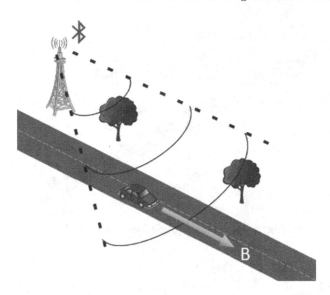

Fig. 3. A decreasing RSSI measure of an unidirectional BLETransmitter. (Color figure online)

So in Figs. 2 and 3:

- the black car is on lane A and is concerned by the message, so it will consume it.
- the red car is on lane B and is not concerned by the message, so it will discard it.

3.2   Solution 2 - Two BLETransmitters

The second solution use two unidirectional BLETransmitters. The main idea of this solution is to use the reception order to establish traffic direction.

The Road Operator just needs to define and save which sequence corresponds for lane A or B.

Case 1: The vehicle is on lane A

In the case presented in Fig. 4, the application will receive the message 1 and after the message 2 that indicates that the vehicle is on lane A.

Case 2: The vehicle is on lane B

In the case presented in Fig. 5, the application will receive the message 2 and after the message 1 that indicates that the vehicle is on lane B.

This solution constrains the operator to put two information in a message:

- a message identifier to establish the "Msg1" and the "Msg2".
- the sequence concerned by the event. "Msg1 then Msg2" or "Msg2 then Msg1" concerns the event.

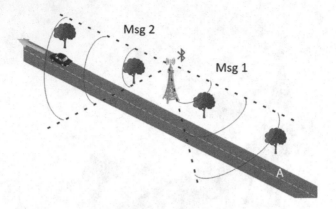

Fig. 4. Receiving two messages on lane A.

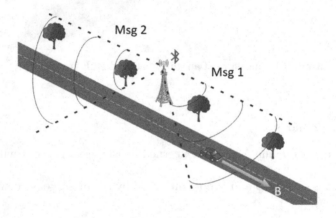

Fig. 5. Receiving two messages on lane B

3.3   Solution 3 - Heading of the Road

The third solution is to give the Heading (angle between a vector and the north) of the lane which is concern by the event where the BLETransmitter is.

When a vehicle receives a BLE message, it compares it to the GPS heading of the vehicle (or compass heading - it depends on enable sensors) within $\pm 90°$ in order to anticipate a potential curve.

Case 1: The vehicle is on lane A

In the case presented in Fig. 6, the Headings of the lane and of the vehicle are the same (more or less 90°). That indicates that the vehicle is on lane A.

Case 2: The vehicle is on lane B

In the case presented in Fig. 7, the Heading of the lane is not the same as the vehicle (more or less X degrees). That indicates that the vehicle is on lane B.

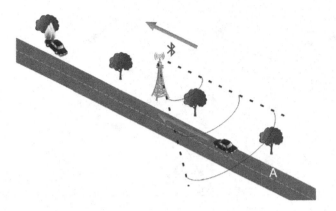

Fig. 6. Corresponding of the road's Heading with the vehicle's Heading.

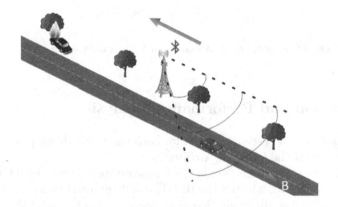

Fig. 7. Opposition between the road's Heading and the vehicle's Heading.

Here, the Road Operator is constrained by the cartographic analysis. Indeed, when it declares a BLE broadcasting, it needs to anticipate, in their internal process, the cartography to establish the correct Heading.

How to compare?

After the reception of a message, a comparison is started. The system will decode the message, extracts the Heading of the lane that is concerned and fetches the vehicle's Heading from the GPS or the compass.

In Fig. 8, we have two Headings: for the vehicle (VH) and the event (EH). They are projected on a trigonometric circle (blue system). Then, the difference of 90° is built, those are angles α and β. In order to make the calculation easy, we rotate the system, and put α on 0°, this action builds two new angles: α' and β' and two new vectors VH' and EH' (red system). The interval α' β' contains the validation area and if the EH' is between them, the event concerns our vehicle.

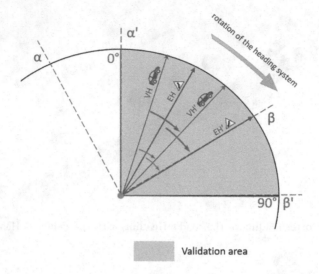

Fig. 8. Rotation of the comparison system in order to validate the event. (Color figure online)

4   Evaluation and Performance Analysis

Here, the purpose is to estimate limits for each solutions, develop and challenge them. We deployed the following architecture.

In Fig. 9, we send orders to the BLETransmitter thanks to TCP connection. The Raspberry Pi, which is the BLETransmitter, constructs the advertising packet and enable the dissemination of it. We can also transmit a "stop" message to stop the broadcast and a "shutdown" message to shutdown the program. For the reception in a vehicle, in a first time, we develop an ad-hoc application which just receives BLE messages, identifies if the message concerns the vehicle and prints it.

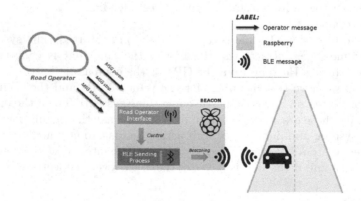

Fig. 9. BLETransmitter architecture in testing phase.

Obviously, we have a Universally Unique Identifier (UUID) in order to distinguish messages sent by other devices. We choose: 00009999-0000-1000-8000-00805f9b34fb.

In order to emulate the unidirectional BLETransmitter, we placed the beacon on a side of a bridge which acted as a shield.

First, we challenge the solution Sect. 3.1 at 130 km/h.

Table 1. RSSI measure during test phase

	Device 1	Device 2	Device 3	Device 4
1st lap	-43 -38	-38 -38	-45 -46 -43 -43-43 -45 -38 -45-43	-38 -37
2nd lap	-45 -45	-38 -38	-42 -43	-38 -32 -33

In the Table 1:

- The Device 1 was powered by a battery.
- The Device 2 was connected to the car.
- The Device 3 and Device 4 were standalone.

The first lap was on the same lane as the DENM and, in theory, the signal should increase. The second lap was on the opposite lane and, in theory, the signal should decrease.

Then we test the solution Sect. 3.2 at 130 km/h. For this session, we put two Raspberry on both sides of the Bridge. They are respectively identified by "1" and "2" in the message.

Table 2. Sequences during test phase

	Beacon code sequence records	Results
1st lap	1 1	Inconclusive
2nd lap	2 2 2	Inconclusive

As we can see in Table 2, we received messages from only one BLETransmitter, none from the Raspberry on the other side of the bridge. It is due to the driving speed.

After we test the solution Sect. 3.3 at 130 km/h.

In Table 3, the event was displayed every time we were on the concerned lane, and we received some duplicate packets.

Table 3. Heading messages during test phase

	Lane concerned	NB messages records	Displayed on screen
1st lap	Yes	2 messages	Yes
2nd lap	No	3 messages	No
3rd lap	Yes	3 messages	Yes
4th lap	No	2 messages	No

4.1 Quantitative Analysis

First, we identify the quantitative cost.

For solution Sect. 3.1, we generally receive between 1 and 3 messages with an RSSI measure too close to determine a correct trend, so, we can not determine if we have an increase or decrease signal power, therefore, we do not know if we are getting closer to the antenna or if we go away from it.

Also with solution Sect. 3.2, as the previous solution, we have not enough message when we are getting closer to the BLETransmitter, so we can not ensure that enough information to determine if the traffic direction correspond with the sequence.

With solution Sect. 3.3, received messages are enough in order to identify the traffic direction of the vehicle, so, identify if an event must be treat or not.

4.2 Implementation Complexity

Now, we see the most complex solution.

In the solution Sect. 3.1, distally, the Road Operator put only an information in the message, and, proximally, we use the advertise data header so we do not have a lot of process but for the Road Operator, it is a little bit complex because it needs to orientate a directional BLETransmitter when it install it.

For the solution Sect. 3.2, distally, two messages must be identified as "message 1" and "message 2" so we need to duplicate and synchronize two BLE-Transmitters from the Road Operator Controller. It also needs to determine and transmit the correct sequence thanks to the cartography. Therefore, proximally, we need to have two directional BLETransmitters installed, which is difficult.

And so, in solution Sect. 3.3, as solution Sect. 3.1 the Road Operator just put an information in the message. Proximally, we totally depend of a embedded system's sensor (compass or gps) but we do not need a directional BLETransmitter.

4.3 Autonomy

We based our analysis on the previous Sect. 4.2.

The solution Sect. 3.1 just needs to determine which is the orientation of the BLETransmitter and an analysis of the cartography, so it is relatively self-contained solution.

For the solution Sect. 3.2, it is totally dependent of the Road Operator process which determines the good sequence relative to the orientation of local BLETransmitters.

Finally, the solution Sect. 3.3 is probably the most standalone solution because, The Road Operator will just determine which lane is concern by the event thanks to the cartography. The rest of the process will be assumed by embedded system's sensor (compass or gps).

5 Conclusion

In this paper we have presented an architecture for intelligent transport system based on the bluetooth protocol. The most important issue of such a study is to show that a simple protocol could be used very simply with low cost to deploy cooperative intelligent transport systems. We have only presented an architecture et as a next step we intend to experiment such a solution on real vehicles within the project SCOOP (supported by the EC).

Acknowledgement. This work was made possible by EC Grant No. INEA/CEF/ TRAN/A2014/1042281 from the INEA Agency for the SCOOP project. The statements made herein are solely the responsibility of the authors.

References

1. European Telecommunications Standards Institute (ETSI). http://www.etsi.org
2. IEEE Draft Standard for Amendment to Standard [for] Information Technology-Telecommunications and information IEEE Std P802.11p/D11.0 April 2010, pp. 1–35, 15 June 2010
3. Intelligent Transport Systems (ITS); Vehicular Communications; GeoNetworking; Part 4: Geographical addressing and forwarding for point-to-point and point-to-multipoint communications; Sub-part 1: Media-Independent Functionality. ETSI EN 302 636-4-1 V1.2.1, July 2014
4. Intelligent Transport Systems (ITS); Vehicular Communications; GeoNetworking; Part 5: Transport Protocols; Sub-part 1: Basic Transport Protocol. ETSI EN 302 636-5-1 V1.2.1, August 2014
5. Intelligent Transport Systems (ITS); Vehicular Communications; Basic Set of Applications; Part 2: Specification of Cooperative Awareness Basic Service. ETSI EN 302 637-2 v.1.3.2, November 2014
6. Weia, C.: V2X communication in Europe: from research projects towards standardisation and field testing of vehicle communication technology. Comput. Netw. **55**(14), 3103–3119 (2011)
7. Santa, J., Fernandez, P.J., Perenaguez-Garcia, F.: Deployment of vehicular networks in highways using 802.11p and IPv6 technologies. Int. JAHUC **24**(1/2), 33–48 (2017)
8. Intelligent Transport Systems (ITS); Vehicular Communications; Basic Set of Applications; Part 3: Specifications of Decentralized Environmental Notification Basic Service. ETSI EN 302 637-3 V1.2.2, November 2014

9. Lochert, C., Hartenstein, H., Tian, J., Fussler, H., Hermann, D., Mauve, M.: A routing strategy for vehicular ad hoc networks in city environments. In: Proceedings of IEEE IV2003 Intelligent Vehicles Symposium (Cat. No. 03TH8683), June 2003, pp. 156–161 (2003)

10. Ayaida, M., Barhoumi, M., Fouchal, H., Ghamri-Doudane, Y., Afilal, L.: PHRHLS: a movement-prediction-based joint routing and hierarchical location service for VANETs. In: IEEE International Conference on Communications (ICC), Budapest, Hungary, May 2013, pp. 1424–1428 (2013)

11. Ayaida, M., Barhoumi, M., Fouchal, H., Ghamri-Doudane, Y., Afilal, L.: HHLS: a hybrid routing technique for VANETs Global Communications Conference (GLOBECOM), Anaheim, December 2012, pp. 44–48. IEEE (2012)

12. Lu, W., Bao, Y., Sun, X., Wang, Z.: Performance evaluation of inter-vehicle communication in a unidirectional dynamic traffic flow with shockwave. In: Proceedings of the International Conference on Ultra Modern Telecommunications, ICUMT 2009, St. Petersburg, Russia, 12–14 October 2009, pp. 1–6 (2009)

13. Lu, W., Han, L.D., Cherry, C.R.: Evaluation of vehicular communication networks in a car sharing system. Int. J. Intell. Transp. Syst. Res. **11**(3), 113–119 (2013)

14. Menouar, H., Lenardi, M., Filali, F.: A movement prediction-based routing protocol for vehicle-to-vehicle communications. In: 1st International Vehicle-to-Vehicle Communications Workshop, Co-located with MobiQuitous 2005, V2VCOM 2005, San Diego, USA, 21 July 2005 (2005)

15. Mir, Z.H., Filali, F.: LTE and IEEE 802.11p for vehicular networking: a performance evaluation. EURASIP J. Wirel. Commun. Netw. **2014**, 89 (2014)

16. Seet, B.-C., Liu, G., Lee, B.-S., Foh, C.-H., Wong, K.-J., Lee, K.-K.: A-STAR: a mobile ad hoc routing strategy for metropolis vehicular communications. In: Mitrou, N., Kontovasilis, K., Rouskas, G.N., Iliadis, I., Merakos, L. (eds.) NETWORKING 2004. LNCS, vol. 3042, pp. 989–999. Springer, Heidelberg (2004). https://doi.org/10.1007/978-3-540-24693-0_81

17. Taleb, T., Ochi, M., Jamalipour, A., Kato, N., Nemoto, Y.: An efficient vehicle-heading based routing protocol for VANET networks. In: Wireless Communications and Networking Conference, WCNC 2006, April 2006, vol. 4, pp. 2199–2204. IEEE (2006)

18. Zeadally, S., Hunt, R., Chen, Y.-S., Irwin, A., Hassan, A.: Vehicular ad hoc networks (VANETs): status, results, and challenges. Telecommun. Syst. **50**(4), 217–241 (2012)

19. Jeong, S., Baek, Y., Son, S.H.: A hybrid V2X system for safety-critical applications in VANET. In: 2016 IEEE 4th International Conference on Cyber-Physical Systems, Networks, and Applications (CPSNA), Nagoya, pp. 13–18 (2016)

20. Bhover, S.U., Tugashetti, A., Rashinkar, P.: V2X communication protocol in VANET for co-operative intelligent transportation system. In: International Conference on Innovative Mechanisms for Industry Applications (ICIMIA), Bangalore, pp. 602–607 (2017)

Teaching and Collaboration

Robots in the Classroom

Mobile Robot Projects in Academic Teaching

Jörg Roth$^{(\boxtimes)}$

Faculty of Computer Science, Nuremberg Institute of Technology,
Nuremberg, Germany
Joerg.Roth@th-nuernberg.de

Abstract. The field of mobile robotics has a long tradition and due to recent developments, we expect a huge potential for the future. Expertise in the area of mobile robotics is important for computer science students. The topic has many connections to different other computer science areas such as computer vision, algorithms, planning, world modeling and machine learning but is also related to basic fields such as mathematics, geometry, statistics, graph theory and optimization techniques. Students have to consider hardware and real-time issues, meanwhile they have to deal with uncertainty of data that are based on sensors. Software development differs from typical desktop, office or client-server developments that often are in focus of computer science studies. As a consequence, academic courses on mobile robotics differ in many ways from other courses. A major issue: we have to get the students very quickly to a point to achieve progress in their projects. Moreover, the teacher has to have an environment to manage the different facets of the complex topics.

Keywords: Mobile robotics · Robot platforms · Robot simulation ·
Academic teaching

1 Introduction

This paper presents ongoing efforts to integrate mobile robot projects in the academic curriculum of computer science degrees programs (Bachelor and Master). The Nuremberg Institute of Technology is of type University of Applied Sciences. This means, its basic task is teaching whereas research, even though strongly encouraged, appears in second place.

Mobile robotics will play a major role in future society and industry. The applications range from household and service robots, medical robots, health care to industrial transport systems and autonomous driving. Besides general development of mechanical platforms, sensors, actuators and computing hardware, we experience great advances in the area of machine learning. For future computer scientist it is essential to have fundamental experience in the area of robotics to be prepared for future tasks.

The computer science degree programs provide a broad education in different areas. Thus, the topic mobile robotics often is an area of specialization. As a consequence, this topic usually is not represented in the student's program mandatory field. At the

K.-H. Lüke et al. (Eds.): I4CS 2019, CCIS 1041, pp. 39–53, 2019.
https://doi.org/10.1007/978-3-030-22482-0_4

Computer Science department of the Nuremberg Institute of Technology the field of robotics can be covered in

- compulsory elective subjects,
- student's projects,
- Bachelor and Master theses.

This means, the topic either occurs in the later part of the studies or in the Master's program. This is reasonable, as mobile robotics require competence in e.g. mathematics, data structures, algorithms, graph theory and programming.

A supervisor of courses on mobile robotics has to deal with different challenges. We identified the following areas:

- *Technical*: A robot platform has to be made available. This includes the actual robot (hardware), but also the environment to develop, test and upload software.
- *Didactic*: The large area of robotics must be tailored to a special amount of knowledge that fits into the respective program.
- *Organizational*: This includes the administration of the (costly) material, service, upgrading, but also supervising safety procedures.

In this paper we describe the experience of several courses in the area of robotics over many years.

2 Robots from the Technical View

2.1 The Robot Platforms

The integration of mobile robots in our courses started 2013 with the *Carbot* robot ([10, 12], Fig. 1, top, left). The main goal was to gather experience with a driving (car-like) robot. In 2017 we introduced a second, legged platform, the hexapod *Bugbot* ([11], Fig. 1, top, right) that additionally makes it possible to address 3D motion problems and gait execution.

The experience with mobile robots in the teaching area actually started some years earlier in 2010 with a first course. At this time, we used Lego NXT sets [1] to teach knowledge about wheeled robot construction and programming. Even though, the courses were a great success from the perspective of students, it was disappointing concerning the richness of contents. The reasons were:

- The mechanical platform mainly consisting of plastic material prevents the construction of precise and stable robots that are able to execute more complex tasks such as exactly driving planned trajectories.
- The sensors supplied with the sets are mainly of simple type (e.g. switches, ultrasonic). The respective output does not enable detailed world modeling.
- The computing power of the so-called 'bricks' (i.e. the computing components) was too weak to execute typical robotics tasks such as sensor data fusion or navigation.

The goal was thus in 2013 to introduce a new robot model, the Carbot. We gave up the ambition to make the robot construction as a part of the course. As this is typically a

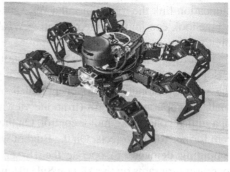
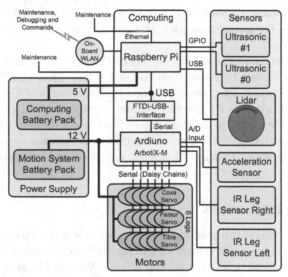

Fig. 1. Carbot (top, left) and Bugbot (top, right), Bugbot architecture (bottom)

mechanical engineering tasks and does not actually enrich the computer science skills, this was reasonable. Thus, the Carbot construction was completely predefined concerning the mechanics, motors and sensors. The students only should extend and modify the software components.

For the Carbot construction we relied on the Tetrix kit – it contained stable metal bars assembled with screws. In addition, strong driving motors, servos and motor controllers were part of the kits. The specific construction was a unique set up, entirely developed in our faculty. For the legged robot Bugbot we used the widely available Trossen Phantom Mark III kit that mainly contained a body, the hexapod legs and a motion control system based on Arduino. This kit provided an empty mounting plate, where we added additional computing boards and sensors.

Figure 1 (bottom) shows the architecture of the Bugbot. One goal was to have fully independent robots concerning power supply and computing power. Both robots carry two batteries – one for the motors, one for the computing board. As the basic communication link the robots install a WLAN access point at startup. The developer's PC or notebook can login to the respective WLAN cell to install new software, debug the robot's software or send task descriptions, e.g. to drive or walk to a specific location.

Both robots have two computing components. One is for higher level tasks such as sensor processing, world modeling and path planning. Currently, this is a Raspberry Pi. The second computing component called the *Motion Subsystem* is represented by a smaller computing platform (from the viewpoint of computing power), but with more capabilities concerning motor control. On the Carbot, we use a NXT brick, well-known from former robot projects. On the Bugbot we use an Arduino that meets the embedded computing demands to operate the 18 servos (three for each of the six legs). The operation programs on the Motion Subsystem computing components are considered as fixed and are usually not subject to changes for e.g. a specific robot tasks. A control interface accepts motion commands (e.g. drive a curve, walk straight) that are autonomously executed. For technical reasons, also some of the sensors are attached to the Motion Subsystem.

Both robots contain a lot of sensors on board. The Carbot is able to map the world with the help of a camera in driving direction and a 360°-Lidar (Light Detection and Ranging). Quick obstacle detection is provided by Ultrasonic and Tactile sensors.

The Bugbot also carries a Lidar and is able to perceive small distance with two Ultrasonic sensors, mounted in different angles. To avoid falling downstairs, the front legs measure the distance to the bottom with two Infrared distance sensors. Both robots use an acceleration sensor to detect tilt angles, collisions and unexpected movements (e.g. falling).

2.2 Simulation Environments

At the time of first course that used the Carbot robot, it was obvious that the hardware was the critical resource. Even though we had three identical Carbots, it was critical to integrate them too careless into the student's work. We quickly gave up the idea of weekly schedules and 'robot hours' to grant access to the three robots for testing. As the schedules had to be synchronized with battery loading times (some hours), the respective slot for testing for a complete class (e.g. with 18 students in 6 groups) would have been too small.

It turned out that an appropriate simulation environment was unavoidable [7]. This should easily be installed on the lab PCs, student's notebook or home computing environment. The real robot should only be used for final testing and result presentation. We had great demands: the developed software should both run on real robot and simulator without modifying the code, even without the need of recompilation. Moreover, simulated motors, sensors and execution environments should be very close to real facilities, concerning timing, precision, errors etc.

Table 1 presents reasons to use a simulation environment in classrooms. Even though we have numerous benefits, we had significant efforts for developing the simulators. Because the respective robot platforms are highly specialized, it is not easy

Table 1. Ten reasons for robot simulation

Reason	Description
1. Convenience	The simulator is very convenient. We may execute runs at any place with a notebook.
2. Valuably of the hardware	Robots are costly (i.e. Bugbot more than 3000€). Some parts are unique or are not produced any more. Assembly of parts is costly in terms of human resources.
3. Number of robots	We have too few robots. In larger courses with e.g. 30 Students it is not possible to provide enough platforms, even if we form groups.
4. Complexity of usage	Real robots are difficult to handle. They are no consumer products. E.g. startup and shutdown require several steps.
5. Danger for users and environment	Even though our robots are no 'killing machines' their motors have a reasonable strength. They can easily harm persons and damage things.
6. Danger for robots themselves	Robots can easily damage themselves, e.g. uncontrolled servo motors can exceed joint limits or break cables.
7. Runtime preparations	The robot often is not prepared when needed. Typical problems: batteries are not loaded, software not updated or sensors not repaired.
8. Serving incomplete robot functions	Real robots only run, if *all* functions run stably, from sensor processing to action planning. Thus, we can only start with a new idea, if all was available. Simulators can replace unavailable functions by their 'ultimate knowledge'. E.g. if real SLAM is currently not working, we can assume an ultimately precise (virtual) SLAM using the simulator's internal robot position.
9. Difficulty of modifications	Modifications of the real robots are difficult. In the simulator we can e.g. add new sensors or change the robot's geometry with only few lines of code.
10. Setting up test environments	To create real test environments for robots is costly and requires a lot of physical space. In the simulator we can e.g. build large mazes or climbing courses with convenient configurations.

to use a simulator of the shelves – the configuration effort would be very high and some functions would even not be possible to realize. We thus fully relied on own developed simulators.

Figure 2 shows a screenshot of the Carbot simulation environment. The main window contains a ground map with the virtual environment and robot, in addition we see the virtual camera image and Lidar scan. Figure 3 shows the more complex Bugbot simulation environment. In contrast to the Carbot, the Bugbot is able to walk over small obstacles and climb small steps, thus we need a physical simulation in three dimensions.

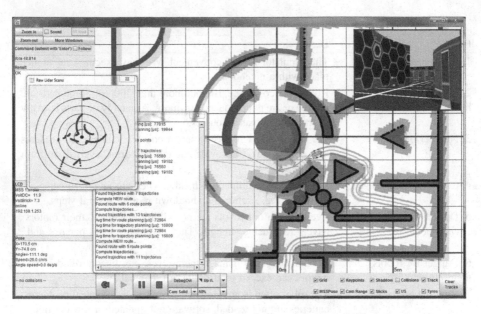

Fig. 2. The Carbot simulation environment

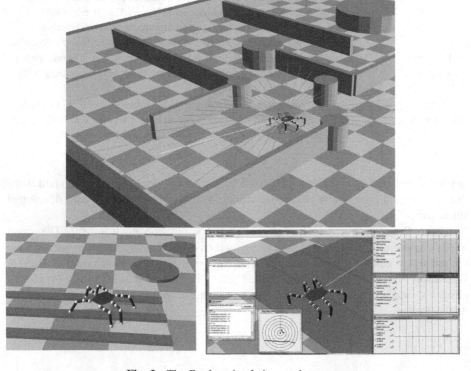

Fig. 3. The Bugbot simulation environment

Both simulators provide the following functions:

- simulation of physical effects, e.g. gravity, friction,
- modeling of virtual environments with obstacles, walls or areas of lower traction,
- scheduling of moving objects that represent, e.g. people who walk through the area,
- simulation of motors and sensors with their specific error and precision properties,
- simulation of virtual cameras – even though also kind of sensors they fundamentally differ in terms of complexity, API and image processing function,
- providing an execution environment for the Motion Subsystem code,
- generating graphical output for the user,
- generating statistics, e.g. measure the virtual damage due to collisions,
- execution of logging and debugging functions,
- state control, e.g. restart the virtual robot, pause a test run.

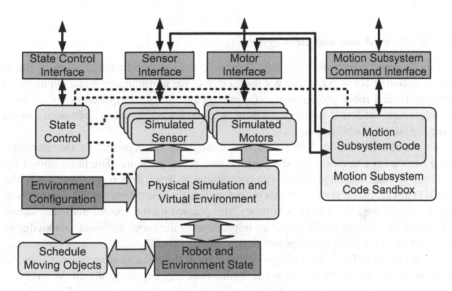

Fig. 4. Structure of the simulation system

Figure 4 shows the simulators' structure. Most important is the physical simulation component. It executes the natural law in the virtual environment, foremost gravity, collision of solid obstacles and friction [5]. It, e.g., lets the Bugbot fall down, if the center of gravity is outside the legs' support polygon. It is also possible to define parts of the bottom as more slippery (e.g. like ice surface) to evaluate, how good the trajectory regulation works. Until now we use an own development for the physical simulation component, but a current student's project tries to replace it by *Bullet Physics Engine* [3].

We simulate the motors on a very fine-grained level of single motor steps. To access the motors on the real environment in the same ways as in the simulator, we make use of the motor interfaces: on the Carbot we have I^2C commands, on the Bugbot a serial protocol to control motors. With sensors we deal in the same way, whereas the way sensors are attached is more heterogeneous. They are attached, e.g. via I^2C bus, GPIO, A/D ports or USB. Thus, for each sensor, a software driver is realized that maps access commands to the hardware or simulation facility. This again ensures same control code between real and simulated robot.

The most complex 'sensor' is the HD camera. As it is too difficult to simulate each access command of the respective hardware interface, we developed a high-level driver to read the image stream from the real or virtual camera.

It is also very complex to embed the Motion Subsystem code into the simulation environment. The problem: both Motion Subsystem computing components have their operating system and runtime libraries – on the Carbot it is *NXJ* (a Java environment for the Lego NXT brick), on the Bugbot it is *Arduino*. In the simulation environment we thus have to reimplement all respective calls and provide equal functions. This is performed by the so-called *Motion Subsystem Code Sandbox* – also an own development.

2.3   Runtime Modes and Debugging

Debugging robot programs is crucial. Typical debugging mechanisms, such as single step execution or break points are not useful due to the multithreading and event-based nature of typical robot programs. Useful debugging information often is not a single variable value but has a geometric nature, e.g. measured distances, positions, world models, grids or visibility graphs.

As a consequence, we integrated two debugging mechanisms in the platform: *debug out* that is a traditional text-based log and *debug painting*. The latter allows the developer to paint simple graphics with coordinates in world dimensions (e.g. cm scale) on a 2D canvas. In the simulator, this output is directly painted on the 2D environment map. In Fig. 2, e.g., we see the occupancy grid painted on the ground map. The debug painting facility is very useful to get an impression of the robot's current knowledge of the world and significantly simplifies debugging of control code.

The usage of debugging facilities is different in the three *runtime modes* (Fig. 5). The *robot controller* is the actual robot application, e.g. exploring the environment or navigating from point to point. In the *simulation mode* the robot controller and execution environment run in the simulator, all together run in a desktop application. From the view of software components, this is the ideal case as all software components run in the same memory.

Running the robot controller on the real robot, we have two cases. We still may use the desktop application for debugging. All debugging calls are redirected through a *debug bridge* that transfers the respective calls via WLAN to the desktop application. The developer can still see all debugging information on a convenient workplace, however, further data such as the (simulated) environment map is not available.

The last mode called *native mode* is the actual mode for real robots. Debug painting calls are directed to empty functions and debug out is passed to a text file for later analyses.

For all modes we have a component called *commander*. This allows a user at runtime to specify the robot's tasks. E.g. a user could specify the position, the robot should drive or walk to. For this, the user enters a command that indicates the

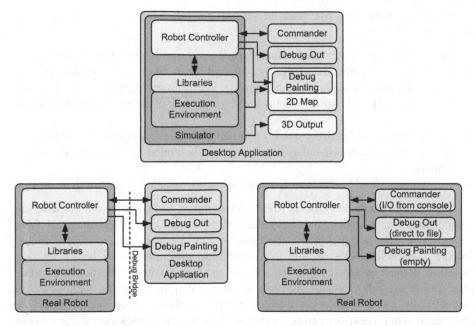

Fig. 5. Runtime modes, simulation (top), real robot with debug bridge (bottom, left), native mode (bottom, right)

movement target and the robot agrees replying 'OK' or disagrees, if the target was out of the reachable area. For more evolved robots, the commander could later be expanded by a convenient user interface, e.g. a touch panel – currently a command-line oriented way is sufficient. Like the debug calls, the commander may communicate with the robot controller in memory, via the debug bridge or, in native mode, via the operating system's console streams.

In robot courses, the commander with its text-oriented nature is ideal for the lecturer to define test cases for the robot controller. They can e.g. be stored in text files (passed via clipboard) or even can be passed by command line at startup.

3 Robots as Subject of Teaching

3.1 Types of Courses and Contributions

The Carbot and Bugbot platforms were created to form an environment for robot research and to teach robotics skills in classes. As a university of applied sciences has teaching as primary task, a professor often has to combine research projects and student projects. Due to a lack of mid-level academic positions (e.g. PhD students) we have to shift some research tasks (e.g. implementing ideas) to students.

In the teaching area, we want to pursue the following goals with our robot platforms:

- They should serve for different course formats, e.g. elective subjects, Master theses.
- We want to transmit knowledge in different areas of mobile robotics such as computer vision, navigation, path planning, world modeling, kinetics [15], sensor data fusion, SLAM (simultaneous localization and mapping) [4] and machine learning.
- The students should get very quickly to a point to achieve progress in their projects. This is an important demand as the (short) time is limited by the respective course formats.
- The students should be able to fade out problems that are not part of their project.

The last two points are crucial. Robots are complex and combine a lot of different components. For a student it is very demanding to get knowledge about all these components in sufficient depth in the short time of a course. E.g. a student should prepare a Bachelor thesis in only five months. In this time she or he should read literature, prepare an approach, implement and test it and write the thesis. For a certain topic inside the robot project, the student should start immediately, without to get distracted by robot components that are not in the focus. Moreover, it should be possible to assume near-optimal performance of these components to evaluate the own work. To give an example: if a student should implement a new navigation algorithm, it is difficult to also consider obstacle detection from camera images. Obstacle detection on real robots often causes errors. As a result, the robot sometimes assumes obstacles at wrong positions. The correction of wrong obstacles would overload the student's project, but they would significantly falsify the evaluation of the navigation approach. This again shows the benefit of the simulation environments. The simulator can provide theoretically correct obstacle detection, as we can put the virtual sensors into error-free mode. In addition, the self-localization can also be set to be optimal. As a result, the students are able to separately test desired effects of the respective approach.

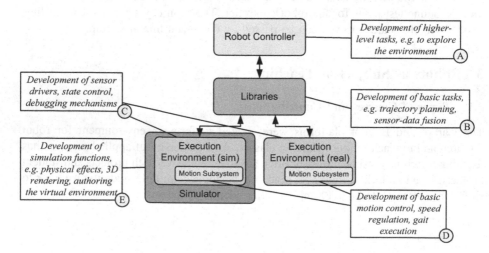

Fig. 6. The robot's software components and potential tasks for students

Figure 6 shows the software components that may be topic of a student's project. The robot controller was already described in Sect. 2.3. From the development point of view it provides a certain service but strongly relies on libraries and is firmly embedded into the runtime environment.

The *Libraries* are a collection of general-purpose functions for mobile robots. They are permanently extended by new projects. Currently, the following functions and algorithms are covered:

- mathematical basics often used for mobile robot projects, e.g. matrix computation, equation systems, zero points of functions, quaternions, Eigen values, covariances;
- geometric and graph functions also often used for mobile robots, e.g. Voronoi diagrams, visibility graphs, intersection of geometric primitives, clothoids, polygonal operations;
- navigation and path planning, e.g. grid based A* [9], trajectory planning, trajectory regulation [13];
- gait modeling and execution, e.g. Tripod, Ripple, Ample gait [14];
- world modeling, e.g. point clouds, spatial indexing [8];
- localization and mapping, e.g. ICP [2], Hector-SLAM [6];
- robot runtime access and life cycle control.

The *Execution Environment* contains access drivers, serial protocols and basic platform services such as logging and debugging. It also contains the *Motion Subsystem*, described in Sect. 2.1. Finally, the *Simulator* maybe subject of extensions by students, e.g. the physical simulation engine can be extended to simulate more effects.

The respective contributions (A)–(E) (Fig. 6) are distributed among the types of courses. At our faculty we have:

- Master thesis: 8 months, single student,
- Bachelor thesis: 5 months, single student,
- Student's project: 12 months, 3–5 students,
- Compulsory elective subject: 15 weeks, 15–30 students.

Table 2 shows the courses of the last years. We see (C) and (D) only rarely occur, as they are very special to our platforms and do not transport general knowledge about robotics. In addition, they are 'mission critical' – errors or problems would significantly hinder future projects. Thus until now, these components are usually developed by the teaching staff and considered as stable.

Contribution of type (A) is ideal for elective subjects over a single term. The benefit: the students build their software upon a stable and well-documented API. In particular they can fade out the structure of the platform and internal components. It also is possible to let the students re-implement available functions that already were integrated into the Libraries. E.g., in one course, the students had to realize a Robot Controller which was able to navigate through unknown environment. As this function already was realized, we deployed a reduced library that did not contain navigation facilities.

Theses mostly were of type (B). Here, we heavily made use of students' projects that also advanced our research – the students often realized new ideas or existing approaches as a basis for comparison with our research ideas.

Table 2. Overview of robot courses

Subject	Type of course	Contribution
Visual SLAM	Master thesis	Carbot (B)
Trajectory planning with clothoids	Master thesis	Carbot (B)
Probabilistic path planning	Master thesis	Carbot (B)
Visual obstacle recognition	Bachelor thesis	Carbot (B)
Vector-based navigation	Bachelor thesis	Carbot (B)
Trajectory regulation	Bachelor thesis	Carbot (B)
Feature extraction	Bachelor thesis	Bugbot & Carbot (B)
Efficient point cloud data structures	Bachelor thesis	Bugbot & Carbot (B)
Incremental navigation	Bachelor thesis	Carbot (B)
Positioning with ISOVIST features	Bachelor thesis	Bugbot & Carbot (B)
Grid-based Lidar-SLAM	Bachelor thesis	Bugbot & Carbot (B)
Kinematics simulation for arthropods	Bachelor thesis	Bugbot (E)
Dynamic simulated obstacles	Bachelor thesis	Carbot (E)
Robot motion building blocks	Student's project	Carbot (D)
Visual processing	Student's project	Carbot (C)
Robot navigation	Student's project	Carbot (B) & (E)
Simulation of a 3D camera view	Student's project	Carbot (E)
Integration of bullet physical engine	Student's project	Bugbot (E)
Programming a navigation tasks	Comp. Elect. subject	Carbot (A) & (B)
Programming an exploration tasks	Comp. Elect. subject	Carbot (A) & (B)

Type (E) also rarely occurs. Similar to the runtime environment, the simulator is a critical resource. Moreover, it is more difficult to identify appropriate internal interfaces. These however are required to define students' projects in a way to made them assessable later. Until now we only have the replacement of the rendering engine and physical engine as project of this type.

3.2   Lessons Learnt

According to our faculty rules, each professor has to evaluate her or his course from the didactical view. However, we did not get enough quantity for meaningful statistics about the special approach. In particular, the evaluation mainly covers teaching qualities (e.g. quality of textbook or slides), not the actual topic of mobile robotic. In addition, it is very difficult to compare the students' feed back between different types of course and the different types of contribution (A)–(E). Finally, even though we get a large total number of projects, the number for a certain combination still is low. Nevertheless, we got a good impression. In this section we will discuss some lessons learnt.

The simplicity of deployment and installation of the simulator was appreciated by students. If the project was to develop a robot-controller (contribution type (A)), the students just have to copy a single binary file (of type .jar) and can start their development and tests. Some students criticized the demands of the tools concerning computing power – actually older notebooks (often used by students) sometimes were too weak to smoothly run the simulator.

None of the courses generated noticeable problems with the robotic topic. In elective subjects all students successfully finished their project, however with different levels of software quality. As a large time of development was performed with the help of the simulator, the students welcomed the flexibility. In particular, the programming could easily be done in groups, partly at home, without waiting for access to the real robot. Also the debugging tools were positively received. Typical robot programs contain a number of threads without a traditional windows-based user interface. Thus, in particular the debug painting facility was a great benefit.

Debug painting is also used for the lecturer to evaluate a student's work. This also is usually very difficult, as the quality of a robot component can either only be evaluated as black box or by code inspection, both with certain drawbacks. If the lecturer requires to students to produce meaningful debug painting output, it is easier to get insights into the student's project and the involved data structures. However, students sometimes complained about the demand of meaningful debug painting output. This is, because this function does not belong to the application task in a closer meaning. Actually, on the real robot, there is no debug painting facility at all – the respective calls are redirected to empty procedures. Thus, debug painting usually means extra coding for the students.

From the teacher's view, the simulation tool also is a great facility. There are longer phases where the students can work without explicit supervision. This in particular is a great benefit, if we think about safety issues. Also costs of damaged parts or even completely damaged robots are an issue. In elective subjects, it is possible to only conduct final tests and presentations on the real robot – which then can easier be supervised by the lecturer.

It also turned out, we strongly benefit from a huge part of own developments. In the stressful time of a course, each interrupt is always a problem for students as well as for the lecturer. E.g. during the period of a Bachelor thesis, the student should not lose time because of technical problems. Deadlines are very tough. Thus, it is a great benefit to solve technical problems in a close loop. This would not be possible, if we strongly relied on third-party software, even if it was open source. Own developments also enable quick adaptations (even though sometimes 'quick and dirty') as a result of unpredicted new demands. These could be a result of adapting projects due to new insights after the course already has started.

The students also appreciated that the simulation may fade out real-world errors during testing and development. This allowed the students to first concentrate on their project's task. However, one student remarked that the navigation project of an elective subject was simplified too much and reminded to 'game development'. As a result, the lecturer must carefully decide, how to fine-tune the project and environment settings to meet the course demands.

Besides the benefits of the described approach, we also have to consider some drawbacks. The major drawback: the development of robots, runtime environments and in particular the simulators were very time-consuming. Until now we coded an amount of approx. 200 000 lines of code, of which only a small part of approx. 10% was contributed by students. Whenever students contribute, a lot of post-processing was required. This was, because the students often do not achieve the level of software quality as required when contributing to long-term libraries. Often, formal corrections were necessary concerning package structures or naming of packages or classes. As student projects usually run parallel, the platform evolved by one project before finishing another. Thus, a costly merge of versions was required. As a rule of thumb, students' contributions are more crucial when 'low-level' (i.e. (D) and (E)) – such work should be avoided as much as possible for student projects.

4   Conclusions

Teaching mobile robotics skills still is a demanding task. Due to the amount of connected fields, it is a challenge to get the students quickly to a point to achieve progress in their projects in the short time of an academic course. Our mobile robots Carbot and Bugbot with their environments form an appropriate basis for a lecturer to offer respective courses. In particular the simulators keep the technical, organizational and safety demands as well as costs under control. Moreover, they help the students to quickly start with their development and keep the hurdle low for first successful experiences with robot programming. Further testing facilities such as debug painting help the students to debug their programs and help the teacher to assess projects.

Dependent on the respective teaching targets, some tasks are still demanding, e.g. development concerning the robot's execution environment, sensor drivers or simulators. Here teachers have to bear serious integration efforts to keep the entire platform stable and manageable.

In the future we want to extend the platforms to more support deep learning technologies. Currently, most of the robot functions are realized in a traditional manner, in particular functions related to sensor data interpretation. We expect many of these functions will be provided by deep neural networks in the future.

References

1. Bagnall, B.: Maximum Lego NXT. Variant Press, Winnipeg (2012)
2. Besl, P.J.: A method for registration of 3-D shapes. IEEE Trans. Pattern Anal. Mach. Intell. **14**(2), 239–256 (1992)
3. Boeing, A., Bräun, T.: Evaluation of real-time physics simulation systems. In: 5th International Conference on Computer graphics and interactive techniques in Australia and Southeast Asia, pp. 281–288
4. Borenstein, J., Everett, H.R., Feng, L.: Where am I? Sensors and methods for mobile robot positioning. Univ Michigan **119**, 27 (1996)
5. Dupont, P.E.: Friction modeling in dynamic robot simulation. In: Proceedings, IEEE International Conference on Robotics and Automation, Cincinnati, 13–18 May 1990
6. Kohlbrecher, S., von Stryk, O., Meyer, J., Klingauf, U.: A flexible and scalable SLAM system with full 3D motion estimation. In: 2011 IEEE International Symposium on Safety, Security, and Rescue Robotics, Kyoto, Japan, 1–5 November 2011

7. Pepper, C., Balakirsky, S., Scrapper, C.: Robot simulation physics validation. In: PerMIS 2007 Proceedings of the 2007 Workshop on Performance Metrics for Intelligent Systems, Washington, D.C., 28–30 August 2007, pp. 97–104 (2007)
8. Pomerleau, F., Colas, F., Siegwart, R.: A Review of Point Cloud Registration Algorithms for Mobile Robotics. Now Publishers, Hanover (2015)
9. Roth, J.: Navigation durch Flächen. In: 13. GI/ITG KuVS Workshop on Location-Based Application and Services, Jena, Germany, 22, 23 September 2016 (in German)
10. Roth, J.: Carbot, Internal Technical Reference, Nuremberg Institute of Technology
11. Roth, J.: Bugbot Kinematics, Internal Technical Reference, Nuremberg Institute of Technology
12. Roth, J.: A novel development paradigm for event-based applications. In: International Conference on Innovations for Community Services (I4CS), Nuremberg, Germany, 8–10 July 2015, pp. 69–75. IEEE xplore (2015)
13. Roth, J.: A viterbi-like approach for trajectory planning with different Maneuvers. In: Strand, M., Dillmann, R., Menegatti, E., Ghidoni, S. (eds.) IAS 2018. AISC, vol. 867, pp. 3–14. Springer, Cham (2019). https://doi.org/10.1007/978-3-030-01370-7_1
14. Roth, J.: Systematic and Complete Enumeration of Statically Stable Multipod Gaits, under review
15. Yoshikawa, T.: Foundations of Robotics: Analysis and Control. MIT Press, Cambridge (2003)

Embedded Systems
for Teaching - Yrobot Evolution

Michal Hodoň[✉], Juraj Miček, Peter Ševčík, and Gabriel Koman

Faculty of Management Science and Informatics, University of Žilina,
Univerzitná 8215/1, 010 26 Žilina, Slovakia
michal.hodon@fri.uniza.sk

Abstract. Robotics and the development of information technologies represent
the trend of the 21st century, which affects all areas of human life. Education, or
learning process, in which efforts to educate younger age students in new
technologies could make a significant contribution to the next era of technological development, is no exception to the use of new technologies. The lim-
itation of education in Slovakia is the lack of financial resources for the
provision of modern educational tools. For this reason, the Yrobot platform was
developed within the project of the Technical Cybernetics Department at the
Faculty of Management Science and Informatics of the University in Žilina. The
Yrobot Platform has been successfully deployed in the educational process
of high schools in cooperation with the Pontis Foundation and Volkswagen
Slovakia. The gradual Yrobot platform development has created conditions for
more effective education of students in electronics, computer science and
computer engineering. This article presents the Yrobot platform development
and location in educational process in slovak schools.

Keywords: Robotics · Yrobot · Education

1 Introduction

The term robotics currently represents several research areas. One of these areas is also
social robotics or social robots [1]. Social Robotics involves engaging robots in certain
forms of social interaction with people using speech, gestures or other means of
communication [2]. The use of robots in social interaction positively helps meeting
their users' needs in different areas of human activities, for example, therapeutic help
for adults and children, etc. [1, 3, 4]. A major area of interest for the deployment and
use of robots is education. In this area, robots can be used to complement existing
teaching structures with aim to provide student support in the learning process (Baxter
et al. 2017). The use of robots in the learning process makes it easier for students to
engage in lessons realized during the process and also has a significant impact on their
social development [5]. The importance of using robots in the learning process is also
confirmed by studies that have shown that physical solutions in a kind of robot form
increase student interest more than their virtual analogies [6–8]. Robots are also perceived by students as better option in terms of interaction, what ultimately leads to a
change in behavior [9–11].

© Springer Nature Switzerland AG 2019
K.-H. Lüke et al. (Eds.): I4CS 2019, CCIS 1041, pp. 54–65, 2019.
https://doi.org/10.1007/978-3-030-22482-0_5

There are different robotic platforms on the market that can be used to support the learning process. Some of these platforms represent separate systems that bring different opportunities for education. For students, it is more attractive to learn literally by playing and testing a real ("live") thing that gives them immediate feedback. However, there are other known platforms (for example Arduino, RPi) that serve as a basis for robot creation but do not contain any moving elements (e.g. wheels, motors, etc.). In order to use these mechanical elements to support the educational process, a new Yrobot platform was developed at the Technical Cybernetics Department at the Faculty of Management Science and Informatics of the University of Žilina. This platform can be considered as a modular education system [12, 13].

This system is related to the idea of an educational system based on Open HW. On this platform, students can acquire primary knowledge and skills in electronics, computer science and computer engineering [14–16]. Students find it attractive when their knowledge during the learning process is demonstrated on a real device which blinks, moves, gives out sounds or any other kind of feedback to them. These facts are very important and positively influencing students' interest and motivation to create something practical and interesting even though this work takes a lot of time and learning challenging techniques to achieve the result [14]. In this context, the true robotic platforms of Open HW play an important role in the learning process [15]. For this reason, this platform has been interesting for developing the Yrobot solution. The difference between the typical OpenHW platform (such as Arduino or Raspberry PI, etc.) and Yrobot platform is, that Yrobot includes a motion subsystem that provides the presentation of the results of the implemented algorithms by direct mechanical expression.

The article presents the evolution of the Yrobot platform and its deployment in education in Slovakia.

2 Yrobot Evolution

Yrobot is a system developed at the Department of Technical Cybernetics of the Faculty of Management Science and Informatics of the University of Žilina to support the education of electronics, informatics, computer science and computer engineering, especially at high schools. An important element of this platform is the ability to work with an open hardware system, i.e., the system is not limited by manufacturer-defined applications and features. It is therefore possible to program and develop new applications or custom extensions. The Yrobot platform is also known in the community as a small robot with yellow wheels. Here you can see that the difference compared to other open platforms is in the opportunity of motion, which presents the algorithm defined by developers.

The central part of the Yrobot platform is represented by a simple 8-bit ATmega16 microcontroller. This microcontroller provides a lower degree of complexity in the development and programming of the Yrobot platform while ensuring communication with the appropriate peripherals of the platform. The choice of microcontrollers for the platform itself therefore corresponds to the requirements of simplicity and availability of development environment and peripherals that ensure effective communication with the environment. To the main components of the Yrobot platform belong:

- Signal LED diodes.
- Two seven-segment displays.
- Acustic signalization.
- Two engines with integrated gearbox. (1:48)
- Wheel angle sensing circuits that are based on CNY70 reflective sensors.
- Button sensors for obstacles detection.
- Power supply for the entire system, which is realized with a 7.5 V or 10 V DC adapter or two Li-Pol 3.7 V 2200 mAh batteries.
- Integrated USB AVR ISP programmer to program the Yrobot platform.

Due to technological advances, the Yrobot platform could be improved and adapted to the growing trend of device connectivity, in particular thanks to the development and price affordability of robotic platforms on the market.

2.1 Yrobot

The first version of the platform was designed in 2010, consisting only of a basement plate with a processor and a 7-segment display. Programming of this platform was realised with a serial port. The platform was later enriched by a temporary steel chassis that contained two engines from CD drives. The wheels for platform movement were adapted from a toy car. Gymnasium of Žilina on Hlinská 29 has shown the interest in this first version already, for the purposes of algorithms presentation on a real object in the educational process.

The new concept of the robotic platform for education support was designed in 2011 under the name of Robot George. This model had a modified design while the baseboard of the solution fulfilled the chassis function. The platform contained new custom-made wheels, which did not allow developers to produce large numbers of robots through serial production. This deficiency was also the reason that led developers to build their own platform. It was caused in particular to by the lack of price-affordable robotic platforms in 2011. Another reason for the development of their own platform was the inconsistency of the available robotic platforms with the requirements and ideas of developers about an open system that was maintained and expanded by the community of high school students.

The Yrobot concept was created in 2012. This concept responded to pedagogical requirements and new development trends. In 2013, the Yrobot prototype was created, which was modified in 2014 in several of today's well-known forms. One of the main changes in this version was also the replacement of the USB connector for programming and adding other robot features. The final version of the Yrobot platform is shown in Fig. 1.

Fig. 1. Yrobot – version 2014

For this platform, additional, different superstructures have been developed that have been designed and created in collaboration with high school students and independent candidates. At the Department of Technical Cybernetics, superstructures were developed to allow a platform:

- Respond to light.
- Detect CO in the air.
- Measure temperature and humidity.
- Broadcast and receive sound.
- Record a video.

These superstructures were put into the educational process and, on their basis, to the students were presented the possibilities of developing Yrobot.

2.2 MYrobot

Given the changing market demands, the Yrobot platform had to be modified. In addition to embedded systems, there are various areas of interest in the market that significantly influence technological developments such as Artificial Intelligence, the Internet of Things, Multi Agent System, and so on [17–19]. In order to ensure the continuity of the learning process in interaction with technological development, it was necessary to modify the Yrobot platform, which enabled the platform to be controlled using the mobile device with Android OS system. A new version of the Yrobot - Myrobot platform (modified Yrobot) was created. The reason for this new platform formation was also to increase students' interest in applications developing for a large number of smart devices on the market. The potential of mobile devices in present is, in particular, to integrate a number of subsystems that can be used in the development of non-traditional applications.

The functionality of the Yrobot platform has been extended with two basic working modes for the MYrobot platform. The first represents a wired connection mode where the smartphone is mounted directly on the platform and with the USB interface communicates and controls the movement of the platform. The second working mode, wireless, provides communication and platform control over Bluetooth. Since the platform is controlled with a mobile device, for the performance of the MCU are very small and are related mainly to interpreting commands for motor movement, sharing information about bends and obstacles. Due to these facts, the MYrobot platform includes these main components:

- ATmega328 microcontroller.
- FT232 USB/UART converter, alternating with HC-05 Bluetooth module.
- Dual H-bridge DRV8833 for control of two DC gear motors.
- Turns sensing circuitry based on CNY70 reflective optical sensors.
- TCRT1000 reflective sensors for obstacles detection.
- Two Lion batteries 18650 with DC/DCconverter.
- The user button can be used for another feedback functions.

In the context of deploying this platform to the learning process, several examples and functions of the MYrobot platform have been developed. These functions for education purposes include:

- Define a robot's route from point A to point B, create a photo, and return to the original position.
- Robot remote control through the internet.
- Send a robot to a specific location with the task of creating video or audio record, and other tasks.

The modified Yrobot platform along with the attached mobile device is shown in Fig. 2.

Fig. 2. Modified Yrobot platform

At present, mobile devices, and especially smartphones, are not only a communication platform, but they are also devices with a complex operating system that provides a number of additional services to the user. The technological progress in the field of mobile devices may be supposed also in the future, so for this reason developers perceive that MYrobot platform as a fun form of developing and presenting applications for modern intelligent smart devices.

2.3   MYrobot

Due to the development in area of mobile devices and the participation of the Department of Technical Cybernetics in the Internet of Things, the modified MYrobot platform was developed to the IoTrobot platform. This platform is based on the idea of implementing a mobile IoT node. The platform was also complemented by an application connector through which the IoT node can be connected to the mobile platform. The connection of IoT and mobile platform opens up new opportunities for developing interesting and fun applications and features such as coordinating multirobotic system activities to meet the task, field exploration, effective environmental monitoring, and so on. The IoTRobot mobile platform is shown in Fig. 3.

Fig. 3. Modified platform IoTrobot

As a result of the mobile devices development, it is clear that the mobile platform complemented by the application connector for the IoT extension module expands the area of solved tasks and enables the development of interesting applications from the mobile sensor field. The modified IoT robot platform is developed on the basis of the 8-bit microcontroller ATmega238P, which controls all platform components. The movement of the platform is ensured by the double H-bridge DRV8833, with which the microcontroller controls the speed of two unidirectional motors. Wheel rotation information microcontroller acquires through two magnetoresistive sensors MRS1 and 2. The intensity of the magnetic flux generated by the magnetic strips glued on the inside of each wheel reads the integrated sensors. The block diagram of the IoTrobot mobile robotic platform is shown in Fig. 4.

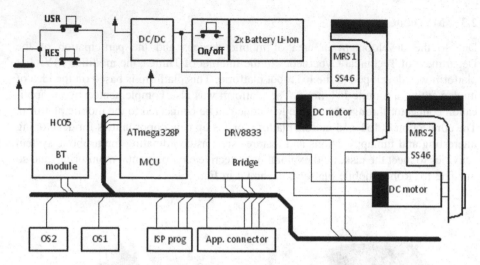

Fig. 4. IoTrobot mobile robotic platform block diagram

The communication between the microcontroller and the Bluetooth module HC05 is secured through the serial communication interface USART MCU. At present for Bluetooth (BL) communication it is possible to use the BL ESP32 module subsystem, which is part of the IoT32 module, so HC05 is available only on request. Two reflective optical sensors are located at the front of the platform to identify obstacles. The device has three buttons RES-restart MCU, USR, i.e. a user button whose function is given by the program, and an on/off button. The MCU can be easily programmed using a standard USBASP programmer connected to a 6-pin ISP connector. The entire platform is powered by two Li-Ion batteries in 18650 case. The application connector serves to extend the system with additional application modules. Nowadays, the IoT32 module is developed and its block diagram is illustrated in Fig. 5.

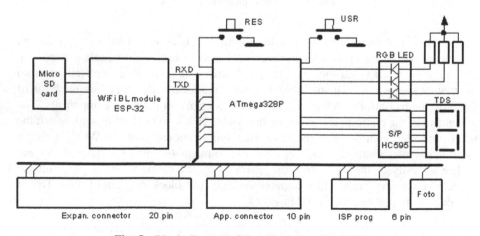

Fig. 5. Block diagram of the robotic module IoT32

The IoT32 module is a sensory node that allows you to scan the selected quantities, pre-process them and send them to the communication network via WiFi or BL. The module contains the control communication subsystem MCU-ATmega328P that consists of an ESP32 module. The module contains indication elements (RGB diode), 7-segment LED display, sensory subsystem (light intensity, temperature), external storage medium (MSD card). The module is powered from a robotic platform via a connector labelled as App.connector. It communicates with the platform using the ISP interface, or SWUART. It is possible to use the module IoT32 autonomous also, but then it is necessary to ensure its power supply with expansion connector, or from the programmer USBASP (ISP prog.).

Thanks to the simple change of the program, this concept provides enough flexibility and at the same time supports the development of a wide range of IoT applications to support the learning process.

2.4   Additional Modules to the Yrobot Platform

As part of Yrobot platform evolution, in addition to the IoT32 module, other modules have been developed and they can be integrated across all YRobot platforms and used by users and pedagogues in the context of specific learning processes (e.g., communication protocols development, audio signal capture, IoT applications and similar).

One of the additional modules developed for the Yrobot platform is the Audiomodule, which allows you to capture audio signals. Audiomodule allows development of applications based on digital processing of the measured signal. From the simplest applications, such as sound intensity measurement to more complex, such as robot acoustic communication. The audiomodule is attached to the robotic platform via an application connector located at the front of the platform. The application connector is one-row with eight outlets. The assignment of connector terminals to individual signals is shown in Fig. 6.

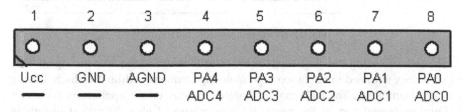

Fig. 6. Application controller

For the audiomodule and microcontroller communication three power outlets and a common ground can be used, the remaining outputs (4 to 8) are used as follows:

- Terminal 4 – PA4/ADC4 enables the control of the signalling light diode D1. If the terminal MCU is set up to output regime (bit DDRA4 = 1), then with logical null record into the bit PORTD4 is possible to light up the diode D1 and with log. 1 record to turn off the diode.

- Terminals 5, 6, 7 – PA3/ADC3, PA2/ADC2 and PA1/ADC1 enable to control the acoustic signal amplification.
- Terminal 8 – PA0/ADC0 represents the zero input of an analogue switch, which is the part of MCU and is located in front of analog-to-digital converter.
- The block diagram of the audiomodule is shown in Fig. 7 and consists of the following blocks:
- Electret microphone is designed to transform acoustic pressure into electrical voltage.
- Correction preamplifier amplifies the small output voltage from the microphone and corrects its frequency dependence on the scanned signal frequency.
- Amplifier with adjustable amplification, allows to customize the audiomodule of varying intensity of the recorded sound.
- Low-pass filters reduce the frequency range of the processed signal.

Low-pass filters 1 a 2 are designed as Butterworth filters second order with a break frequency 3600 Hz. They are realized with Sallen-Key topology. Low-pass filter 3 is first order passive filter with break frequency 4020 Hz.

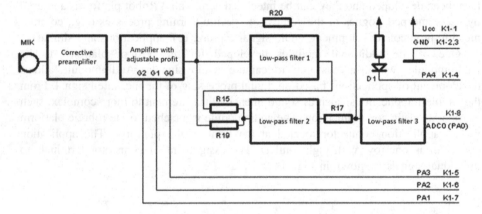

Fig. 7. Block audiomodule diagram

The task of analog low-pass filters is to limit the width of the acoustic signal zone so that it does not need to select too high sampling frequency while it is discreditizing over time (sampling). The audiomode is located directly on the application connector platform, in frontal part of the robot. For this reason, it also detects all disturbing sounds generated by the moving robot (motors, wheels, vibrations). All this can significantly exceed the level of the useful acoustic signal (operator commands, signals from the second robot's acoustic signal, and so on). For this reason, it is advisable to carry out the first applications when the robot does not move.

Other modules that extend the features of Yrobot platforms are modules for wireless connection such as the bluetooth module (Y-BT) and wifi module (Y-WiFi).

Platform Yrobot and module Y-BT interconnection provides the communication interface USART. The connection of USART connectors of Yrobot modules is as follows:

- Pin VIN on Y-BT with connector VIN on module Yrobot.
- Pin TXD on Y-BT with connector TXD on module Yrobot.
- Pin RXD on Y-BT with connector RXD on module Yrobot.
- Pin GND on Y-BT with connector GND on module Yrobot.

The communication between Yrobot platform and module Y-WiFi is provided by SPI or communication interface USART. The Y-WiFi module is designed to be directly connected to the Yrobot platform without additional cables.

Stated additional modules extend the features of the original Yrobot platform and open new opportunities in algorithm creation to developers and users for providing education using modern approaches and methods that are defined by the marketplace and enable them to acquire the technical knowledge and skills that are usable in current practice.

3 Conclusion

The area of interest in using the Yrobot platform to support education are high schools in Slovakia. The effort of this platform developers' team is to encourage students' interest in electronics, programming and computer engineering, what will ultimately create a community of active members with an interest in robotics, open hardware, and joint education in these areas. Due to the Yrobot platform development it is obvious that the developers of this platform have seen its success in the educational process in Slovakia. This fact is confirmed by the location of the Yrobot platform in education at 24 schools in the Slovak Republic. These schools purchased the Yrobot platform for educational purposes, or they gained it thanks to the partnership with the Faculty of Management Science and Informatics. Figure 8 shows a map of schools in Slovakia where the Yrobot Learning Support Platform is located.

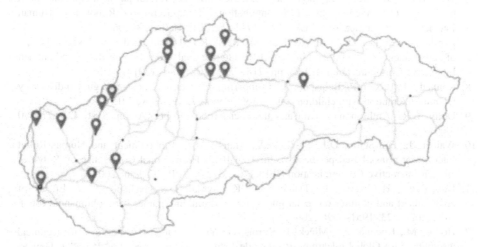

Fig. 8. Map of schools in the SR using the Yrobot Platform for education

Based on the successful Yrobot platform implementation and testing at schools, it is possible to assume the importance of this platform in the educational process also in the future. In order to support a more intense implementation of the Yrobot platform, it is necessary to extend in particular the set of examples, capabilities and functions of the current platform and to modify the platform according to the needs and direction of the market, i.e. in Mobile Applications, the Internet of Things, Industry 4.0 etc. At the same time, it is necessary to create a community of platform users who are the source of new ideas and interesting solutions for using and developing the Yrobot platform. The team of Yrobot developers assumes that the ongoing development and modification of the Yrobot platform is a way to expand the community of people interested in this platform, which can ultimately lead to a more robust implementation of the Yrobot platform within the educational process focusing on electronics, informatics and computer engineering also at other schools in the Slovak Republic.

References

1. Conti, D., Nuovo, S.N., Buono, S., Nuovo, A.D.: Robots in education and care of children with developmental disabilities: a study on acceptance by experienced and future professionals. Int. J. Soc. Robot. **9**, 51–62 (2017)
2. Fong, T., Nourbakhsh, I., Dautenhahn, K.: A survey of socially interactive robots. Robot Auton. Syst. **42**, 143–166 (2003)
3. Feil-Seifer, D., Mataric, M.J.: Defining socially assistive robotics. In: IEEE 9th International Conference on Rehabilitation Robotics, pp. 465–468. IEEE, Chicago (2005)
4. Sridhar, A.N., Briggs, T.P., Kelly, J.D., Nathan, S.: Training in robotic surgeryan overview. Curr. Urol. Rep. **18**, 1–8 (2017)
5. Baxter, P., Ashurst, E., Read, R., Kennedy, J., Belpaeme, T.: Robot education peers in a situated primary school study: personalisation promotes child learning. Public Libr. Sci. **12**, 1–23 (2017)
6. Wainer, J., Feil-seifer, D.J., Shell, D.A., Mataric, M.J.: The role of physical embodiment in human-robot interaction. In: IEEE International Symposium on Robot and Human Interactive Communication (IEEE), pp. 117–122. IEEE, Hatfield (2006)
7. Looije, R., Van Der Zalm, A., Neerincx, M., Beun, R.J.: Help, I need some body: the effect of embodiment on playful learning. In: IEEE International Workshop on Robot and Human Interactive Communication (IEEE), pp. 718–724. IEEE, Paris (2012)
8. Kennedy, J., Baxter, P., Belpaeme, T.: Comparing robot embodiments in a guided discovery learning interaction with children. Int. J. Soc. Robot. **7**, 293–308 (2015)
9. Duffy, B.R.: Anthropomorphism and the social robot. Robot. Auton. Syst. **42**, 177–190 (2003)
10. Wainer, J., Feil-Seifer, D.J., Shell, D.A., Matari, M.J.: Embodiment and Human-Robot Interaction: a task-based perspective. In: 16th IEEE International Conference on Robot & Human Interactive Communication (IEEE), pp. 872–877. IEEE, Jeju (2007)
11. Kose-Bagci, H., Ferrari, E., Dautenhahn, K., Syrdal, D.S., Nehaniv, C.L.: Effects of embodiment and gestures on social interaction in drumming games with a humanoid robot. Adv. Robot. **23**, 1951–1996 (2009)
12. Hodoň, M., Kochláň, M., Miček, J., Karpiš, O.: Yrobot. Open HW platform for technical disciplines. In: Global e-learning (Centro de Estudios Financieros), pp. 257–274. Universidad a distancia de madrid, Madrid (2015)

13. Kochláň, M., Hodoň, M.: Open hardware modular educational robotic platform - Yrobot. In: 23rd international conference on robotics in Alpe-Adria-Danube region, pp. 1–6. Institute of Electrical and Electronics Engineers Inc., Smolenice, Slovakia (2016)
14. Yoon, H.: A relation between young children's computer utilization and their use of education robots. In: 6th International Conference on Human-Robot, Lausanne, Switzerland, pp. 291–292 (2011)
15. Wang, W.: A mini experiment of offering STEM education to several age groups through the use of robots. In: 6th IEEE Integrated STEM Education Conference, Princeton, NJ, USA, pp. 120–127 (2016)
16. Mandoda, F., Bonani, M., Riedo, F.: Bringing robotics to formal education: the Thymio open-source hardware robot. IEEE Robot. Autom. Mag. **24**, 77–85 (2017)
17. Tornow, M., Al-Hamadi, A., Borrmann, V.: A multi-agent mobile robot system with environment perception and HMI capabilities. In: International Conference on Signal and Image Processing Applications, Melaka, Malaysia, pp. 252–257 (2013)
18. Chovanec, M., Cechovic, L., Mandak, L.: Aeris - robotics laboratory with dynamics environment. Adv. Intell. Syst. Comput. **457**, 169–180 (2016)
19. Hodoň, M., Miček, J., Kochláň, M.: Networking extension module for Yrobot - a modular educational robotic platform. Adv. Intell. Syst. Comput. **457**, 159–167 (2016)

Smart Contract Based Decentralized Parking Management in ITS

Pranav Kumar Singh[1,2]([✉]), Roshan Singh[2], Sunit Kumar Nandi[1,3],
and Sukumar Nandi[1]

[1] Department of CSE, Indian Institute of Technology Guwahati,
Guwahati 781039, India
sunitnandi834@gmail.com, sukumar@iitg.ac.in
[2] Department of CSE, Central Institute of Technology Kokrajhar,
Kokrajhar 783370, Assam, India
snghpranav@gmail.com, roshansingh3000@gmail.com
[3] Department of CSE, National Institute of Technology, Arunachal Pradesh,
Papum Pare 791112, India

Abstract. Providing a better experience to the drivers is one of the core objectives of implementing Intelligent Transportation Systems (ITS). ITS aims to offer a range of services for making the life of drivers more comfortable. However, the way these ITS related services are implemented until now is centralized and is somewhat cumbersome. Centralized approach for implementing ITS services make the customers and the stakeholders of the services trust and depend on various intermediaries. Moreover, such an approach is often prone to a single point of failure which affects the availability of the services. Decentralized technologies such as Blockchain and Smart Contracts can help address such issues. In this paper, we study the scope of Blockchain Technology in implementing ITS related services. We design a decentralized system for Parking Management in ITS using Smart Contracts. We implement our proposed system on the Ethereum blockchain platform to demonstrate its feasibility.

1 Introduction

With the rise in the number of smart vehicles on the road, Intelligent Transportation Systems (*ITS*) is becoming a necessity. *ITS* is the application of information and communication technologies which enhances transportation safety, mobility, reduces traffic congestions and pollution [17]. *ITS* provide drivers better driving experience by providing a range of communication services such as travel and traffic management services, electronic payment services and infotainment services to name a few. With time the number of smart vehicles on the road is increasing, and so the parking-related problem is [6]. The problem is much more prominent in urban areas where finding space for parking is much more difficult and frustrating to the drivers. Often drivers need to circle a parking area several times before finding a vacant lot to park their vehicle. It is one of the major causes of increasing traffic congestion and air pollution in cities.

To counter the problem of parking, many parking management systems have been developed over the years. These systems provide real-time parking lot availability status with features of booking these parking lots by the users. Most of these systems are centralized which make the drivers dependent upon the service providers for accessing the services. These centralized systems do not provide drivers with the flexibility of comparing the services provided by various parking lot providers such as the parking charges charged by different parking zones within a locality. Also, the installation and management of such systems are costly. However, there has not been much work done in implementing *ITS* related services such as parking service using decentralized technologies like Blockchain [4]. In the future, there will be a high demand for efficient and robust parking services because of urbanization. Thus, this paper presents a decentralized approach for efficient parking management using blockchain and smart contracts.

2 Related Work

There exist a significant number of work done for parking management using technologies such as Wi-Fi, WSNs and RFID. In [10], the authors propose an RFID based parking management system for handling the management, controlling, transaction reporting and operation tasks for parking lots. Works exploring WSNs for parking management can be found in [12,15], and [18]. In [12], the authors describe an intelligent car parking system with low-cost WSN. An integrated approach of using WSN along with the web-based application for parking management is described in [15]. A Wi-Fi and WSN based approach for parking management is discussed in [16]. The system uses WSN for identifying vacant lots and Wi-Fi for navigation. The development in the field of IoT in recent years has drawn the attention of the research community as well as industry. Some popular works based on IoT can be found in [3,5,14]. A VANET based parking system is proposed in [7]. In [1], authors proposed a new decentralized architecture where the intelligence is deployed in a distributed manner to achieve scalability. The authors [8] introduced an agent-based simulation system and constructed a framework of parking charge and reservation. With this framework, the authors analyzed comprehensive benefit and comparison of charges and reservation mechanisms for parking. However, we could not find much significant contribution in the domain of parking management systems using decentralized technologies such as blockchain [2]. We believe that blockchain technology along with smart contracts has the potential to felicitate security (from inside and outside attack), availability, reliability, and trust in the parking systems. To this end, our proposal is one such contribution.

3 Background

In this section, we briefly describe *ITS* architecture and give an overview of the blockchain, smart contracts and Ethereum the technologies used in our system.

3.1   ITS Architecture

ITS architecture provides a common framework for planning, defining, and integrating intelligent transportation systems. It specifies how the different *ITS* components would interact with each other to solve transportation related problems. It identifies and describes various functions and assigns responsibilities to multiple stakeholders of the system. The *ITS* architecture facilitates in implementing a broad range of services such as route guidance, e-payments, traffic control, etc. Fig. 1 shows the architecture of an ITS.

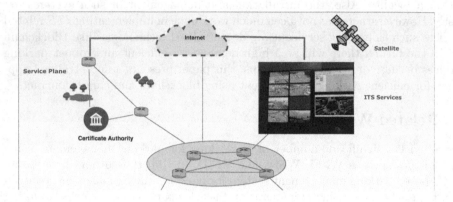

Fig. 1. ITS architecture

3.2   Blockchain

A blockchain as its name suggests is a sequence of blocks where each block is linked with its previous one. The blocks are linked with each other using cryptographic hashes. Blockchain gained popularity with the introduction of Bitcoin [9], a decentralized peer to peer cryptocurrency. A block is formed of zero or more data elements known as transactions and is created by certain special nodes in the network called as miner nodes. It uses Public Key Infrastructure (*PKI*) for the verification of the transactions. A blockchain is an append-only ledger where the data can only be added in a sequence. This property of the blockchain makes the data on the blockchain immutable. A blockchain is maintained by a network of nodes. Each full node on the network maintains a local copy of the global blockchain. Every time when a new block comes in the network the full node checks for the validity of the block by verifying the transactions in the block. If the block is found to be valid, the full node updates its local copy of the blockchain by adding the block onto the chain. This procedure is performed by all the full nodes in the network. Decentralization is another unique feature of the blockchain. A blockchain will continue to function even if a single miner node exists in the system. That's the reason blockchain based systems provide high availability. A blockchain can be used to establish trust among set untrusted nodes. Blockchain assumes the nodes in the network to be untrusted. It utilizes a consensus mechanism to make these untrusted node agree on one particular state of the blockchain.

3.3 Smart Contracts

Smart Contracts [11] are a bunch of self-executable code sitting on top of a blockchain. It consists of well-defined conditions and their corresponding actions. The condition specifies the actions to be performed when it turns out to be true. A smart contract works on the data present on the blockchain. It is also immutable that means once deployed on the chain the content of the contract cannot be changed. This ensures bias-free implementation of the contract which helps to minimize the need for trust.

3.4 Ethereum Framework

Ethereum [13] is a public blockchain platform. Unlike Bitcoin blockchain, Ethereum supports smart contracts. That means snippets of code can be written and deployed on the Ethereum blockchain. The Ethereum blockchain is based upon state transition model, where each node executes a set of transactions in the same order to reach a common consensus.

Ethereum also facilitates to run its private and permission instance of the blockchain. Ethereum blockchain supports two kinds of accounts: externally owned account and contract account. Externally owned account (EOA) are those accounts which are owned by the users of the system. These accounts are capable of sending and receiving ether to another EOA or a contract account. The contract account is an address where the smart contract code resides.

4   System Model

Our system model as shown in Fig. 2 consists of the Traffic Authority (TA), Road Side Units ($RSUs$) an On-Board Unit (OBU) which is built in the vehicle, and an IoT device placed in the parking lot. The TA deploys the smart contract on the blockchain. A Graphical User Interface (GUI) is provided at the vehicle end for interacting with the smart contract (SC). Our system also has an entity named Parking Zone Manager (PZM). PZM is the owner of a parking zone. A parking zone can have one or more parking lots.

Similarly, a PZM can be an individual or an organization. PZM can set the charges of the parking lot which it owns. All the payments in the system are done with the help of a cryptocurrency ether this is the only unit of exchange in our system. The $RSUs$ deployed by the TA are responsible for maintaining the blockchain. The RSUs maintain the blockchain by performing a computationally expensive procedure called mining. Mining refers to the process of solving certain cryptographic problems for generating the blocks of the blockchain. Beside the $RSUs$, the $PZMs$ can also install their mining equipment and can contribute to maintaining the blockchain by participating in the mining procedure thus making the system truly decentralized.

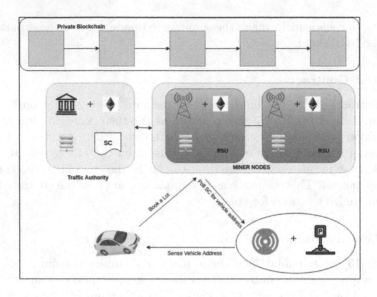

Fig. 2. Proposed system model

5   Implementation

The core logic of the implementation is based on the smart contract, which in the real world can be deployed by the TA. The smart contract logic of our implementation is explained as follows. The *TA* adds a parking zone along with the *PZM* of the zone onto the blockchain by calling the method *configurePZ*. A driver can poll the blockchain to get the information about different parking zones available in a particular area by using the ZIP/PIN code of the area. For this, our contract provides a getter method called *checkAvailiabilty*. Depending upon its choice and availability a driver can book a parking lot by calling *book-MyLot*. On being called the method results in a successful transaction if there exist enough parking lots available in the parking zone; otherwise, the transaction gets reverted. In the case of a successful transaction, the vehicle is allocated a lot in the parking zone. The vehicle is also provided with a randomly generated passkey which it has to use for entering into the parking lot. The parking lot is equipped with an IoT device which continuously polls the smart contract for checking the address of the vehicle and the provided passkey. If the address and the passkey provided by the vehicle trying to park in the lot matches with the credentials of the vehicle in the *SC* which has booked the lot then the vehicle is allowed to park otherwise not. The smart contract maintains a timer to specify the duration of time the parking lot was occupied by the vehicle. The timer starts as soon as the vehicle books a lot and ends when it exists from the lot. A vehicle can exit a lot by calling the method *exitParking*. Upon resulting in a successful transaction the timer associated with the vehicle gets off and the parking lot occupied by the vehicle in the contract gets free. The vehicle can now pay the parking bill. It checks the amount to be paid by invoking the method *myParkingBill*. The method returns the amount to be paid as the bill in ether (the cryptocurrency unit provided on Ethereum blockchain). In our proposed system the parking bill to be paid is calculated as follows.

$$ParkingBill = Duration\ of\ Parking * Rate\ of\ Parking$$

After getting the parking bill the driver can pay the bill by invoking the method *payMyBill*. Our smart contract restricts further booking of parking lots by the driver of a vehicle if the vehicle has got pending dues. Our smart contract also provides the facility of canceling a booked lot by a driver. However, to deal with the notorious drivers trying to book and cancel the lots uselessly, we have taken certain preventive measures.

- A booked lot can only be canceled by a vehicle which has booked it. The *SC* specifies the duration during which the cancellation of the reserved lot can be made. A driver cannot cancel a reserved lot beyond a threshold duration of time.
- To discourage any vehicle from frequent canceling of lots we also imposed a cancellation charge.

A *PZM* is allowed to make changes in the parking rate via the *SC* only. It can increase or decrease the parking rates. For this *PZM* needs to notify the upcoming changes prior to its implementation. To curb the menace of a *PZM* who often fluctuates the parking rates, we incorporate appropriate logic in the smart contract that restricts the *PZM* to make frequent changes in the rates.

6 Experimental Setup

We demonstrate the feasibility of our system with a prototype implementation using the Ethereum blockchain platform. We run a private and permissioned instance of the blockchain. The proposed system consists of three types of nodes, i.e., full nodes, light nodes, and miner nodes.

- Full Node: A full node is a node on the blockchain network which has the full copy of the blockchain downloaded and available. It has all the blocks available locally starting from the genesis block. It is required for the full node to have sufficient storage space to accommodate these blocks. In our system *RSU*s and the TA are considered as full nodes.
- Miners: A miner is a full node on the blockchain network that participates in the creation of blocks. Miners compete with each other to generate a block, usually by solving some complex cryptographic problems. Since miners invest their resources for maintaining the blockchain they are incentivized with mining rewards. The stability and immutability of a blockchain highly depend upon the miners present in the network. In our system *RSU*s are considered to be the miners, whereas TA can participate in the mining procedure voluntarily.

– Light Nodes: A light node is a node on the blockchain network that does not have an entire copy of the blockchain but gets the part it cares about from someone it trusts. This allows users to transact on the blockchain without downloading an entire copy of the blockchain. It's always suggested for the low capacity devices to join as a light node to be a part of the blockchain network.

Table 1. Devices and their Role

Device name	No. of device	Geth version	Role
Dell-Vostro (8 GB RAM, i7-7700 CPU, 1 TB HDD)	1	v1.8.17-stable release	RSU/TA
Lenovo G-5080 laptop (4 GB RAM, Intel Core i5 processor, 1 TB HDD)	1	geth-linux-amd64-1.8.22	RSU
Raspberry Pi 3	1	geth 1.8.18 ARMv7	Vehicle OBU
nodeMCU	1		IoT device

In our proposed system, *TA* and the *RSU*s are the full nodes, *RSU*s are also considered as the miner nodes whereas the *OBU* installed in the vehicle is deemed to be as a light node. Figure 3 illustrates the setup containing 2 full/miner nodes. As shown in Figs. 4 and 5, we use Raspberry Pi as the *OBU* of the vehicle and a nodeMCU (a micro-controller unit with onboard Wi-Fi module) as an IoT device at the parking lot, respectively. We used D-Link WiFi for connecting these devices. For writing the *SC*, we used Solidity (a programming language for writing smart contracts on Ethereum blockchain). We use the Remix integrated development environment (IDE), a browser-based IDE for compiling and testing the *SC*. Table 1 lists the devices used and their roles in our implementation.

We performed experiments on our setup blockchain network where a driver books a parking lot using the provided web-based GUI in the vehicle. For accessing the GUI, we use a display screen which is connected to the Raspberry Pi acting as the *OBU* of the vehicle. We developed a web-based GUI application as shown in Fig. 6 for the driver to book the lots and perform other transactions.

The GUI communicates with the Ethereum blockchain using web3.js API. The booking results in a transaction that is mined by our miner nodes. We modeled the parking lot scenario with the help of led indicators which are connected with the nodeMCU acting as an IoT device at the parking lot. Initially, when the lot is free for parking a red indicator glows continuously.

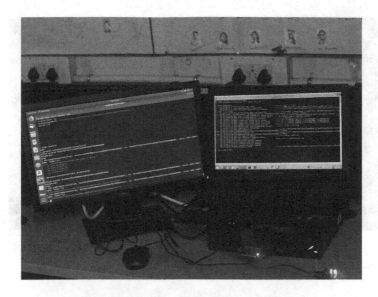

Fig. 3. Full node and miner setup

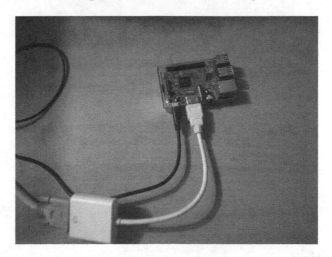

Fig. 4. Vehicle OBU

The IoT device continuously polls the SC to get the booking status of the lot. A vehicle which has booked the lot approaches the parking lot and calls the method *enterLot* if the address and the passkey provided by the vehicle matches with the values stored in the smart contract then the red led turns off and the green led glows indicating the vehicle to park in the lot.

Fig. 5. IoT device at parking lot

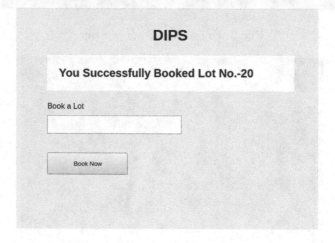

Fig. 6. GUI at the vehicle end

7   Evaluation

We evaluate our blockchain and smart contract based decentralized approach for parking management by comparing it with existing traditional approaches and by analyzing the performance of the system:

7.1   Comparative Analysis:

1. Transparency and Immutability: All the procedures involved in our developed system are committed on the blockchain as in the form of mined transactions. With our system, neither it is possible for the driver for parking its vehicle

without paying the parking fees, nor it is possible for the *PZM* to charge higher rates for parking.

2. Availability: As compared to the centralized approach our system always guarantee the availability of service as long as a full node exit in the system. This ensures that one can always do a transaction with our system.
3. Trust: In traditional approaches, the parties involved in the parking scenario need to trust each other. These parties are highly untrusted and often try to cheat each other. Like the *PZM* who may be greedy about higher parking rates to have more income. The facility provided by our system to the drivers for comparing and choosing parking lots help to eliminate blind trust on these untrusted parties.

7.2 Performance Analysis

We analyze the performance of our system by evaluating the average throughput. We consider throughput as the number of successful transactions per second starting from the first transaction deployment time.

Average throughput is calculated as an average of throughput over execution time. Figure 7 shows average throughput plot. The average throughput was calculated over the batch of 1, 10, 50, 100, 250, 500, 750, 1000, 1100, 1200, 1300, 1400 and 1500 transactions. The transactions were executed on our blockchain network is maintained by two miner nodes as shown in Fig. 3. All the transactions were of type *bookMyLot*. The average was calculated over five independent runs for each set of transactions. The average throughput for a set of 1 transaction was found to be 0.423 and 12.33 for a set of 1500 transactions.

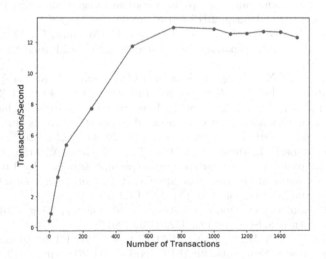

Fig. 7. Average throughput

8 Conclusion

In this paper, we proposed a decentralized approach for parking management using blockchain and smart contracts. We implemented our proposed system on an Ethereum private network. Our proposed system help drivers find the best parking lot of their choice. At the same time, it also helps various *PZM*s by providing them with a common platform to get more vehicles to use their parking area thus helping them to generate more money. The approach also does not need any sensing requirement at the parking lot for letting the vehicle in and out. All of these objectives are achieved with the smart contract itself. We find that the use of smart contracts and blockchain help reduce blind trust upon untrusted parties and increase the availability of the service. The system will remain decentralized as long as not more than 50% of the nodes maintaining the blockchain are compromised. Our system guarantees decentralization and high availability of services as it is practically infeasible for an attacker to gain control over more than half of the nodes in an ITS scenario. However, the lower transaction throughput and the power consuming PoW based consensus mechanism used for maintaining Ethereum blockchain can be a bottleneck in its public grade implementation. As future work, we will try to integrate more features in our current system and will introduce more decentralized *ITS* related services. We will also explore other low power consuming consensus mechanism for implementation.

References

1. Alam, M., et al.: Real-time smart parking systems integration in distributed its for smart cities. J. Adv. Transp. **2018** (2018)
2. Amato, G., Carrara, F., Falchi, F., Gennaro, C., Meghini, C., Vairo, C.: Deep learning for decentralized parking lot occupancy detection. Expert Syst. Appl. **72**, 327–334 (2017)
3. Kong, X.T., Xu, S.X., Cheng, M., Huang, G.Q.: Iot-enabled parking space sharing and allocation mechanisms. IEEE Trans. Autom. Sci. Eng. **99**, 1–11 (2018)
4. Kosba, A., Miller, A., Shi, E., Wen, Z., Papamanthou, C.: Hawk: The blockchain model of cryptography and privacy-preserving smart contracts. In: 2016 IEEE Symposium on Security and Privacy (SP), pp. 839–858. IEEE (2016)
5. Kubler, S., Robert, J., Hefnawy, A., Cherifi, C., Bouras, A., Främling, K.: IoT-based smart parking system for sporting event management. In: Proceedings of the 13th International Conference on Mobile and Ubiquitous Systems: Computing, Networking and Services, pp. 104–114. ACM (2016)
6. Lin, T., Rivano, H., Le Mouël, F.: A survey of smart parking solutions. IEEE Trans. Intell Transp. Syst. **18**(12), 3229–3253 (2017)
7. Lu, R., Lin, X., Zhu, H., Shen, X.: SPARK: a new VANET-based smart parking scheme for large parking lots. In: IEEE INFOCOM 2009, pp. 1413–1421. IEEE (2009)
8. Mei, Z., Feng, C., Ding, W., Zhang, L., Wang, D.: Better lucky than rich? Comparative analysis of parking reservation and parking charge. Transp. Policy **75**, 47–56 (2019)

9. Nakamoto, S., et al.: Bitcoin: a peer-to-peer electronic cash system (2008)
10. Pala, Z., Inanc, N.: Utilizing RFID for smart parking applications. Facta Univ.-Ser. Mech. Eng. **7**(1), 101–118 (2009)
11. Szabo, N.: Formalizing and securing relationships on public networks. First Monday **2**(9), (1997)
12. Tang, V.W., Zheng, Y., Cao, J.: An intelligent car park management system based on wireless sensor networks. In: 2006 First International Symposium on Pervasive Computing and Applications, pp. 65–70. IEEE (2006)
13. Wood, G.: Ethereum: a secure decentralised generalised transaction ledger. Ethereum Proj. Yellow Pap. **151**, 1–32 (2014)
14. Yan, G., Yang, W., Rawat, D.B., Olariu, S.: Smartparking: a secure and intelligent parking system. IEEE Intell. Transp. Syst. Mag. **3**(1), 18–30 (2011)
15. Yang, J., Portilla, J., Riesgo, T.: Smart parking service based on wireless sensor networks. In: 38th Annual Conference on IEEE Industrial Electronics Society, IECON 2012, pp. 6029–6034. IEEE (2012)
16. Yuan, C., Fei, L., Jianxin, C., Wei, J.: A smart parking system using WiFi and wireless sensor network. In: 2016 IEEE International Conference on Consumer Electronics-Taiwan (ICCE-TW), pp. 1–2. IEEE (2016)
17. Zhang, J., Wang, F.Y., Wang, K., Lin, W.H., Xu, X., Chen, C.: Data-driven intelligent transportation systems: a survey. IEEE Trans. Intell. Transp. Syst. **12**(4), 1624–1639 (2011)
18. Zhang, Z., Li, X., Yuan, H., Yu, F.: A street parking system using wireless sensor networks. Int. J. Distrib. Sens. Netw. **9**(6), 107975 (2013)

Smart Cities

Multi-Service Capacitated Facility Location Problem with Partial Covering in Smart Cities

Gerbrich Hoekstra[1,2] and Frank Phillipson[2(✉)]

[1] University Groningen, Groningen, The Netherlands
[2] TNO, The Hague, The Netherlands
frank.phillipson@tno.nl

Abstract. We consider the problem of distributing various services over urban areas. In this work we introduce the Multi-Service Capacitated Facility Location Problem with Partial Covering (MSCFLP-PC), which extends the MSCFLP by allowing for partial satisfaction of demand, where a penalty has to be paid for the uncovered demand. We present some practical results by solving the problem as an Integer Linear Programming Problem on various real urban areas. Experiments indicate that partial covering is an effective means to lower costs. This study is the first to formulate and solve the partial covering extension of the MSCFLP.

Keywords: Smart city infrastructure planning · Multi service · Coverage · Partial coverage

1 Introduction

In this paper we look at smart city access network planning from the side of offering multiple services to the inhabitants of a city. The smart city access network should be efficient in covering the demand of all the services together. For this, in [13], the Multi-Service Location Set Covering Problem was introduced, in which multiple services, such as WiFi, smart transportation, alarm, video etc., are distributed over a set of locations. As potential locations for offering smart city services, lampposts are used. This distribution is done such that all demand is covered, for all services at minimal costs. Next, in [5,6] this model is extended with capacity constraints resulting in the Multi-Service Capacitated Facility Location Problem (MSCFLP).

In this paper, we will introduce an extension of the MSCFLP. This new problem extends the MSCFLP by introducing partial covering to it and this problem will be referred to as the Multi-Service Capacitated Facility Location Problem with Partial Covering (MSCFLP-PC). Rather than satisfying demand of all points, it is allowed to cover only a fraction of the demand points, where there has to be paid a penalty for all uncovered demand. This penalty can be a

© Springer Nature Switzerland AG 2019
K.-H. Lüke et al. (Eds.): I4CS 2019, CCIS 1041, pp. 81–96, 2019.
https://doi.org/10.1007/978-3-030-22482-0_7

real amount that a service provider has to pay to the government, or it can be seen as some indirect or social costs. It yields a more efficient location assignment in which a small number of demand points, that are very expensive to serve, are excluded from the service set. In general, Facility Location Problems (FLPs) are studied in a setting in which all customer demand need to be satisfied. However, the authors in [1] argue that very distant customers could influence the final solution disproportionately, yielding unsatisfactory solutions. Serving such customers drives up the total costs and lacks to improve the service level to the majority of customers. Another motivation for partial covering concerns the fact that 'satisfying all requirements' could imply that the problem becomes unsolvable (see [9]).

In this paper a formal description and formulation of the MSCFLP-PC is provided. First we will give a short overview of the relation of this research to the existing literature in Sect. 2. Next, in Sect. 3 we give a formal description of the problem. In Sect. 4 we describe the test instances we used for the analysis. Results on these instances are presented in Sect. 5, and their sensitivity to certain parameters is shown in Sect. 6. We conclude with a short discussion in Sect. 7.

2   Partial Covering Problems in Literature

There have been various studies on the combination of partial covering and Set Cover Problems (SCP) (e.g. [4]), and partial covering in the context of FLPs (e.g. [7]). As a result, various model approaches are suggested in literature.

Partial covering has been of interest in other problems as well, including FLPs, maximal covering models, and Partial Vertex Cover Problems. Vasko et al. [11] introduce the Partial Coverage Uncapacitated Facility Location Problem (PCUFLP). The aim of the PCUFLP is to determine which ware-houses should be opened in order to satisfy the demand of some of the locations, such that the total costs, representing the summation of fixed opening costs and variable costs, are minimised. In line with this research, Monabbati [7] developed the Uncapacitated Facility Location Problem with self-serving demands (UFLP-SS). It generalises the UFLP by introducing demand-side servers. Such a server is located at one of the demand points, and can exclusively serve the corresponding demand point. A demand point that can be served from both a demand-side server, and the facilities, is called a self-serving demand point.

Maximal covering models are another stream in literature in which the concept of partial covering has been investigated. Church et al. [2] formulated the Maximal Covering (Location) Problem, which aims at maximising demand coverage within the specified service distances by using a fixed number of facilities. In this context, partial covering is not considered a relaxation of some demand covering constraint as in other partial covering problems, but rather the main criteria to be maximised. In a similar fashion, partial covering problems can be considered as optimisation versions of the Dominating Set Problem, and the Vertex Cover Problem as argued by [3].

To the best of our knowledge, partial covering has not been previously researched in the context of CFLPs and also not in the context of multiple services.

3 Partial Coverage Model

In this section we introduce the generalisation of the MSCFLP, which is called the Multi-Service Capacitated Facility Location Problem with Partial Covering (MSCFLP-PC). The goal of this problem is to 'cover' the demand of only a fractional part of the demand points, rather than covering all demand points as in the MSCFLP while minimising total costs.

Our approach is inspired by the work of [7] and [11], who deal with related partial covering problems. Both studies put an upper bound on the number of unserved demand points by introducing an additional service location or service possibility. As stated earlier, Monabbati [7] introduces demand-side servers as a second service option. When a server is present at such a demand-side, the demand point can either be served by the server, or by one of the facilities as in general FLPs. Vakso et al. [11] use a different formulation of the problem to incorporate partial covering. However, similar to [7] an additional service possibility is introduced. In their work, a 'universal warehouse' is introduced, which is a 'dummy' warehouse that allows a feasible solution to not cover all demand points. When a demand point is 'served' by this additional warehouse, it implies that the demand point is not served by another (real) warehouse, and thus it is left unserved in the solution. This warehouse can serve all demand points, and its fixed opening cost is equal zero. The variable cost of serving a demand point by the dummy warehouse is similar to the lost sales cost of the demand point. In line with the optimality criterion of the MSCFLP, the optimality criterion of the MSCFLP-PC is the total costs of the solution, which is the sum of both the total opening costs of the locations and service, and the total penalty costs.

To come to a formulation of our problem, first a universal access location is introduced, which has infinite capacity and range, and a variable cost equal to the lost sales cost of a demand point. Due to its infinite capacity and range, the universal access location can serve all demand points. This implies that for relatively low lost sales costs, the majority of the demand points are served by the universal access location, which might be considered as unsatisfactory in some situations. Setting the variable cost of the universal access location relatively high, optimal solutions of the extended problem are equivalent to optimal solutions of the MSCFLP.

In Table 1 an overview of the notation is presented. The problem consists of a set of demand points, locations, and services. Each demand point $i \in \mathcal{G}^u$ has some potential demand d_i^u for service $u \in \mathcal{F}$. A demand point $i \in \mathcal{G}^u$ is characterised by its location and its demand for service $u \in \mathcal{F}$. Similarly, a location $j \in \mathcal{L}$ is characterised by its location, and its connected services. A service $u \in \mathcal{F}$ is characterised by its range and its capacity η_j^u, which is defined as the maximum number of connections that it can hold simultaneously.

Table 1. Parameters and decision variables of the MSCFLP.

General Notation	
$\mathcal{L}$	Set of all locations
$\mathcal{F}$	Set of all services
$\mathcal{G}^u$	Set of all demand points for service $u \in \mathcal{F}$
$|\mathcal{X}|$	Cardinality of the set $\mathcal{X}$
Indices	
i	Demand point, $i \in \mathcal{G}^u$ for service $u \in \mathcal{F}$
j	Location, $j \in \mathcal{L}$
u	Service, $u \in \mathcal{F}$
Parameters	
$a_{ij}^u = \begin{cases} 1, & \text{if demand point } i \in \mathcal{G}^u \text{ can be served from location } j \in \mathcal{L} \text{ for service } u \in \mathcal{F} \\ 0, & \text{otherwise} \end{cases}$	
c_j^u	Cost of equipping location $j \in \mathcal{L}$ with service $u \in \mathcal{F}$, $c_j^u > 0$
f_j	Cost of opening location $j \in \mathcal{L}$, $f_j > 0$
d_i^u	Demand of demand point $i \in \mathcal{G}^u$ for service $u \in \mathcal{F}$, $d_i^u \in \mathbb{N}$
η_j^u	Maximum number of connections access location $j \in \mathcal{L}$ can release for service $u \in \mathcal{F}$, $\eta_j^u \in \mathbb{N}^+$
M	A large number, $M > 0$
Decision variables	
s_{ij}^u	The number of connections made between access location $j \in \mathcal{L}$ and demand point $i \in \mathcal{G}^u$, $s_{ij}^u \in \mathbb{N}$
$x_j^u = \begin{cases} 1, & \text{if access location } j \in \mathcal{L} \text{ is a service access point for service } u \in \mathcal{F} \\ 0, & \text{otherwise} \end{cases}$	
$y_j = \begin{cases} 1, & \text{if location } j \in \mathcal{L} \text{ is an access location} \\ 0, & \text{otherwise} \end{cases}$	

Starting from the formulation in [5], the proposed mathematical formulation is as follows. First of all, let the universal access location be denoted by j', and replace the demand covering constraint as defined in [5] by the system of constraints given in Constraint set (1), where $s_{ij'}^u$ is a binary variable that is equal to one if demand point i is served by the universal access location. That is, if a demand point $i \in \mathcal{G}^u$ having demand for service $u \in \mathcal{F}$ is served by the universal access location (i.e., $s_{ij'}^u = 1$), the demand point is unserved in the solution. In turn, the objective function should be rewritten to Eq. (2), which includes the lost sales cost p_i^u for all demand points $i \in \mathcal{G}^u$ and for all services $u \in \mathcal{F}$. As the fixed opening cost of both the location and the services is zero for the universal access location, the universal access location is only part of the objective function through the penalty cost summation.

$$\begin{cases} \sum_{j \in \{\mathcal{L}, j'\}} s_{ij}^u \geq d_i^u, & \forall i \in \mathcal{G}^u, \forall u \in \mathcal{F} \\ s_{ij'}^u \in \mathbb{N}, & \forall i \in \mathcal{G}^u, \forall u \in \mathcal{F} \end{cases} \tag{1}$$

Now, the Integer Linear Programming problem (ILP) for the MSCFLP-PC is formulated as follows:

$$\min \sum_{j \in \mathcal{L}} \sum_{u \in \mathcal{F}} c_j^u x_j^u + \sum_{j \in \mathcal{L}} f_j y_j + \sum_{u \in \mathcal{F}} \sum_{i \in \mathcal{G}^u} p_i^u s_{ij'}^u, \tag{2}$$

subject to

$$x_j^u \leq y_j \qquad \forall j \in \{\mathcal{L}, j'\}, \forall u \in \mathcal{F}, \qquad (3)$$

$$\sum_{i \in \mathcal{G}^u} s_{ij}^u \leq \eta_j^u x_j^u \qquad \forall j \in \mathcal{L}, \forall u \in \mathcal{F}, \qquad (4)$$

$$\sum_{j \in \{\mathcal{L}, j'\}} s_{ij}^u \geq d_i^u \qquad \forall i \in \mathcal{G}^u, \forall u \in \mathcal{F}, \qquad (5)$$

$$s_{ij}^u \leq a_{ij}^u M \qquad \forall i \in \mathcal{G}^u, \forall j \in \mathcal{L}, \forall u \in \mathcal{F}, \qquad (6)$$

$$s_{ij}^u \in \mathbb{N} \qquad \forall i \in \mathcal{G}^u, \forall j \in \{\mathcal{L}, j'\}, \forall u \in \mathcal{F}, \qquad (7)$$

$$x_j^u \in \{0, 1\} \qquad \forall j \in \{\mathcal{L}, j'\}, \forall u \in \mathcal{F}, \qquad (8)$$

$$y_j \in \{0, 1\} \qquad \forall j \in \{\mathcal{L}, j'\}. \qquad (9)$$

Objective (2) minimises the total costs, which is defined as the sum of the opening costs of the services, the overall penalty costs and the opening costs of the access locations. Constraint (3) ensures that only access locations can be equipped with services. Capacity restrictions are taken into account by including Constraint (4). It limits the number of connections that an access location can release for a specific service. When an access location is not equipped with some service, the capacity of this service is set equal to zero, which ensures that for the service at this location no connections can be made. Constraint (5) ensures that the demand of every demand point is satisfied by one of the real or by the dummy access location, and Constraint (6) implies that a connection can only be established between demand point $i \in \mathcal{G}^u$ and access location $j \in \mathcal{L}$ for service $u \in \mathcal{F}$, when the demand point is located in the range of the service ($a_{ij}^u = 1$). Lastly, constraints (7)–(9) specify the solution space.

The universal access location is uncapacitated, and thus no capacity constraint needs to be taken into account for it. Similarly, due to its infinite range, $s_{ij'}^u$ is not bounded from above by $a_{ij'}^u$ for any $i \in \mathcal{G}^u$, and thus Constraint (6) does not need to be defined for location j'. Stated differently, $a_{ij'}^u$ is equal to one for all $i \in \mathcal{G}^u$.

The problem formulation consists of

$$2|\mathcal{L}||\mathcal{F}| + |\mathcal{G}|(|\mathcal{L}| + 1) \quad \text{constraints and} \qquad (10)$$

$$|\mathcal{G}||\mathcal{L}| + |\mathcal{L}|(|\mathcal{F}| + 1) \quad \text{variables.} \qquad (11)$$

A major advantage of this formulation is the fact that the problem always has a feasible solution, and thus it can be solved on each and every problem instance. Namely, since the universal access location has infinite capacity and range, a solution in which all demand points are served by the universal access location is always a feasible solution.

4 Experimental Design

In this section we present the experimental design of the various conducted experiments, which are identical to the conducted experiments in [5].

4.1   Software and Hardware

The problem has been implemented in, and the experiments are conducted by MATLAB version R2016b. It is a programming language published by Math-Works, which allows for a wide range of computations, and other data processing. The problems are solved by use of the external solver CPLEX, using its standard options, using a Branch and Cut algorithm. IBM ILOG CPLEX Optimisation Studio (COS) is a solver developed by IBM. It is an optimisation software package for solving linear programs, mixed integer programs, and quadratic programs. The free student 12.7.1 version of the package has been used to generate the results. The experiments are performed on a DELL E7240 laptop with an Intel(R) Core(TM) i5-4310U CPU 2.00 GHz 2.60 GHz processor. The laptop is operational on a 64-bit operating system.

4.2   Input Parameters

In this section all parameter values and the various characteristics of the test instances will be discussed. We describe the parameter settings for the locations, services, and the demand points.

Locations. The lighting system is used as a set of candidate access locations which can be equipped with services. Data on the locations of lampposts in the Netherlands is publicly available via Dataplatform, which is an initiative of Civity to share data from organisations. The test instances describe various subareas of the city of Amsterdam, as shown in Table 2. In total, nine test instances are considered, of which instance 1 to 7 are the small instances. The fixed opening costs of a location are taken $f_j = 5,000$ for every location $j \in \mathcal{L}$. A mapping of all locations (lamp posts) of some small subarea of the city of Amsterdam can be found in Fig. 1.

Table 2. Overview of the test instances.

Inst.	No. Locations $|\mathcal{L}|$	No. Demand points			Tot. $|\mathcal{G}|$
		$|\mathcal{G}^1|$	$|\mathcal{G}^2|$	$|\mathcal{G}^3|$	
1	33	47	3	9	59
2	77	73	8	15	96
3	99	260	9	13	282
4	102	462	8	15	485
5	400	111	20	25	156
6	782	21	93	104	218
7	516	1,241	42	46	1,329
8	6,079	8,106	397	326	8,829
9	6,981	10,122	528	431	11,081

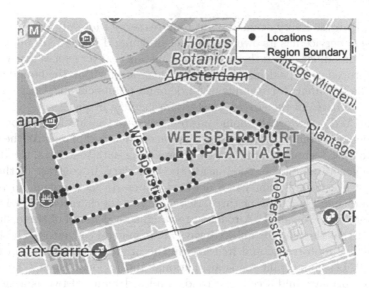

Fig. 1. Mapping of all access locations in some small subarea of the city of Amsterdam.

Services. In total three services will be considered for the test instances. The various services and their parameter values are based on the works of [14], and [12]. As previously stated, a service is characterised by its range and its capacity. The capacity is defined as the maximum number of connections it could have at the same time. It is assumed that every service has a circular coverage area. In practice every range is applicable, resulting from all kind of other (propagation) models. Given the range, the coverage matrix with elements a_{ij}^u can be filled. For every service, information is provided in Table 3 on the range, capacity, and opening costs of the service. The first service is a WiFi service. It has a range of 100 m, can serve up to a maximum of 30 demand points, and its opening cost is equal to 300. The second service is a Smart Vehicle Communication (SVC) service, which aims at providing data to drivers. It has a range of 200 m, a capacity of 15 connections, and an opening cost of 300. The last service is an Alarm service, which has an unlimited capacity. This service has a range of 300 m, and opening cost equal to 150. The Alarm service aims at providing a loud signal to warn humans about dangers. As the service provision is independent on the number of humans within the range of the access location, the capacity of the service is unlimited.

Table 3. Overview of the considered services for the test instances.

Service	Range	Capacity η_j^u	Open. cost c_j^u	Penalty cost p_i^u
$u = 1$: WiFi	100	$30 \; \forall j \in \mathcal{L}$	$300 \; \forall j \in \mathcal{L}$	$500 \; \forall i \in \mathcal{G}^1$
$u = 2$: SVC	200	$15 \; \forall j \in \mathcal{L}$	$350 \; \forall j \in \mathcal{L}$	$250 \; \forall i \in \mathcal{G}^2$
$u = 3$: Alarm	300	$\infty \; \forall j \in \mathcal{L}$	$150 \; \forall j \in \mathcal{L}$	$1,500 \; \forall i \in \mathcal{G}^3$

Demand Points. Every demand point requires service for only one service, and in turn every service has its own disjoint set of demand points. Although sets of demand points differ across the various test instances, every set is generated by the same procedure. The demand points are generated within the boundary that specifies the test area. An example of all demand points classified per service in some small subarea of the city of Amsterdam is given in Fig. 2.

For the WiFi service, the home addresses located inside the boundary are taken as demand points. All houses are assigned a demand of one. As the second service is a SVC technique, which aims at providing data to drivers, the demand points are generated on the roads inside the boundary. In contrast to the WiFi service, not every road point has a demand of one. In fact, a demand point is assigned a demand one, two, or three, depending on its characteristics. Demand points referring to so called "A-roads" are assigned a demand of three, simulating the fact that these important highways are in general congested. These roads are labelled as motorways, and freeways in the original documentation (Open-StreetMap). Less important roads are national and regional roads. These roads are labelled primary and secondary roads, and a demand of two is assigned to demand points on such roads. All other roads are of least importance, and in turn are assigned a demand equal to one.

The last service is the Alarm service. As it has an infinite capacity, serving its demand points can be approached as a covering problem instead of some capacitated supply problem. In line with this approach, the demand points of the alarm are intersections of a grid. It is indicated in [8] that this approach works best with regard to computational efficiency. For more information on the generation of the grid, we refer to Section 6.3 of [14]. Similar to the WiFi service, a

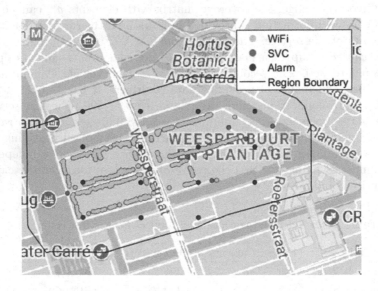

Fig. 2. Plot of the demand points per service of some small area in Amsterdam.

demand of one is assigned to every demand point. However, the optimal solution is the same for other demand values, as the Alarm service has an unlimited capacity. Hence, for efficiency reasons, a demand of one is assigned.

Note that the demand points, that are not located in range of at least one location, are excluded from the set of demand points. That is, when there is no location in the neighbourhood of a demand point, it is deleted from the set of demand points.

5 Results and Analysis

The proposed MSCFLP-PC extends the MSCFLP by relaxing the demand fulfilment constraint. The problem optimises the location assignments of the various services simultaneously, and allows for some demand points to remain unserved in the optimal solution. When a demand point is left unserved, a fixed penalty needs to be incurred. By this, it is tried not to serve demand points, that influence the multi-service location assignment disproportionately. In turn, the solution balances the total opening costs of locations and services on the one hand, and the total penalty costs on the other hand.

The optimality criterion of the MSCFLP-PC is the total costs of the solution, which consists of both the opening costs of the access locations and the service access points, and the overall penalty costs. Next to this optimality criterion, the solution is evaluated with respect to the service levels of the various services. The service level s_u of service $u \in \mathcal{F}$ is defined as the percentage of demand that is satisfied in the solution. It is mathematically defined in Eq. (12).

$$s_u = \frac{\sum\limits_{i \in \mathcal{G}^u} \sum\limits_{j \in \mathcal{L}} s_{ij}^u}{\sum\limits_{i \in \mathcal{G}^u} d_i^u} \cdot 100\%, \quad \forall u \in \mathcal{F} \tag{12}$$

In Table 4, the results of the MSCFLP-PC are displayed. It shows for every instance the service levels, the objective value, the gap, and the time until the solver has been terminated. Furthermore, it displays the cost savings that are obtained by introducing partial covering to the problem relative to the MSCFLP solution. The penalty parameters are equal to 500, 250, and 1,500 as provided in Table 3.

Different conclusions can be drawn from the results of Table 4. First of all, we see that for instances 1 and 3 a similar solution as the MSCFLP in [6] is obtained. Here all service levels are 100%. Most likely this result is caused by the size of the instances. The instances are relatively small, as only a limited number of services are opened in the MSCFLP solution. Only one service access point of the Alarm service can cover the whole subarea, and in turn it can serve all Alarm demand points. From this observation, combined with the fact that the penalty for the Alarm service is high, we conclude that it is optimal to open one Alarm service. Given that at least one location needs to be opened, the other services can be offered cheaply, and thus it will not be optimal to serve the customers partially.

In contrast, the solution of instance 2 differs from the MSCFLP solution despite the fact that the instance is also small in size. Particularly, in the best found solution of this instance, one of the WiFi demand points is left unserved. In the MSCFLP solution a relatively expensive WiFi service access point serving only four demand points has been opened. Thus, it is reasonable to close one of the access locations, and serve the demand points only partially. Since a single WiFi demand point is unserved in the MSCFLP-PC solution instead of four, it can be concluded that three of the demand points could be served by another service access point, which results in a cost saving of $5,000 + 300 - 500 = 4,800$.

Furthermore, from Table 4 it can be concluded that partial covering is useful for the SVC service in the solution of instance 4. It yields a cost saving of 100. The solution of the MSCFLP and the solution of the MSCFLP-PC for instance 4 are geographically displayed in Figs. 3(a) and (b). For instance 4 it holds true that a single SVC service access point cannot serve all SVC demand points, because it cannot reach all demand points from a single access location. However, by excluding one of the SVC demand points, that has a demand of one, a single service access point can serve and reach all SVC demand points. Since the penalty cost parameter exceeds the opening cost parameter of the SVC service by a 100, it is optimal to not satisfy the demand of the demand point. In turn, fewer SVC service access points need to be opened compared to the MSCFLP solution.

From the first four instances it can be concluded that it is mainly the surface and the shape of the subarea that determines whether it is optimal to apply partial covering. For these areas it holds true that a single Alarm service can cover the whole surface and thus partial covering is not applied that often. From instance 4 onwards the instances span a larger area and contain more demand points, which implies that partial covering is of greater value. Especially

Table 4. Results of the MSCFLP-PC. It lists for every instance and every service the service levels, objective value of the solution, the running time of the solver, and the cost savings that are obtained compared to the MSCFLP solution of [6].

Inst.	s_1 (%)	s_2 (%)	s_3 (%)	Obj.	Gap (%)	Time (s)	Cost sav. (%)
1	100.0	100.0	100.0	11,100	0.0	1.8	0.0
2	98.6	100.0	100.0	16,900	0.0	28.4	22.1
3	100.0	100.0	100.0	48,200[a]	3.7	4.3	0.0
4	100.0	88.9	100.0	85,550[a]	3.9	6.0	0.1
5	93.7	64.5	96.0	29,950[a]	6.6	43,200.0	21.5
6	38.1	55.1	98.1	69,900[a]	4.3	228.0	30.2
7	99.5	97.9	100.0	228,700[a]	1.9	266.7	1.3
8	99.1	86.2	100.0	1,595,350[a]	4.2	43,200.0	7.2
9	99.3	89.8	99.8	2,003,800[a]	4.6	42,297.7	8.6

[a]The solver is terminated according to the stopping criteria as defined in [5].

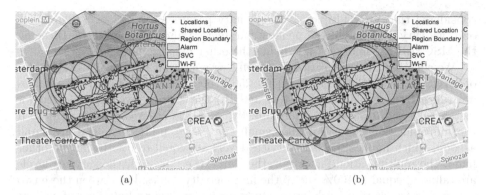

Fig. 3. In this figure both the solution of the MSCFLP (a) and the solution of the MSCFLP-PC (b) are geographically displayed for instance 4. The yellow stars, dots, and circles, correspond to the service access points, demand points, and the covered area of the WiFi service. Similarly, the red, and blue objects of the figure correspond to the SVC, and Alarm service, respectively. (Color figure online)

in instance 6, where the service level of the WiFi service drops to 38.1%. The WiFi demand points in instance 7 are much more clustered compared to instance 6, which makes it reasonable that its service level will exceed the service level of the WiFi service in instance 6.

Lastly, some demand points of instances 8 and 9 are left unserved in the solution of the MSCFLP-PC. Especially SVC demand points are left unserved in the MSCFLP-PC, which is reasonable since both instances contain demand points that have high demands. This observation, combined with the fact that these demand points are not always located near a set of WiFi demand points, implies that an additional access location should be opened. In turn, this access location is a service access point for the SVC service only, so high cost savings are obtained in the MSCFLP-PC solution by serving only a fractional part of the set of SVC demand points.

6   Sensitivity Analysis

We start our sensitivity analysis by investigating the effect of $f_j > 0$ on the solution, which is the opening cost of location $j \in \mathcal{L}$. A fixed value is set for all locations. Second, the impact of the penalty cost parameter p_i^u is evaluated, which is the penalty cost of service $u \in \mathcal{F}$ for not meeting demand of demand point $i \in \mathcal{G}^u$. Similarly, fixed values are chosen for the penalty cost parameters and both the effects of individual as well as simultaneous increases in the penalty costs are evaluated.

The penalty parameters p_i^u are rather arbitrarily selected in Sect. 4.2. Therefore, in this section the effect of these parameters on the MSCFLP-PC solution is investigated by use of two approaches. First, various penalty parameters are considered that are multiples of the penalty parameter values of Table 3. Second, we vary over one of the penalty parameters and investigate the effect on the MSCFLP-PC solution while fixing the other penalty parameters.

We consider a multiplication factor $m \in \mathbb{Q}$ such that the penalty cost vector of services $u \in \mathcal{F}$ equals $p_i^u = m[500; 250; 1, 500]$. All other parameters values are taken from Table 3. In Fig. 4(a) and (b) the service levels are plotted for instances 7 and 8, respectively. Again, two extreme cases can be identified. If the multiplication factor is rather small (i.e., $m \leq 0.11$), penalties are small as well, which implies that the services levels are equal to 0%. If, on the other hand, the multiplication factor is rather large (i.e., $m \geq 2$), the services levels are (almost) equal to 100% due to the high penalty values. In between these two extreme cases, service levels are monotonically increasing functions of m (see Fig. 4).

For $m \geq 0.12$ nonzero services levels are achieved. This results from the fact that both instances contain some location, that can serve many demand points. As an example, consider instance 7. In this instance there is an access location that can reach a set of demand points consisting of 30 WiFi demand points, 20 Alarm demand points, and 11 SVC demand points which have a total demand of 14. For $m \leq 0.11$ the total penalty costs for this set of demand points is smaller are equal to $5, 335$, which falls short on the sum of all opening costs, i.e. $f_j + \sum_{u \in \mathcal{F}} c_j^u = 5, 800$. Thus, for $m \leq 0.11$ it is optimal to not serve all demand points. However, for $m = 0.12$ the total penalty costs of the set of demand points are equal to $5, 820 > 5, 800$, so it is optimal to serve at least some of the demand points. Services levels are monotonically increasing functions of the multiplication parameter m and they converge to 100%.

We continue to explore the impact of the penalty parameters by varying one penalty parameter while fixing the other penalties at the values provided in Table 3. Again instance 7 is taken to compare the different penalties. The penalty parameters are evaluated on the interval $[0, f_j + c_j^u + 1]$. The cost of serving a demand point i having demand for service u from an access location j, that is a service access point of this service only and serves only this demand point, is equal to $f_j + c_j^u$. Whenever the penalty parameter exceeds this value, it is optimal to serve all demand points having demand for service $u \in \mathcal{F}$. In turn, a penalty parameter exceeding the right boundary of the interval yields a service level of 100% for service u, and thus the service level will converge on the considered interval.

In Fig. 5 the service levels are plotted for various values of the penalty parameter of the WiFi service (a), the SVC service (b), and the Alarm service (c). From the different figures it can be concluded that the service levels are monotonically increasing functions of the penalty parameters. Figure 5(b) shows that the SVC penalty parameter p_i^2 has no impact on the service level of both the WiFi and Alarm service. For $p_i^2 \geq 0$ the service levels are equal to $s_1 = 99.92\%$ and $s_3 = 100.00\%$.

Contrary to the SVC service, the penalty parameters of the WiFi and Alarm service do affect the service levels of the other services (see Figs. 5(a) and (c)). Furthermore, Fig. 5(c) shows that relatively high service levels are attained for the WiFi and SVC service (i.e., $s_1 = 99.92\%$ and $s_2 = 95.74\%$) when the penalty parameter of the Alarm service is equal to 0. This result may be caused by the fact that the WiFi demand points in instance 7 are highly clustered and SVC demand points are in general located in the neighbourhood of WiFi demand points. This implies that SVC demands can be served from the same access location as WiFi demand points, and thereby serving both set of demand points is cheap. The fact that on average 29.5 WiFi demand points are served per service access point if $p_i^3 = 0$ underpins this conjecture. Similarly, Fig. 5(a) shows that the service level of the Alarm service is high (i.e., $s_3 = 97.83\%$) for $p_i^1 = 0$. This result is easily explained by the fact that the penalty parameter of the Alarm service is high (i.e., $p_i^3 = 1,500$), and thereby it is efficient to serve almost all Alarm demand points. Lastly, Figs. 5(a) and (c) show that the service level of the SVC service converges to a limit of 97.87% for the various values of p_i^1 and p_i^3. This result is easily explained by the fact that instance 7 contains one remote SVC demand point, which corresponds to 2.13% of the total SVC demand.

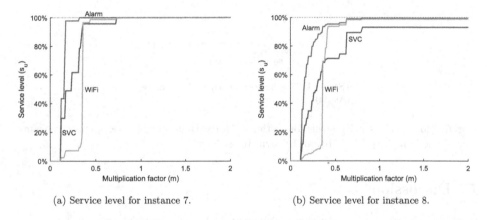

(a) Service level for instance 7.   (b) Service level for instance 8.

Fig. 4. Plot of the service levels for instance 7 (a) and instance 8 (b) for various values of the multiplication factor m.

Summarising, relatively high service levels are achieved for the current set of penalty parameters. Multiplying the vector of penalty costs with a number close to one has only a small effect on the solution. If, on the other hand, individual changes are considered, the WiFi penalty parameter particularly has an effect on the service levels of the other services. Contrary to the WiFi penalty parameter, the SVC penalty parameter does not affect the service levels of the other services.

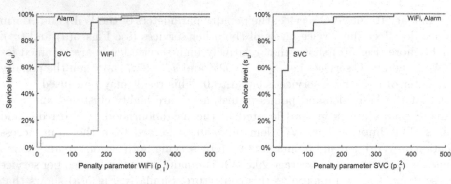

(a) Service level as function of penalty for instance 7 (WiFi).

(b) Service level as function of penalty for instance 7 (SVC).

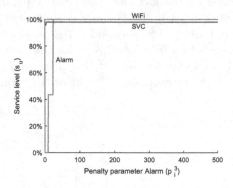

(c) Service level as function of penalty for instance 7 (Alarm).

Fig. 5. Plots of the service levels for instance 7 for various values of the penalty parameter of the WiFi (a), SVC (b), and Alarm (c) service.

7 Discussion

In this paper we considered the problem of assigning multiple services to access points. We extended the Multi-Service Capacitated Facility Location Problem (MSCFLP) by allowing for partial satisfaction of demand. For this extended problem, the Multi-Service Capacitated Facility Location Problem with Partial Covering (MSCFLP-PC) is introduced and defined. It extends the MSCFLP by relaxing the limitations on demand fulfilment and associating penalty costs with it. We analysed the performance of the solution of a number of cases and performed some simulations to analyse the impact of cost parameters on the solution.

Results show that partial covering is an effective means to lower costs. Even discarding only a couple of demand points for service can yield large cost benefits. By allowing for partial covering, cost benefits are obtained for some experiments that improves the location assignment, while service levels are decreased by only a relatively small percentage. Our sensitivity analysis shows that small changes in the current set of location cost and penalty cost parameters will only have a minor effect on the solution.

Future work could focus on the alternative problem formulations for the extended model. Although it is believed that the current formulation suits the problem best in general, there might be situations in which one of the following alternative formulations would be preferred. One different approach is to include a universal access location, that has a finite capacity, but infinite range and lost sales costs equal to zero. This implies that only a fixed number of demand points can be served by the universal access location, which results in an upper bound on the number of unserved demand points, and thus a lower bound on the service level. The second alternative problem formulation is based on the model procedure in which (at least) k-out of n constraints should hold. This is a generalisation of the either-or modelling procedure in which either one of two constraints should hold, but not both. It introduces an additional binary variable for each constraint and an additional constraint on these binary variables. Two papers in literature in which this procedure is used to incorporate partial covering are the papers by [4] and [10]. An alternative here is using penalty constraints. The third and last proposed research direction is the use of goal programming. This is an approach in multi-objective optimisation, which extends linear programming to deal with multiple (probably conflicting) optimisation criteria. To every criteria a goal (target value) is assigned, and undesirable deviations from this goal are minimised in the objective function.

References

1. Charikar, M., Khuller, S., Mount, D., Narasimhan, G.: Algorithms for facility location problems with outliers. In: Proceedings of Symposium on Discrete Algorithms (SODA), pp. 642–651 (2001)
2. Church, R., ReVelle, C.: The maximal covering location problem. Pap. Reg. Sci. Assoc. **32**, 101–118 (1974)
3. Fomin, F., Lokshtanov, D., Raman, V., Saurabh, S.: Subexponential algorithms for partial cover problems. In: FSTTCS, pp. 193–201 (2009)
4. Gandhi, R., Khuller, S., Srinivasan, A.: Approximation algorithms for partial covering problems. J. Algorithms **53**(1), 55–84 (2004)
5. Hoekstra, G., Phillipson, F.: Location assignment of capacitated services in smart cities. In: Renault, É., Boumerdassi, S., Bouzefrane, S. (eds.) MSPN 2018, vol. 11005. Springer, Cham (2018). https://doi.org/10.1007/978-3-030-03101-5
6. Hoekstra, G., Phillipson, F.: Heuristic approaches for location assignment of capacitated services in smart cities. Computers **7**(4), 67 (2018)
7. Monabbati, E.: Uncapacitated facility location problem with self-serving demands. ORiON **29**(2), 169–180 (2003)
8. Murray, A.T., OKelly, M.E., Church, R.L.: Regional service coverage modelling. Comput. Oper. Res. **35**(2), 339–355 (2008)
9. Shi, Y., Zhang, Z., Du, D.Z.: Randomized bicriteria approximation algorithm for minimum submodular cost partial multi-cover problem. arXiv preprint arXiv:1701.05339 (2017)

10. Takazawa, Y., Mizuno, S., Kitahara, T.: An approximation algorithm for the partial covering 0-1 interger program (July 2017, revised)
11. Vasko, F., Newhart, D., Stott, K., Wolf, F.: A large-scale application of the partial coverage uncapacitated facility location problem. J. Oper. Res. Soc. **54**(1), 11–20 (2003)
12. Verhoek, M.: Optimising the placement of access points for smart city services with stochastic demand. Master's thesis, Groningen University, the Netherlands (2017)
13. Vos, T., Phillipson, F.: Dense multi-service planning in smart cities. In: International Conference on Information Society and Smart Cities (2018)
14. Vos, T.: Using Lamppost to provide urban areas with multiple services. Master's thesis, Erasmus University, Rotterdam, the Netherlands (2016)

Multi Service Modular Capacitated Facility Location Problem for Smart Cities

Bert Veerman[1,2] and Frank Phillipson[2(✉)]

[1] VU University Amsterdam, Amsterdam, The Netherlands
[2] TNO, The Hague, The Netherlands
frank.phillipson@tno.nl

Abstract. This paper introduces the Multi Service Modular Capacitated Facility Location Problem, which extends the Multi Service Capacitated Facility Location Problem by allowing for modular capacities. This extension can lead to significant costs benefits, especially in dense areas. Two heuristics are proposed to solve the problem: the *Extended Pricing Heuristic (EPH)* and the *Extended Covering Heuristic (ECH)*. The *ECH* gives better results, but its feasibility is dependent on the choice of the parameters. The *EPH* does not have this problem and has lower computation times for large instances.

Keywords: Smart city infrastructure planning · Multi service ·
Coverage · Modular systems

1 Introduction

In smart cities a variety of services will be provided to inhabitants. The range of applications will be found on service directions such as energy, sanitation, health care, transportation, farming, governance, automation, manufacturing etc. [1]. Internet of Things (loT) provides for intelligent Machine-to-Machine (M2M) and Machine-to-User (M2U) communication and enables provision of the essential services. A set of such services and the intelligent infrastructure form the basis of what is now known as Smart Cities. The basis for this intelligent infrastructure is the access network, which connects access points by fibres to a core network. The smart city access network should be efficient in covering the demand, for all the services together. The demand can be seen as the set of clients spread over a city requiring a certain service. Examples of services are Wi-Fi, motion detection, alarms, air quality meters and traffic density meters. For this, the Multi-Service Location Set Covering Problem was introduced by Vos and Phillipson [15], in which multiple service-providing boxes are placed across the city. Lamppost are used as potential spots for offering smart city services. This distribution is done such that the demand of all clients is covered, for all services, at minimal costs. Hoekstra and Phillipson [10,11] extended this problem formulation with

© Springer Nature Switzerland AG 2019
K.-H. Lüke et al. (Eds.): I4CS 2019, CCIS 1041, pp. 97–108, 2019.
https://doi.org/10.1007/978-3-030-22482-0_8

capacity constraints resulting in the Multi Service Capacitated Facility Location Problem (MSCFLP). This means that the number of clients that one box can serve is limited. Solutions were obtained by sequentially distributing the boxes by a series of Integer Linear Problems (ILP).

The capacitated problem can be seen as the problem where only one box per service can be placed at every spot, having a specific capacity. However, in practice it is often possible to place multiple boxes of a service at the same spot or to enlarge the capacity of a box with discrete steps. For this practical application, this paper introduces the Multi Service Modular Capacitated Facility Location Problem (MSMCFLP) which extends the MSCFLP by allowing for modular capacities. This problem was not studied earlier. Two heuristics are proposed to solve this problem: the *Extended Pricing Heuristic (EPH)* and the *Extended Covering Heuristic (ECH)*. The EPH is an extension of a greedy heuristic, whereas the ECH is an extension of a Lagrangian heuristic. First of all, a literature review is given in Sect. 2. In Sect. 3, the problem formulation is introduced whereafter the heuristics will be presented in Sect. 4. The results are discussed in Sect. 5 and finally the conclusion is given in Sect. 6.

2 Literature Review

The MSCFLP is introduced by Hoekstra and Phillipson [10] and not studied elsewhere. Most studies focus on one service and elaborates on the Capacitated Facility Location Problem (CFLP), for which many extensions exists. A short overview on this topic is given. Besides, the Set Covering Problem (SCP) is regarded in this review, because it is used in one of the heuristics.

The Facility Location Problem (FLP) is an extensively studied problem in literature. The objective is to minimise the costs while serving all customers. The costs consists of the placement costs of facilities and the transportation costs between the facilities and the demand points. There are two versions: the capacitated (CFLP) [13] and the uncapacitated (UFLP) [6] one. Both problems are known to be NP-hard, which can be proved by a reduction from Vertex Cover [8]. The capacitated version puts an additional restriction on the capacity of the facilities. Both the UFLP and the CFLP allow that multiple facilities serve a fraction of the demand. Of course, adding the integrality constraint will make the problem more difficult. This results in the Single-Source Capacitated Facility Location Problem (SSCFLP) for which many heuristics are proposed in literature. Most heuristics are Lagrangian in which a constraint is relaxed. Examples are the relaxation of the capacity constraint as in [12] and the relaxation of the assignment constraint as in [14]. Besides, several meta-heuristics are proposed such as the *iterated tabu search* in [9].

There are many extensions of the CFLP. An example is the Modular Capacitated Location Problem (MCLP) in which different facility types can be chosen [4]. In this work, different ILP formulations are given, which resulted in different Lagrangian relaxation procedures. These heuristic methods provide satisfactory results regarding optimality gap and computation time. In addition, this problem was extended with the single source property in [5] which resulted in the

Single Source Modular Capacitated Plant Location Problem (SSMCPLP). A Lagrangian heuristic was used and improved by *tabu search* and *local search* algorithms. Also for this problem, satisfactory results were obtained.

The SCP is a simplification of the SSCFLP, which can be obtained by omitting the capacity constraint and setting all connection costs c_{ij} equal to zero. Nevertheless, Garey and Johnson [7] proved that the problem is NP-hard. The SCP is an extensively studied problem in literature, for which many heuristics exist. An example is the Lagrangian heuristic of Beasley [2], which is shown to be very efficient. The Lagrangian parameter λ is updated by *subgradient optimisation*. However, for large instances the computation times are still high. Ceria et al. [3] showed that the computation times can be reduced by defining the core problem. This is nothing more than only regarding the sets with the lowest costs, while keeping all items included in a minimum number of sets. Vos and Phillipson [15] showed that this combination of Lagrangian relaxation and defining the core problem performed very well on the Multi Service Location Set Cover Problem (MSLSCP).

3   Problem Formulation

In this section, the Multi Service Modular Capacitated Facility Location Problem (MSMCFLP) is introduced. First of all, some definitions are needed.

- A demand point requires a certain quantity of one service and is given by coordinates. For example, a home address where a Wi-Fi connection of a certain bandwidth is needed.
- A location is a potential spot from where services could be provided. A location is given by coordinates and can for instance be a lamppost.
- An access location is a location that is opened to equip with one or more services. For example, a lamppost that is connected by fibre and has a electricity connection.
- A service access point is a box providing a certain service and can only be placed on access locations. This can for instance be a Wi-Fi router.

In the MSCFLP only one service access point for each service is allowed on every access location, which has a strict capacity. However, in practice one could expect that multiple service access points of the same service can be placed on one access location, enlarging the capacity in modular steps. This extension is in literature only studied by considering one service. Allowing modular capacities may also lead to significant costs savings in the multi-service context. Therefore, a new problem is introduced in this paper, the Multi Service Modular Capacitated Facility Location Problem (MSMCFLP).

Let $\mathcal{L}$ be the set of all locations, $\mathcal{F}$ the set of all services and $\mathcal{G}^u$ the set of all demand points for service $u \in \mathcal{F}$. The sets $\mathcal{G}^u$ are disjoint which implies that all demand points have demand for only one service. The parameters are defined in Table 1.

Table 1. Parameters of the MSCFLP

Parameter	Range	Description
a_{ij}^u	$\{0,1\}$	$\begin{cases} 1 \text{ if demand point } i \in \mathcal{G}^u \text{ can be served from location } j \in \mathcal{L} \text{ for service } u \in \mathcal{F} \\ 0 \text{ otherwise} \end{cases}$
f_j	$[0,\infty)$	opening costs of location $j \in \mathcal{L}$
c_j^u	$[0,\infty)$	equipping costs of one service access point of service $u \in \mathcal{F}$ on location $j \in \mathcal{L}$
d_i^u	$\mathbb{N}^+$	demand of demand point $i \in \mathcal{G}^u$ for service $u \in \mathcal{F}$
η_j^u	$\mathbb{N}^+$	capacity of one service access point of service $u \in \mathcal{F}$ on location $j \in \mathcal{L}$
κ_j^u	$\mathbb{N}^+$	maximum number of service access points of service $u \in \mathcal{F}$ on location $j \in \mathcal{L}$

Note that d_i^u, η_j^u and κ_j^u are restricted to be a positive integer. A demand point or location can be removed if respectively the demand, capacity or maximum number of service access points is equal to zero. It is assumed that the total equipping costs are linear in the number of service access points, which means c_j^u is constant. Furthermore, κ_j^u can be determined based on practical reasons. This setup is very general to allow for different sizes of locations and service access points. The MSCFLP is equal to the MSMCFLP with the additional constraint that $\kappa_j^u = 1$, $\forall j \in \mathcal{L}, \forall u \in \mathcal{F}$. In this way, the MSLSCP is equal to the MSCFLP without the capacity constraint.

The decision variables are presented in Table 2.

Note that the upper bounds of x_j^u and s_{ij}^u are induced by the choice of the parameters. By this construction, the decision variables x_j^u are binary in the MSCFLP. The formulation of the ILP is as follows:

$$\min \sum_{u \in \mathcal{F}} \sum_{j \in \mathcal{L}} c_j^u x_j^u + \sum_{j \in \mathcal{L}} f_j y_j, \tag{1a}$$

such that

$$x_j^u \le \kappa_j^u y_j \qquad\qquad \forall j \in \mathcal{L}, \forall u \in \mathcal{F}, \tag{1b}$$

$$\sum_{i \in \mathcal{G}^u} s_{ij}^u \le \eta_j^u x_j^u \qquad\qquad \forall j \in \mathcal{L}, \forall u \in \mathcal{F}, \tag{1c}$$

$$\sum_{j \in \mathcal{L}} s_{ij}^u \ge d_i^u \qquad\qquad \forall i \in \mathcal{G}^u, \forall u \in \mathcal{F}, \tag{1d}$$

$$s_{ij}^u \le a_{ij}^u d_u^i \qquad\qquad \forall i \in \mathcal{G}^u, \forall j \in \mathcal{L}, \forall u \in \mathcal{F}, \tag{1e}$$

$$s_{ij}^u \in \{0,1,\ldots,d_u^i\} \qquad\qquad \forall i \in \mathcal{G}^u, \forall j \in \mathcal{L}, \forall u \in \mathcal{F}, \tag{1f}$$

$$x_j^u \in \{0,1,\ldots,\kappa_j^u\} \qquad\qquad \forall j \in \mathcal{L}, \forall u \in \mathcal{F}, \tag{1g}$$

$$y_j \in \{0,1\} \qquad\qquad \forall j \in \mathcal{L}, \tag{1h}$$

The goal is to minimise the total costs (Eq. 1a), which consists of the costs regarding the opening and equipping of locations. Important to notice is that there are no connection costs involved, since it is assumed that these are zero. Constraint 1b ensures that only access locations can be equipped and restricts the maximum number of service access points on an access location. The capacity

Table 2. Decision variables of the MSMCFLP

Variable	Range	Description
y_j	$\{0,1\}$	$\begin{cases} 1 \text{ if location } j \in \mathcal{L} \text{ is an access location} \\ 0 \text{ otherwise} \end{cases}$
x_j^u	$\{0,1,\ldots,\kappa_j^u\}$	number of service access points of service $u \in \mathcal{F}$ on access location $j \in \mathcal{L}$
s_{ij}^u	$\{0,1,\ldots,d_u^i\}$	quantity of service $u \in \mathcal{F}$ from location $j \in \mathcal{L}$ to demand point $i \in \mathcal{G}^u$

constraint is forced by Constraint 1c. Constraint 1d ensures that all demand is served. Constraint 1e restricts that service access points can only serve demand points in their corresponding range. Note that this formulation allows that the demand of a demand point can be served by multiple service access points, each serving a unitary fraction of the demand. The solution space is given by Constraints 1f, 1g and 1h. The solution space can be decreased by removing the variables s_{ij}^u for which $a_{ij}^u = 0$. By doing this, the number of decision variables decreases and Constraint 1e becomes redundant.

4 Heuristics

In Hoekstra and Phillipson [10], it is shown that the computation times of large instances using ILP-solvers for the MSCFLP is high. Besides, there are relative high gaps between lower bounds and objective values, even after long computation times. It is expected that this remains the case for the MSMCFLP, since this problem contains a larger solution space. Therefore, two heuristics are proposed to solve the MSMCFLP: the *Extended Pricing Heuristic (EPH)* and the *Extended Covering Heuristic (ECH)*. They are explained in Subsect. 4.1 and 4.2, respectively. In addition, an expectation of their performance is given in each subsection.

4.1 Extended Pricing Heuristic

This heuristic consists of the following two phases.

1. Find a feasible solution for the MSMCFLP using the *Pricing Heuristic*.
2. Solve the MSMCFLP using the exact method on the restricted problem with the opened locations obtained in the first phase.

In the first phase, the *Pricing Heuristic* finds a feasible solution for the whole problem in a greedy way. Thereafter, the ILP formulation (Eq. 1) is applied to the restricted problem to improve the number of service access points and access locations. The restricted problem contains all the demand points and only the locations that are opened in the first phase. Note that the second phase always gives a feasible solution, since the solution of the first phase is already feasible. On the other hand, the *Pricing Heuristic* is not expected to give the best results in the first phase by its greedy nature. The second phase gives optimal solutions for the restricted problem by an ILP solver. However, this can result in high computation times, especially for large instances.

The *Pricing Heuristic* iteratively equips access locations with 'cheap' service access points till all demand points are served. An overview of the algorithm can be found in Algorithm 1.

Algorithm 1. Pricing Heuristic

---

1 **while** *Not every demand point is served* **do**
2   Calculate price of service access points;
3   Equip access location with cheapest service access point;
4   Sort demand points of selected service access point on their reachability;
5   **while** *Capacity of selected service access point is not exceeded* **do**
6   Serve least reachable demand points by selected service access point;
7   **end**
8   Update costs, demand points, service access points;
9 **end**

The price of a service access point of service u on location j is calculated as in Eq. 2.

$$P_j^u = \frac{\text{number of unserved demand points of service } u \text{ in range of location } j}{\text{costs of equipping location } j \text{ with service } u}$$

(2)

The reachability of a demand point is calculated as the number of possible service access points that can still serve the demand point. The last step in the algorithm consists of updating the variables. The costs are updated, since the opening costs only have to be paid once for each location. This means that after this step only equipping costs have to be paid at this location. The served demand points are left in the next iteration. Finally, if location j is already equipped with κ_j^u service access points of service u, no more service access points of that service can be placed on location j.

4.2 Extended Covering Heuristic

This heuristic also consists of two phases, but the first phase is different.

1. Find a feasible solution for the MSLSCP (no capacity constraints).
2. Solve the MSMCFLP using the exact method on the restricted problem with the opened locations obtained in the first phase.

In other words, a coverage of the demand points is found in the first phase. In the second phase the capacity restriction is incorporated by solving the ILP formulation on the restricted problem, which boils down to adding multiple service access points to the access locations. It is important to remark that a low κ_j^u can lead to infeasible solutions as not enough service access points can be placed to serve all demand points. Different methods can be applied to find a solution in the first phase. In this paper the *Sequential Set Covering Heuristic* of Vos and Phillipson [15] is used. Similar to the *ECH*, the second phase gives optimal solutions for the restricted problem by an ILP solver.

5   Results

First of all, the experimental design is addressed in Subsect. 5.1. In Subsect. 5.2, the effects of allowing for modular capacities are presented. Finally, a comparison is made between the results of the *EPH* and the *ECH* in Subsect. 5.3.

5.1   Experimental Design

The same experimental design is used as in Hoekstra and Phillipson [10]. Lampposts are taken as locations which can be equipped with three services: Wi-Fi, Smart Vehicle Communication (SVC) and Alarm. Every service has its own set of demand points and every demand point requires only one service. The coordinates of the locations and demand points are based on real data. All demand points are located inside the region boundary that is based on the lampposts. Home addresses are taken as Wi-Fi demand points, all with demand equal to one. The SVC demand points are based on the roads. The demand of these points can vary between one, two and three, depending on the traffic density of the road. The Alarm demand points are equally spread over the region boundary and have a demand equal to one. The instances differ from each other in size and density. The sizes of the instances can be found in Table 3. Instances 1–7 are referred to as small, whereas instance 8 and 9 are referred to as large.

The number of locations is relatively high compared to the number of demand points, taking into account the above defined capacities. For example, one Wi-Fi

Table 3. Overview of the sizes of the instances.

| Instance | # Locations | # Demand points | | | |
		Wi-Fi	SVC	Alarm	Total
1	33	47	3	9	59
2	77	73	8	15	96
3	99	260	9	13	282
4	102	462	8	15	485
5	400	111	20	25	156
6	782	21	93	104	218
7	516	1,241	42	46	1,329
8	6,079	8,106	397	326	8,829
9	6,981	10,122	528	431	11,081

access point can serve thirty demand points, which implies that many locations will not be opened. However, this is only the case for dense instances in which the demand points and locations are close to each other. It is expected that relatively more locations are opened in sparse instances. An overview of the properties of the services can be found in Table 4. It is chosen to take the parameters equal for all locations.

Table 4. Overview of the parameters of the services.

Number u	Name	Range	Costs c_j^u	Capacity η_j^u	Demand d_i^u
1	Wi-Fi	100	300	30	1
2	SVC	200	350	15	1, 2, 3
3	Alarm	300	150	∞	1

Note that the range is defined in metres and it is assumed that the coverage area of every service is circular. This allows us to determine the coverage elements a_{ij}^u based on the haversine distance between the locations and demand points. The opening costs of a lamppost are taken equal to $f_j = 5,000$ for all locations. For simplicity, it is chosen to take $\kappa_j^u = \kappa$ the same for every location and service. Consequently, κ is set equal to 10 to enhance the feasibility of the ECH. This means that every access location can be equipped with ten service access points of every service.

Finally, the heuristics are programmed in MATLAB. The CPLEX solver is used to solve the ILP in the second phase of both heuristics using a *branch-and-bound* algorithm. The solver is terminated when the gap between the lower bound and objective value is less than 0.1%.

5.2   Effects of Modular Capacities

In this subsection, the effects of allowing for modular capacities are discussed. The results of the exact method on the MSCFLP, the EPH on the MSMCFLP and the *ECH* on the MSMCFLP can be found in Tables 5, 6 and 7, respectively.

The exact method only has low computation times for the very small instances. The number of access locations is in most cases (almost) equal to the number of Wi-Fi access points. The number of service access points for SVC and Alarm are much lower, which means that many access locations are only equipped with one Wi-Fi access point. This stipulates the potential cost benefit, by allowing for modular capacities.

The *EPH* has low computation times for instances 1–7 and higher computation times for instance 8 and 9. However, this is proportional in the instance size. One could see that multiple service access points are opened on one access location. Take for example instance 1, one access locations is equipped with two Wi-Fi, one SVC and one Alarm access points.

Table 5. Objective values, computation times and number of service access points and access locations of the exact method on the MSCFLP. Instances marked with a † did not terminate within 12 h.

Instance	Objective	Time (s)	# Access locations	# Service access points		
				Wi-Fi	SVC	Alarm
1	11,100	1.1	2	2	1	1
2	21,700	22.1	4	4	1	1
3	48,200	4.9	9	9	1	1
4	85,650	6.4	16	16	2	1
5†	38,150	43,200.0	7	6	3	2
6	100,200	171.8	18	11	15	11
7	231,600	316.6	43	43	8	6
8†	1,718,450	43,200.0	319	310	69	42
9†	2,192,800	43,200.0	408	386	83	53

Table 6. Objective values, computation times and number of service access points and access locations of the *EPH* on the MSMCFLP with $\kappa = 10$.

Instance	Objective	Time (s)	# Access locations		# Service access points		
			Intermediate	Final	Wi-Fi	SVC	Alarm
1	6,100	1.8	1	1	2	1	1
2	17,050	1.8	4	3	4	2	1
3	23,200	1.7	5	4	9	1	1
4	30,650	1.9	5	5	16	2	1
5	34,100	1.6	7	6	8	4	2
6	131,250	2.2	24	24	11	18	11
7	126,250	2.9	22	22	44	7	4
8	907,800	32.7	167	158	306	61	31
9	1,167,850	38.0	211	204	375	83	42

The benefit of allowing for modular capacities can be seen by comparing Table 5 with Table 6. The objective values of the *EPH* are lower than the objective values of the (non-modular) exact method for almost all instances. This can be explained by the difference between the number of access locations. Both methods need a similar number of service access points, but the number of access locations is lower for the *EPH*. The high opening costs f_j compared to the equipping costs c_j^u, result in the significant difference between the objective values. The exception is instance 6, in which the *EPH* needs more access locations which yield in a higher objective value. This is due to the sparseness of the demand in this instance.

Table 7. Objective values, computation times and number of service access points and access locations of the *ECH* on the MSMCFLP with $\kappa = 10$.

			# Access locations		# Service access points		
Instance	Objective	Time (s)	Intermediate	Final	Wi-Fi	SVC	Alarm
1	6,100	3.5	1	1	2	1	1
2	17,050	3.2	3	3	4	2	1
3	23,200	4.2	4	4	9	1	1
4	30,650	3.1	5	5	16	2	1
5	38,450	3.0	7	7	7	3	2
6	110,050	3.4	21	20	10	15	12
7	111,900	4.0	19	19	45	8	4
8	804,200	571.2	138	137	309	62	32
9	1,028,900	286.1	180	177	366	79	43

For illustrating purposes, the graphical representation of both solutions on instance 1 can be found in Figs. 1 and 2. The exact method needs two access locations for two Wi-Fi service access points to satisfy the demand. This induces the two Wi-Fi ranges in Fig. 2. On the other hand, the two Wi-Fi access points are placed on one access location in the *EPH*. All demand points can be reached from that location, but two Wi-Fi access points are needed to satisfy the capacity restriction. The saved access location results in a cost benefit of $f_j = 5,000$.

To be fair, the comparison between the exact method on the MSCFLP and the *EPH* on the MSMCFLP is not consistent, because the problems are not equivalent. However, it cannot be denied that allowing modular capacities results in high costs benefits and makes the problem, surprisingly, easier to solve. The disadvantage of the *EPH* is that is not known whether it is practically applicable to equip an access location with multiple service access points of the same service.

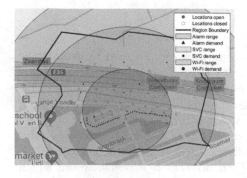

Fig. 1. *EPH* on the MSMCFLP

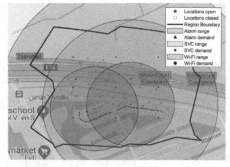

Fig. 2. Exact method on the MSCFLP

5.3 Comparison of Heuristics

One could easily see that the objective values of the *ECH* are higher than those obtained by the *EPH*, especially for the large instances. On the other hand, the computation times of these instances are higher for the *ECH*, which is caused by the *Sequential Set Covering Heuristic* in the first phase. Interesting to see is the difference between the number of access locations after phase 1 (intermediate) and in the final solution. The *ECH* almost needs all locations to satisfy the capacity constraint after the covering in the first phase. The opposite happens for the *EPH*, this method starts with a greedy solution which is optimised by an ILP. Therefore, more access locations are saved in the second phase. Although the number of access locations is lower for the *ECH*, approximately the same number of service access points are used in both methods. This means that the *ECH* is better able to choose locations, but the same number of service access points are needed to serve all demand.

As said before, the advantage of the *EPH* is that it will always lead to feasible solutions, regardless of the choice of the κ. The *ECH* can only produce feasible solutions for sufficiently high κ. In instance 9, some access locations are equipped with eight Wi-Fi service access points. Therefore, taking $\kappa < 8$ can result in infeasibility, if the demand points cannot be served by other service access points. Trial-and-error showed that this is already the case for $\kappa = 6$. On the other hand, the *EPH* solves instance 9 for $\kappa = 6$ with an objective value of 1,177,800. Naturally, this is higher than the objective value in Table 6, but the difference is only small.

6 Conclusion

In this paper, the MSMCFLP is introduced, which extends the MSCFLP by allowing for modular capacities. It is shown that this extension can lead to significant costs benefits in case of a high κ. The benefits are also dependent on the density of the demand points. Otherwise, there is no reason for placing multiple service access point on one access location. Two heuristics are proposed to solve the problem: the *EPH* and the *ECH*. The *ECH* gives lower objective values, but has higher computation times. Another disadvantage of this method is its dependency on the choice of κ. To conclude, for sufficient high κ, the *ECH* gives the best results. When regarding large instances or low values of κ, the *EPH* will be the best method to solve the MSMCFLP.

A suggestion for further research would be to include a restriction on the combination of service access points of different services on one access location. An example of this can be seen in Eq. 3.

$$\sum_{u \in \mathcal{F}} \alpha^u x_j^u \leq \tau_j y_j \qquad\qquad \forall j \in \mathcal{L} \qquad (3)$$

The parameters can be chosen based on practical reasons. For example, either a large service or two small services can be placed on an access location. In that case, the α^u for the large service should be twice as large as the one of the small service. Furthermore, note that for consistency reasons the following should hold.

$$\left\lfloor \frac{\tau_j}{\alpha^u} \right\rfloor \leq \kappa_j^u \qquad\qquad \forall j \in \mathcal{L}, \forall u \in \mathcal{F} \qquad (4)$$

By this construction, Constraint 1b becomes redundant and can be removed. A sensitivity analysis could be performed on the parameters to obtain the effect on the objective value.

References

1. Balakrishna, C.: Enabling technologies for smart city services and applications. In: 2012 Sixth International Conference on Next Seneration Mobile Applications, Services and Technologies, pp. 223–227. IEEE (2012)
2. Beasley, J.: A lagrangian heuristic for set-covering problems. Nav. Res. Logistics **37**, 151–164 (1990)
3. Ceria, S., Nobili, P., Sassano, A.: A lagrangian-based heuristic for large-scale set covering problems. Math. Program. **81**, 215–228 (1998)
4. Correia, I., Captivo, M.: A lagrangean heuristic for a modular capacitated location problem. Ann. Oper. Res. **122**, 141–161 (2003)
5. Correia, I., Captivo, M.: Bounds for the single source modular capacitated plant location problem. Comput. Oper. Res. **33**, 2991–3003 (2006)
6. Dileep, R.: Simple methods for uncapacitated facility location/allocation problems. J. Oper. Manag. **1**(4), 215–223 (1981)
7. Garey, M., Johnson, D.: Computers and Intractability: A Auide to the Theory of NP-Completeness. W.H. Freeman & Co., New York (1979). iSBN 0716710447
8. Guha, S., Khuller, S.: Greedy strikes back: improved facility location algorithms. J. Algorithms **31**, 228–248 (1999)
9. Ho, S.: An iterated tabu search heuristic for the single source capacitated facility location problem. Appl. Soft Comput. **27**, 169–178 (2015)
10. Hoekstra, G., Phillipson, F.: Location assignment of capacitated services in smart cities. In: The 4th International Conference on Mobile, Secure and Programmable Networking (MSPN 2018), Paris, France (2018)
11. Hoekstra, G., Phillipson, F.: Heuristic approaches for location assignment of capacitated services in smart cities. Computers **7**(4), 67 (2018)
12. Klincewicz, J., Luss, H.: A lagrangian relaxation heuristic for capacitated facility location with single-source constraints. J. Oper. Res. Soc. **37**, 495–500 (1986)
13. Nauss, R.: An improved algorithm for the capacitated facility location problem. J. Oper. Res. Soc. **19**(12), 1195–1201 (1978)
14. Pirkul, H.: Efficient algorithms for the capacitated concentrator problem. Comput. Oper. Res. **14**, 197–208 (1987)
15. Vos, T., Phillipson, F.: Dense multi-service planning in smart cities. In: International Conference on Information Society and Smart Cities (2018)

A Smart City Ecosystem Enabling Open Innovation

Dirk Ahlers[1]([✉]), Leendert W. M. Wienhofen[2], Sobah Abbas Petersen[3],
and Mohsen Anvaari[4]

[1] Department of Architecture and Planning,
NTNU – Norwegian University of Science and Technology, Trondheim, Norway
dirk.ahlers@ntnu.no
[2] Trondheim kommune, IT-tjenesten, Trondheim, Norway
leendert.wienhofen@trondheim.kommune.no
[3] Department of Computer Science, NTNU – Norwegian University of Science
and Technology, Trondheim, Norway
sobah.a.petersen@ntnu.no
[4] ITARK consulting, Trondheim, Norway
mohsen.anvaari@itark.no

Abstract. In this position paper we present IT-centered challenges that lie in designing an architecture for a flexible, open, transferable, and replicable smart city ecosystem spanning a plethora of suppliers and systems. The background is the smart city and energy project +Cityx-Change. Its vision is to enable the co-creation and development of Positive Energy Blocks in smart sustainable cities. It will include the development of a framework and supporting tools to enable a common energy market, supported by a connected community and city integration. It will explore influences of the energy transition into city operations and urban planning, the integration of e-Mobility as a Service (eMaaS) into positive energy communities, and the growth of local trading markets and new business models. Digitalization, open architectures, and open data need to support these processes for open urban innovation in the ICT-enabled city.

Keywords: Smart city · Data architecture · ICT ecosystem ·
Enterprise architecture · Open data · Positive energy districts ·
Energy transition · Energy informatics · eMaaS ·
Community engagement

1 Introduction

Smart Cities are becoming a pervasive topic of research and practice in a number of disciplines. Smart City itself is in our understanding a strong multidisciplinary field, combining many different stakeholder views and city-related disciplines with digitalization and ICT support for more livable and sustainable cities.

© Springer Nature Switzerland AG 2019
K.-H. Lüke et al. (Eds.): I4CS 2019, CCIS 1041, pp. 109–122, 2019.
https://doi.org/10.1007/978-3-030-22482-0_9

It combines cities, their inhabitants, smart digitalization, and societal aspects [1,4,14,19,23].

We focus here on the ICT aspects in Smart Cities, and in particular, on how to define a large-scale smart city IT architecture that spans multiple actors in an open and collaborative way through an ecosystem approach. This means we are not just aiming at an architecture for the operation of city systems in a strict municipal sense, but rather at an open system approach that can include actors from municipalities, public services, utilities, external companies, societal groups, academia etc. into an open ecosystem.

The background and motivation for this paper is the EU H2020 funded +CityxChange project that aims to develop Positive Energy Blocks (PEBs) in smart cities and communities as part of emission reductions to reach the Paris Climate Goals. The project background is described in Sect. 2.

We use approaches from the fields of complex systems, large-scale systems, data platforms, and Enterprise Architecture (EA). Our conceptual approach acknowledges the inherent complexity of smart cities and is designed to be open to additional stakeholders in and around a city, and to enable smart city evolution as an ongoing process. This goes hand in hand with an open innovation approach [7,10] that follows a quadruple helix participation model of collaboration between cities and public bodies, industry and business, research and academia, and citizens and civic society.

In this paper we thus focus on these communities, specifically on professional stakeholders to enable them to connect and build upon the ecosystem, and on citizens and private stakeholders to be able to participate in smart city development, benefit from open systems and open data, and for all stakeholders to make it easier to participate in smart city systems with lower entry barriers. We understand the ICT landscape as a complex systems-of-systems, forming an evolving ecosystem enabling openness and innovation. Based on these considerations, a decision was made for a loosely coupled, distributed, service-based ecosystem architecture instead of a monolithic, centralised, closed approach. Through this, we focus on system integration and data exchange, open standards, and a reference architecture supported by Enterprise Architecture methods to ensure autonomy of individual systems, while providing overall guidance and cohesion for the important collaboration and coordination aspects.

Open data, standards, IoT, etc. are a part of a smart city's ICT landscape, but many individual system specifications and data streams can be the responsibility of individual systems and partners, based on a separation of concerns. Finding the threshold between individual and overall responsibility and concern is an interesting challenge. Then the overarching task focuses on the interplay and orchestration of the different systems, coordination, joint data sources, joint open standards, overall monitoring and evaluation. Then the ecosystem approach becomes as much a technical challenge as one of stakeholder engagement, participation, and coordination for a comprehensive smart city project.

The main objective of this paper is to discuss challenges, principles, and solutions in developing an open ecosystem for Smart Cities that supports open innovation through openness, access, and stakeholders' awareness throughout its architecture.

The rest of this paper is structured as follows: Sect. 2 provides the background and describes the +CityxChange project; Sect. 3 describes the technological challenges of ICT support for smart cities: Sect. 4 describes EA in the project and provides an overview of its main methods; Sect. 5 describes the +CityxChange ecosystem-of-services architecture approach. Section 6 provides a conclusion and an outlook to future work.

2   Project Background

The +CityxChange project[1] is developing and deploying Positive Energy Blocks and Districts (PEB/PED) and scale these out as part of the European Clean Energy Transition in cities. 32 partners, including 7 cities and industry and research partners have joined forces to co-create these future energy systems. It follows an integrative approach with a strong focus on city integration, open innovation and replication ability. The approach combines:

- Integrated Planning and Design of Cities;
- Creation and Enabling of a Common Energy Market;
- CommunityxChange with all stakeholders of the city to create connected and engaged communities.

The project is funded by the EU H2020 Smart Cities and Communities topic SCC-1.[2] The call revolves around the sustainable energy transition in cities that should realize Europe wide deployment of Positive Energy Districts by 2050 through highly integrated and highly efficient innovative energy systems. Of interest are not only the direct technical solutions, but the interaction and integration between buildings, users, cities, the larger energy system, and the implications and impact on city planning, city systems, energy trading, citizen involvement, regulations, big data, digitalization, and socio-economic issues. A Positive Energy Blocks is defined by the EU as several buildings that actively manage their energy consumption and the energy flow between them and the wider energy system. They achieve an annual positive energy balance through use, optimization, and integration of advanced materials, energy reduction, local renewable energy production and storage, smart energy grids, demand-response, energy management of electricity, heating, and cooling, user involvement, and ICT. PEBs/PEDs are designed as an integral part of the district energy system. They should be intrinsically scalable up to positive energy districts and cities and are well embedded in the spatial, economic, technical, environmental and social context (see Footnote 2).

---

[1] Positive City exChange http://cityxchange.eu/.
[2] Smart Cities and Communities H2020-LC-SC3-2018-2019-2020, https://ec.europa. eu/info/funding-tenders/opportunities/portal/screen/opportunities/topic-details/ lc-sc3-scc-1-2018-2019-2020.

Solutions and demonstration projects will be first demonstrated in the Lighthouse Cities (Limerick, Ireland and Trondheim, Norway) and will be replicated in five Follower Cities (Alba Iulia, Romania; Sestao, Spain; Písek, Czech Republic; Smolyan, Bulgaria and Võru, Estonia).

New forms of integrated spatial, social, political, economic, regulatory, legal, and technological innovations will deliver citizen observatories, innovation playgrounds and regulatory sandboxes linked to urban living labs, and Bold City Visions to engage civil society, local authorities, industry, and RTOs to scale up from PEBs to Positive Energy Cities, supported by a distributed and modular energy system architecture.

3   Technology Objectives

The +CityxChange project spans many different objectives, however, in this paper we focus on the technical objectives. Regulatory issues, citizen-centered approaches, replication, or business models are out of scope. On the technical and physical side, the underlying approaches and systems that drive the ICT view are:

- development and deployment of PEBs,
- integration of local distributed renewable energy sources, and energy storage;
- connection of buildings and building systems to energy communities and markets;
- optimized energy system operation;
- connection to energy and district heating systems;
- smart metering;
- integration of electric vehicles;
- better mobility solutions by offering eMaaS;
- integrated planning and design; [17]
- digital platforms for community and stakeholder engagement;
- integration with city systems;
- open innovation supported by open data, hackathons, prototyping, etc.;
- monitoring and evaluation of the project through KPI data processing and analysis;

Out of these arise the objectives for the ICT ecosystem architecture. The project needs to create an overall ICT architecture and service-based ecosystem to ensure that service providers of the +CityxChange project will develop, deploy and test their services through integrated and interconnected approaches that maintain an open approach.

In addition, the project needs to ensure that data can be transferred in an open, accessible, interoperable, and secure manner through data integration and exchange, and will further investigate new and emerging technologies such a Distributed Ledger Technologies, e.g., IOTA and the generation blockchain as additions to existing transfer, payment or transaction methods.

4   Enterprise Architecture

Enterprise Architecture [15] can be a very powerful facilitator for complex projects by playing an advisory role in the strategic level and a guiding role in the implementation, and most importantly, helping to bridge between these two levels in an enterprise or a project.

The Open Group in its EA Framework TOGAF describes EA as an activity focused on "understanding all of the different components that make up the enterprise and how those components inter-relate"[3]. The Gartner Group's definition further highlights EA as a process that facilitates change, through "principles and models that describe the enterprise's future state and enabling its evolution and transformation"[4]. EA is thus more than system architecture. It's concern is the overall ICT landscape and aligns the organizational business strategy and its ICT implementation. That means EA is a full stack of business architecture, data architecture, application architecture, technology architecture, and security architecture. Traditional EA frameworks assume that it is possible to describe in detail all ICT applications since they are usually deployed in-house [6]. Thus, these frameworks may be challenged when EA is considered as an open ecosystem which encompass several stakeholders, services, and cities that do not necessarily have a central or purely hierarchical control.

We take the understanding that also a smart city or a smart city project suits the enterprise view of EA to benefit from its framework and approach. Here we model the project with its different actors in smart cities through an EA approach, which is a viable approach if leaving out certain overly detailed descriptions [12, 16].

In the context of the +CityxChange project, the project-wide enterprise architecture is then the process of translating the project's cities' visions into demo projects and their development, implementation, and deployment by developing principles, requirements, models, and guidelines that enable the consistent development of various components of demo projects and ensuring that project deliveries are in compliance with the project's and cities' visions and needs and contribute to the overall goals. EA can further help bridge between the overall more strict development model of an H2020 project and the more agile approaches for individual components and for the engagement of external stakeholders.

Enterprise architecture can play at least four roles in the project: (1) as a decision-support tool it can advise the project coordinators and task leaders to manage the service portfolio of the project more efficiently by conducting realistic gap analyses and overviews, (2) as an integration and interoperability tool it can ensure that various stakeholders, service providers and ICT systems are efficiently communicating with each other (ensuring organizational, semantic and technical interoperability), (3) as a quality assurance tool it can monitor whether

---

[3] http://pubs.opengroup.org/architecture/togaf8-doc/arch/.
[4] https://www.gartner.com/it-glossary/enterprise-architecture-ea/.

development of different ICT components in the project are in compliance with project guidelines and city visions, and (4) as a communication tool it can ensure the knowledge reusability and replicability within and outside of the project.

Performed thoroughly, EA can produce a huge number of artefacts that all have their use in a large enterprise. Selecting the right ones for specific projects is a challenging process. One of the most comprehensive taxonomies for describing the artefacts from the views of the different stakeholders is provided by the Zachman Framework[5]. More recently, TOGAF has become popular as it not only recommends what to capture and describe, but also a process to conduct EA projects. The TOGAF project Application Development Process (ADM) also supports the evolution of the EA and change management process. For example, care has to be taken to select the ICT solutions and artefacts with the maximum impact to reduce overhead and deliver the most value in line with the business objectives. TOGAF considers EA as a continuum and describes how architectures can continuously evolve. This also aligns well with the smart city approach, as shown in Fig. 1 and discussed below. It provides a set of foundation (or reference) architectures (for the Business, Application, Data and Technology architectures), which provide good starting points for EA.

It is then possible to adapt and refine a generic foundation architecture to suit the domain or specific needs of the enterprise. An overview and comparison of the main EA methods are provided in [21].

5   +CityxChange Ecosystem Approach

In this section, we describe our technical concept and framework towards a reference architecture for the +CityxChange development and implementation. The overall ecosystem will need to address the technical objectives detailed in the previous section through a number of principles and challenges discussed below.

The current situation of many smart city ICT systems is to go for a large single-vendor solution. We do not find this optimal and not in line with iterative municipal system approaches and hence, motivated by the city needs and the project challenges, we propose to not build one centralised urban monolithic platform, but instead to develop a flexible distributed service-oriented ecosystem. It will focus on system integration, orchestration, and collaboration, through open systems, integration of open data, and an Enterprise Architecture and open ecosystem approach.

---

[5] https://zachman.com/about-the-zachman-framework,
https://www.zachman.com/resources/ea-articles-reference/327-the-framework-for-enterprise-architecture-background-description-and-utility-by-john-a-zachman.

5.1 Principles and Challenges

In order to reach the objectives set forward in the previous section, we design a +CityxChange ecosystem that builds on the following principles:

API-driven and distributed service-oriented architecture as architecture style for the ecosystem.

Loose coupling of components supports the previous point through independent components, defined interfaces, encapsulation and information hiding of internal structures of other components [18]. It offers flexibility and reusability around adding, replacing, changing, and evolving components and a reduction in system-wide effects.

Separation of concerns in the same line ensure that there is no need to run everything on a common platform but allows for distribution of systems and responsibilities. This also mandates the ability and necessity to use open standards and interoperability of systems. It also allows for easier replicability of individual parts of the project. This is a driving force for the project.

Individual system and data responsibility to ensure separation of concerns and domain-specific systems working independently.

Enterprise architecture view to include the whole city context as discussed in detail in Sect. 4.

Interoperability through Open standards and open APIs, open documentation, open data models etc.

Replicability As a main objective, replicability means that solutions are generic enough that they can be deployed in other cities and contexts, that the overall solutions are sufficiently modularised, and that interfaces are well defined and open to enable a solution work within a different deployment landscape.

Joint guidelines and data governance to ensure project-wide consistency and joint understanding of the approach and needs.

Open by default is the approach taken by the project to ensure maximised transparency and replicability. It should be reflected in all project work.

Open data open city data, open research data, etc. in line with FAIR principles (making research data findable, accessible, interoperable and re-usable)[6].

Enabling and facilitating systems open for everyone to ensure access not only to data, but also to frameworks and systems as much as possible.

Citizen engagement Engagement of citizens and external stakeholders through workshops, co-creation activities, early involvement, hackathons, open data, etc. is an open-ended tasks. Being able to integrate any unexpected results in an agile manner is a benefit and needs to be enabled properly

Open innovation as a guiding principle to enable meaningful connections and contributions from city and citizens, industry, academia, and other stakeholders [7, 8, 10].

---

[6] Guidelines on Data Management in Horizon 2020, http://ec.europa.eu/research/participants/data/ref/h2020/grants_manual/hi/oa_pilot/h2020-hi-oa-data-mgt_en.pdf.

Sustainability in both the ecological use of ICT [2] and the technical sustainability of solutions for long-term use and migration options for after the project.

Opening up and connecting silos is important since many existing systems to be used may be rather closed. Making them open and interoperable is a benefit for the project, but also for future work by others.

Reuse of existing knowledge from other Smart City and ecosystem project, reusing existing frameworks, standards, etc. See the overview in Sect. 5.2.

Transformation and change, smart city projects as a hub and trigger for change, as well as using existing transition projects to realise co-benefits [3]

Supporting digitalization and digital transformation.

Migration and integration of relevant parts after the project.

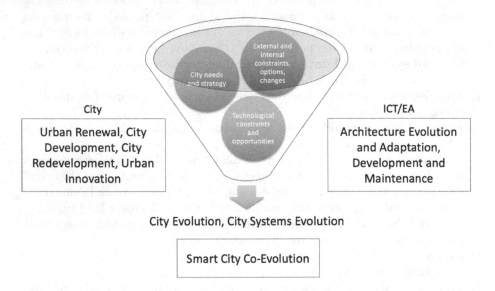

Fig. 1. Smart city co-evolution through city and ICT/EA views. Adapted from [11]

At their core, many smart city initiatives are change projects and part of the digital transformation. This in turn means that frameworks and architectures need to address issues of large-scale system evolution and transition [3]. This also hold true for new smart city projects, as they do not operate on a blank slate. Figure 1 shows a few key concepts around this, based on [11] and adapted to this project space. It highlights the importance of including the city needs and strategies, the internal and external constraints and stakeholders, and the technological constraints and opportunities towards smart city co-evolution. The depicted concept is strongly linked to open innovation and stakeholder engagement through quadruple helix approaches, as discussed in Sect. 1.

5.2   Ecosystem Architecture

Following the definition of an ICT ecosystem from the Open ePolicy Group [13], the service-oriented ecosystem of +CityxChange encompasses not only the data, applications and technologies, but also the policies, regulations, processes, and stakeholders that together constitute the larger technology environment for implementing +CityxChange solutions in each of the cities.

The overall ecosystem will need to address different scales of granularity of systems and components ensuring interoperability and operation: individual partner and city systems (existing and new, posing different interoperability and integration challenges); individual demo projects; demo areas and sites within cities; general project within a city; overall project, integrating all cities. In addition, it needs to address the challenges raised above in Sects. 3 and 5.1.

We choose to follow an architecture style that moves away from central monolithic systems to distributed service-oriented ecosystems in a systems-of-systems thinking. We see this move in many other places. Foe example, the European SCC-1 project calls are evolving. As one of the latest changes, there has been a move away from central project-based systems. In part this is also based on the expectation that partners are mature enough for the next step in the energy transition and that smart cities will already have their own data platforms. This opens the path towards a distributed architecture, which allows all partners to operate their own systems towards a common project goal by focusing on an ecosystem approach with suitable interfaces between systems.

Additionally, common architecture styles that follow layered and distributed structures are being used more often, including for smart cities [22]. The TOGAF method can be represented as a layered architecture, where the different views (Business, Applications and Technology) could be considered as a layer. Thus, it is not surprising that some of the smart city architectures reported in the literature use a TOGAF-inspired layered approach.

The ESPRESSO Smart City Reference Architecture[7] [9] is a major EU-funded initiative. It is partly based on the TOGAF methodology and has selected relevant architecture artefacts for Smart Cities, similar to our project. As shown in Fig. 2, its conceptual reference architecture starts from the consumers of the services at the top. It then identifies the services provided by the enterprise (business services), the applications to support the services, the data services and the data sources. The bottom layers include physical sensing devices to capture real-time and survey data and their physical positions. Several cross-cutting services, such as the security, auditing, communication, and collaboration services, as well as integration, business intelligence, master data management etc. are linked to all the layers. We in turn have drawn inspiration from the ESPRESSO layered architecture and ability for decentralization.

---

[7] ESPRESSO, systEmic Standardization apPRoach to Empower Smart citieS and cOmmunities, 2016 http://espresso-project.eu/.

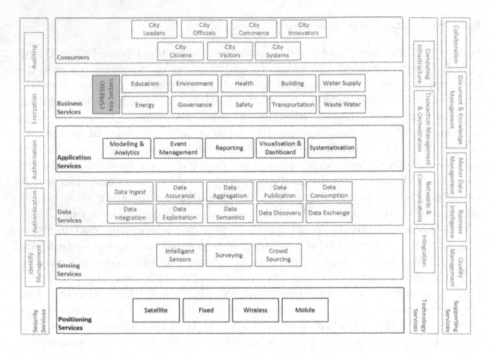

Fig. 2. ESPRESSO smart city reference architecture. (Source: [9])

The ITU meta-architecture [11] follows a similar multi-tier or layered model. It uses hard and soft infrastructure and surrounding layers defined as Natural Environment; Hard Infrastructure (Non ICT-based, such as urban infrastructure); Hard Infrastructure (ICT-based); Services (smart city services); Soft Infrastructure (people, governance, software and data).

Closer towards concrete implementation, data models, and exchange formats, FIWARE[8] [20] is an extensive framework and library of a networked architecture and an extensive list of data models for numerous entities and sensors/actuators within a smart city and will help to ensure standard-compliance, along with other relevant standards. It is a European project in line with the Digital Single Market strategy, and ensures portability, interoperability and openness of services across Europe.

Both Lighthouse Cities, Limerick and Trondheim, are part of the international smart city network Open & Agile Smart Cities (OASC[9]). OASC has the goal of creating and shaping the nascent global smart city data and services market and, as our project, is driven by implementation and focused on open platforms and citizen engagement. The Minimal Interoperability Mechanisms (MIMs) approach inspires the replication task in our project, as MIMs are simple and transparent mechanisms, ready to use in any city, regardless of size or

---

[8] https://www.fiware.org/developers/.
[9] https://oascities.org.

capacity. In practice, the OASC MIMs are a set of common (realtime) APIs to access data, context information to structure data, and a common, but optional, data platform to store and serve data. In addition, a reference architecture and a reference implementation complete the set of MIMs.

5.3   Proposed Solution

The conceptual view of the service ecosystem high-level architecture for the +CityxChange project is shown in Fig. 3. Following the ESPRESSO inspiration and adopting the TOGAF approach, the consumers of the services are described on the top layer, followed by the business services, which in this case are the actual demonstration projects around energy, modeling, and citizen engagement. This is followed by a governance, regulations, economy, and business model layer. Considering the focus on energy markets and prosumers of energy, this is an essential part of the service ecosystem of the +CityxChange project. As a side not, a lot of the resulting business models and value creation are also based on ICT approaches [5], but will be more than that and arise out of all aspects, including participation. Below this, the soft ICT services such as models, applications, data services, storage, and systems are described. The hard ICT components such as cloud infrastructure, smart grid, sensors, and other devices are found below the soft ICT layer. At the bottom, a non-ICT layer is described, identifying the physical context such as the energy hardware and controllers, buildings, other infrastructure, or public spaces. Furthermore, components in the service ecosystem are structured vertically according to the three themes of the project, ((i) integrated planning and design, (ii) common energy market and

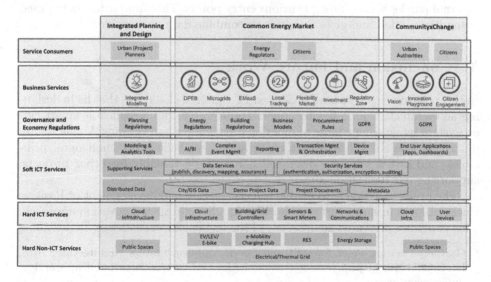

Fig. 3. Conceptual view of the +CityxChange service ecosystem high-level architecture. (Source: +CityxChange project)

(iii) CommunityxChange). On the side of this, and not pictured, is an EA cross-cutting concern, comprising data and API repositories, user journeys, overall interface and architecture guidelines and other resources of use for the overall project development.

A recent Gartner report[10] notes that the digital transformation requires organizations to choose new modern architecture styles and suggests service-oriented application architectures (SOA) Different styles of APIs, such as REST, SOAP, enterprise buses and others such as microservices or miniservices allow to abstract from individual partner and component details and easier include other digital services and assets. This forces an agreement on communication and interface definitions, structures, and workflows between systems, abstracting from implementation details. This supports our choices, as well as the large-scale software systems engineering literature that we do not go into detail at this time.

An open data platform will be established, supporting the "open by design" driver. KPIs stemming from the project will be published in the overall KPI system and by some cities in open data portals[11]. Note that the data to be published there is not limited to the KPIs. Trondheim municipality intends to open up as much data as possible, within legal boundaries, so third parties can use this data to develop innovative solutions. Also, it aims to become a good source of data for the university so students can work with real life data and real life scenarios rather than textbook examples. The work with the open data platform will not only be guided by the project, but will also find inspiration in other distributed open data platforms and aims to combine data from many different sources, some open, some national, some private. Partly to support open data, and partly to support the projects decision support, open APIs, with a clear description of the data models and functionality, will be provided, giving external parties access through various entry points. This approach is being used by multiple cities, and gives a chance to combine data nationwide.

6   Conclusion and Future Work

In this position paper we have presented IT-centered challenges that lie in design-ing an architecture for a flexible, open, transferable, and a replicable smart city ecosystem integrating a large number of stakeholders and systems. While we are describing one EU H2020 smart city project, we believe the challenges, prin-ciples, and initial solutions discussed here can be valuable for other projects, supporting our replication aim.

The project's vision is to enable the co-creation and development of Positive Energy Blocks in smart sustainable cities in a holistic open innovation approach. This paper has presented an overview of the technological challenges in designing

---

[10] Gartner, Decision Point for API and Service Implementation Architecture, 2018, ID G00351010, https://www.gartner.com/doc/3879865/decision-point-api-service-implementation.

[11] For example for Trondheim at data.trondheim.kommune.no; the link to the reposi-tory will become available during 2019.

an overall ICT architecture and service-based ecosystem to enable this and other technological challenges and stakeholder integration.

The +CityxChange project is in its first few months and thus the work described in this paper is being discussed and refined and ideas for the detailed implementation are reviewed. Some of the main activities in the near future will be to instantiate the descriptions and ecosystem architecture provided in this paper, develop and maintain the repository for the lifecycle management of APIs, data models, vocabularies, etc. to support API discovery and registration, the identification and mapping of the data, data types and meta data and indeed the description of services and designing seamless integration of the multiple applications and data to support the demonstrations and their replication through architecture and interaction blueprints.

Acknowledgements. +CityxChange (Positive City ExChange) is a smart city project under the Smart Cities and Communities topic that has been granted funding from the European Union's Horizon 2020 research and innovation programme under Grant Agreement No. 824260. The main content of this paper corresponds to work that has been performed before the project start, as project development, requirements gathering, and aligning with project, city, and partner visions and approaches. It further includes initial refinements and findings within the project.

We thank our colleagues and project team members Markus Helfert, University of Limerick, and John Krogstie, NTNU, as well as the whole +CityxChange project and project preparation team for valuable discussions and contributions.

References

1. Ahlers, D., Driscoll, P., Löfström, E., Krogstie, J., Wyckmans, A.: Understanding smart cities as social machines. In: Workshop on the Theory and Practice of Social Machines, WWW 2016 Companion, IW3C2, pp. 759–764 (2016). https://doi.org/10.1145/2872518.2890594
2. Anthopoulos, L.: Defining smart city architecture for sustainability. In: Proceedings of 14th Electronic Government and 7th Electronic Participation Conference (IFIP2015), pp. 140–147 (2015)
3. Anvaari, M., Cruzes, D.S., Conradi, R.: Smart grid software applications as an ultra-large-scale system: challenges for evolution. In: Proceedings of the 2012 IEEE PES Innovative Smart Grid Technologies, ISGT 2012, pp. 1–6. IEEE (2012). https://doi.org/10.1109/ISGT.2012.6175687
4. Appio, F.P., Lima, M., Paroutis, S.: Understanding smart cities: innovation ecosystems, technological advancements, and societal challenges. Technol. Forecast. Soc. Chang. **142**, 1–14 (2019). https://doi.org/10.1016/j.techfore.2018.12.018
5. Baldwin, E., Curley, M.: Managing IT Innovation for Business Value: Practical Strategies for IT and Business Managers. Intel Press (2007)
6. Bellman, B., Griesi, K., Bergman, M.: Agile enterprise architecture: oxymoron or new vision. In: Proceedings of ISPIM 2015 (2015)
7. Chesbrough, H.W.: Open Innovation: The New Imperative for Creating and Profiting from Technology. Harvard Business Press, Brighton (2003)
8. Chesbrough, H.W., Vanhaverbeke, W., West, J.: Open Innovation: Researching a New Paradigm. Oxford University Press, Oxford (2006)

9. Cox, A., Parslow, P., Lathouwer, B.D., Klien, E., Kempen, B., Lonien, J.: D4.2 – Definition of Smart City Reference Architecture. Technical report, ESPRESSO systEmic Standardisation apPRoach to Empower Smart citieS and cOmmunities (2016)
10. Curley, M., Salmelin, B.: Open Innovation 2.0: The New Mode of Digital Innovation for Prosperity and Sustainability. Springer, Cham (2017). https://doi.org/10.1007/978-3-319-62878-3
11. ITU-T Focus Group on Smart Sustainable Cities: Setting the framework for an ICT architecture of a smart sustainable city. Technical report, International Telecommunications Union (ITU) (2015)
12. Kakarontzas, G., Anthopoulos, L., Chatzakou, D., Vakali, A.: A conceptual enterprise architecture framework for smart cities: a survey based approach. In: 2014 11th International Conference on e-Business (ICE-B), pp. 47–54, August 2014
13. Kaplan, J.: Roadmap for open ICT ecosystems. Technical report, Open ePolicy Group, Berkman Center for Internet and Society, Cambridge, MA (2005)
14. Khatoun, R., Zeadally, S.: Smart cities: concepts, architectures, research opportunities. Commun. ACM 59(8), 46–57 (2016). https://doi.org/10.1145/2858789
15. Lankhorst, M.: Enterprise Architecture at Work. Springer, Heidelberg (2017). https://doi.org/10.1007/978-3-662-53933-0
16. Mamkaitis, A., Bezbradica, M., Helfert, M.: Urban enterprise: a review of smart city frameworks from an enterprise architecture perspective. In: 2016 IEEE International Smart Cities Conference (ISC2), pp. 1–5. IEEE (2016)
17. Nielsen, B.F., Baer, D., Lindkvist, C.: Identifying and supporting exploratory and exploitative models of innovation in municipal urban planning; key challenges from seven norwegian energy ambitious neighborhood pilots. Technol. Forecast. Soc. Chang. 142, 142–153 (2019). https://doi.org/10.1016/j.techfore.2018.11.007
18. Pautasso, C., Wilde, E.: Why is the web loosely coupled?: A multi-faceted metric for service design. In: Proceedings of the 18th International Conference on World Wide Web, WWW 2009, pp. 911–920. ACM (2009). https://doi.org/10.1145/1526709.1526832
19. Ratti, C., Claudel, M.: The City of Tomorrow: Sensors, Networks, Hackers, and the Future of Urban Life. Yale University Press, New Haven (2016)
20. Salhofer, P., Joanneum, F.: Evaluating the FIWARE platform: A case-study on implementing smart application with FIWARE. In: Proceedings of the 51st Hawaii International Conference on System Sciences, pp. 5797–5805 (2018)
21. Sessions, R.: A comparison of the top four enterprise-architecture methodologies. Technical report, ObjectWatch Inc. (2007)
22. Tomas, G.H.R.P., et al.: Smart cities architectures: A systematic review. In: ICEIS 2013 - 15th International Conference on Enterprise Information Systems (2013)
23. Townsend, A.M.: Smart Cities: Big Data, Civic Hackers, and the Quest for a New Utopia. W.W. Norton & Company, New York (2013)

Innovations and Digital Transformation

Innovation Management Methods in the Automotive Industry

Karl-Heinz Lüke[1]([⊠]), Johannes Walther[2], Daniel Wäldchen[2],
and Denis Royer[1]

[1] Ostfalia University of Applied Sciences, Wolfsburg, Germany
{ka.lueke,d.royer}@ostfalia.de
[2] IPM AG, Hannover, Germany
{j.w,d.w}@ipm.ag

Abstract. The automotive industry is mainly characterized by shorter product life cycles, ever-growing competitive pressure, significant technological advances and massive changes in the political, technological and sociocultural environment. Therefore, innovation management as an enabler for product, process and business model innovations is becoming more and more important in the automotive industry, a statement which is confirmed by massive increase in innovation expenditure. This paper discusses specific innovation methods related to three cooperation fields: supplier, customer and in-house. The research project, presented in this paper, ascertains their particular implementation level in the automotive industry. One of the findings is the growing significance of the in-house innovation method Big Data as a result of enormous data volume increase. Consequently, the Automotive Big Data Platform (ABDP) Reference Architecture is presented in this paper. Big Data will enable the automotive industry to cope with the challenges.

Keywords: Innovation management · Open innovation ·
Automotive industry · Big Data · Requirements · Architecture concept

1 Current Situation and Motivation

The great and unbroken significance of innovations is particularly confirmed by increased innovation expenditure. The top 1000 innovators worldwide have almost doubled their investments in innovation, since 2005 [1]. This development is remarkable, but not surprising. After all, companies are coming under increasing pressure due to shorter product life cycles, ever-growing competitive pressure and significant technological advances [2].

This is particularly true for the automotive industry. Caused by the drive system electrification, the automobile and the industry are facing the biggest change since the introduction of mass production. It is expected that the share of diesel and gasoline engines worldwide will decline from currently 14% and 78% respectively to 5% and 47%, in 2030 [3, 4]. At the same time, the share of electric vehicles will rise from currently 1% to 14%, and the share of hybrid vehicles from 7% to 34% [3, 4]. In unison, the production capacity of the battery cell production will more than triple

K.-H. Lüke et al. (Eds.): I4CS 2019, CCIS 1041, pp. 125–141, 2019.
https://doi.org/10.1007/978-3-030-22482-0_10

between 2017 and 2020 from 93 to 313 gigawatt hours [3]. Advances in information and communication technologies allow self-driving cars to become a reality, in the near future. Forecasts show that the number of cars registered and driven by people themselves will fall by 40% by 2030 [3, 4].

Radical technological change favors the emergence of new market players who do not have to take existing corporate structures into account and who are driving the industry change taking great risk. Established car manufacturers are challenged by companies such as Tesla and BYD, and the fact that 41% of all electric cars were produced in China in 2017 [3]. The industry needs to rethink its business models in the course of digitization. Younger generations in urban areas in particular want to use the automobile, but do not necessarily want to own it [5]. It is expected that the share of worldwide car sharing users will more than quintuple between 2015 and 2025 from 7 to 36 million users. In the same period, the fleet size of car sharing providers is expected to increase almost fourfold from 112,000 to 427,000 vehicles [3, 4]. Here, too, new mobility providers are emerging such as Uber and the Google subsidiary Waymo.

Against this background, innovations and their management are a top priority for the decision-makers of OEMs and suppliers [6]. The recent positive market environment creates the financial scope for investments in research and development (R&D). New passenger car registrations worldwide will reach a new high of 79.23 million vehicles, in 2019 [3, 4]. At the same time, the ten largest automobile manufacturers, with one exception, were able to increase their previous year's sales, when comparing 2016 to 2017 [3, 4]. Nevertheless, maximum efforts and efficient use of resources are required to master the upcoming change. It is not surprising that of the 20 companies that invest most in innovation across all sectors, six are from the automotive industry, and four have increased their innovation expenditure, comparing 2018 to 2017 (Table 1).

Table 1. Expenditure of Automotive Top R&D spenders [1]

	2018 USD Billions	% of revenue	Difference to 2017
Volkswagen AG	USD 15.8	5.7%	14.1%
Toyota	USD 10.0	3.9%	2.6%
Ford	USD 8.0	5.1%	9.6%
General motors	USD 7.3	5.0%	−9.9%
Daimler	USD 7.1	3.6%	−9.2%
Honda	USD 7.1	5.4%	8.7%
Average	USD 9.2	4.8%	2.7%

To generate new and more efficient ways to innovate, the automotive industry also relies on innovations from and in cooperation with suppliers [7]. OEMs are increasingly trying to gain access to innovations from their suppliers. This innovation process is also known as "Open Innovation" and it means to open up to external innovation sources and users [8]. To this end, strategic partnerships are established such as the

Volkswagen Group's FAST (Future Automotive Supply Tracks) program. This approach seems to make sense in particular in the automotive industry. Over the past decades, the value-added structure has become the shape of a pyramid including various Tier levels of suppliers and OEMs. It shows 62% of the added value is generated by suppliers [2]. This suggests that there is enormous potential for innovation.

The idea of this study is to take a closer look at the innovation management tools that are already applied in the automotive industry to drive transformation and changes and those which can be transferred from other industries or academia.

2 Research Need

When searching for the two keywords innovation and automotive industry, the EBSCO host database shows 603 hits for scientific articles in English, published between 2009 and 2019.[1] This number is remarkably high, as only 142 hits show up for the aviation industry ceteris paribus.

Of the 603 hits found for the automotive industry, however, only 50 contributions additionally refer to methods (Table 2), of which only two articles actually focus on innovation methods. This result corresponds with Ili et al. statement from 2010 that research on innovation in the automotive industry is mostly based on explorative case studies, but rarely on surveys [7].

Table 2. Keyword hits for academic journals targeting innovation methods in the automotive industry between 2009 and 2019

Year	2009	2010	2011	2012	2013	2014	2015	2016	2017	2018	2019
# Research articles	2	5	3	2	4	3	8	6	9	6	2

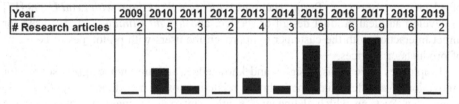

The automotive industry is an economically important factor in the Triad countries in general, and in Germany in particular [3, 4]. It is often regarded as a pioneering industry [9]. The authors of this study are therefore convinced that it is relevant to specifically analyze the innovation management methods applied in the automotive industry. From a scientific point of view, it makes sense to fill the research gap that is emerging here, specifically since surveys are rarely the methodology of choice.

---

[1] EBSCO Host Business Source Premier, selection: Title, Abstract or Keywords

3 Innovation Methods Evaluation

3.1 Innovation Management Methods

The significance of efficient innovation management as an enabler of product, process and business model innovations is growing rapidly in the automotive industry. This paper discusses specific innovation management methods which are related to the cooperation fields supplier, customer and in-house [10].

There are many ways to innovate and create value. To involve suppliers and enable collaboration is one of it. We differentiate the supplier related innovation methods: *Cooperation with Universities* to initiate knowledge transfer, *External Contest for Ideas* e.g. with suppliers, universities and research facilities [11], *Start-up Identification and Co-operation* (e.g. start-up scouting, start-up pitching, innovation competition) and co-operation on various intensity levels, *Innovation Scouting* implying systematic and continuous search for innovations and innovative solutions outside the company [12], *Value-added Networks (strategic alliances)* consisting of legally independent but economically dependent companies [13] and *Innovation Communities* [14] that are related to a task and are pushing forward certain innovation projects (e.g. open source).

The customer of today is looking for innovative products and services to simplify and enrich life. To get ideas what customers do need and want is essential. We differentiate the customer related innovation methods [10]: *Megatrend Studies* to identify the impact of sociocultural, political and technological trends in the long run, *Day-in-Life Visits* [15], involving functional teams that visit customers and observe them in their environment, and *Test Markets* [16] being simulated in virtual environments or in laboratories, *Field Tests* in order to introduce innovations to a chosen local test market of selected test users (e.g., Berlin, Hamburg), *Ideation Workshops with Lead Users* [17] to develop an ideal product design or service, and *Insight Clinique* [18, 19] used for direct interaction with the customer to approach the users with prototypes or concepts of products or services.

Employees have ideas, insights and knowledge, and are another great source for innovation. We differentiate the in-house related innovation methods [10]: *Employee Suggestion Systems* which define and employ internal business processes for the evaluation of process improvements and product innovations [20], *Internal Ideation Contests* inviting staff to provide ideas and suggestions to a specific innovation field [21], and *Internal Ideation Workshops* [22] to provide ideas for a new product or service, *Scenario Engineering* [23] used to select strategies and to raise awareness about probable future events, *Roadmap Development* [24] applied in project management, especially for projects that take a slightly longer time horizon, and *Big Data* [25] to analyze large data sets of structured, semi-structured or unstructured data.

3.2 Evaluation Criteria

This research project "Innovation Management in the Automotive Industry" spotlights the innovation management methods applied in the automotive industry. It is based on a questionnaire which is asking the participants to indicate the application level of open innovation methods in their company on a five-level ordinal scale (very high (5) to very low (1)). The findings are mapped in separate innovation radars that focus on the cooperation fields supplier, customer and in-house [10].

The survey (online questionnaire in German and English) was conducted in February 2018. 460 companies from the automotive industry took part (respondent rate 4,74%), 358 questionnaires could be evaluated. Most of the participants operate as OEM, 1st-tier or 2nd-tier suppliers (89%) and generate sales of less than EUR 500 million (59%). The participating companies primarily implement product innovations (76%), secondary apply process innovations (68%) and finally use business model innovations (66%). More than half of the respondents classified the maturity rate of their innovation management as high or very high (60%).

3.3 Analysis of Applied Methods/Innovation Radar

The innovation radars [26, 27] for the cooperation fields supplier, customer and in-house show the results of this research project.

The innovation radar "supplier" shows that the automotive industry applies the supplier originated innovation methods (Fig. 1) "Value-added Networks (strategic alliances)" (3,25) and "Co-operation with universities" (3,23) most frequently. The supplier originated innovation methods "External Contest for Ideas" (2,36), "Start-up Identification and Co-operation" (2,61) and "Innovation Communities" (2,75) are less relevant in the automotive industry.

The innovation radar for "customer" integration (Fig. 2) shows that the automotive industry predominantly applies the innovation methods "Ideation Workshop with Lead Users" (3,11) and "Megatrend Study" (2,88), while "Day-in-Life-Visits" (2,05), "Test Market" (2,34) and "Field Test" (2,50) are applied on a smaller scale.

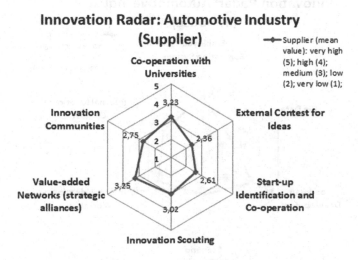

Fig. 1. Innovation radar: supplier

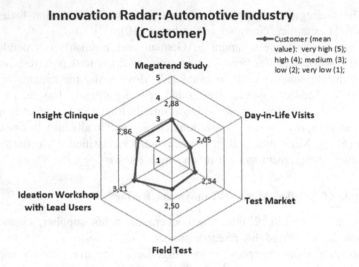

Fig. 2. Innovation radar: customer

The innovation radar for "in-house" integration (Fig. 3) shows that the innovation sources "Employee Suggestion System" (3,68) and "Roadmap Development" (3,61) are paramount in the automotive industry. "Big Data" (2,44), "Scenario Engineering" (2,90) and "Internal Ideation Contest (3,19)" are of minor importance in the automotive industry.

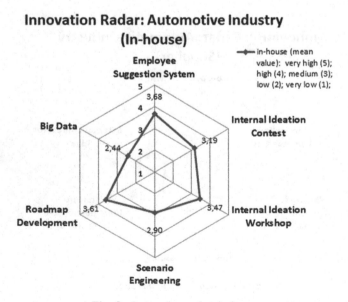

Fig. 3. Innovation radar: in-house

3.4   Detailed Evaluation of Innovation Methods

Further conclusions can be drawn by a deeper quantitative analysis of the empirical data sets. The study distinguishes automotive companies according to relevant characteristics such as revenue, value chain, innovation type and number of employees and divides them into "customer segments". The study is taking these customer segments into account to gain deeper understanding of the innovation preferences of the different automotive companies with the idea of discovering what each customer segment finds most valuable, to more accurately tailor innovation methods toward that customer segment:

- The analysis of the customer segments *revenue class* (less than 50 million, 50–500 million and more than 500 million) focusses on the economic aspect [10],
- the deeper analysis of the customer segments *supply chain class* (OEM, Tier 1, Tier 2, Tier 3-n) considers the company's position in the supply chain [10],
- the analysis of the customer segments *innovation type class* (process, product, business, hybrid form (process, product and business)) considers the type of innovation that is mainly applied at the company, and
- the analysis of the customer segments *number of employees' class* (1 to 50, 51–500, 501–5000, over 5000) considers the number of employees of the company that applies certain innovation methods.

Figure 4(a) shows a list of the mean value of all innovation methods for all investigated customer segments. Figure 4(b) lists the mean value of the customer segment *number of employees' class* (1–50).

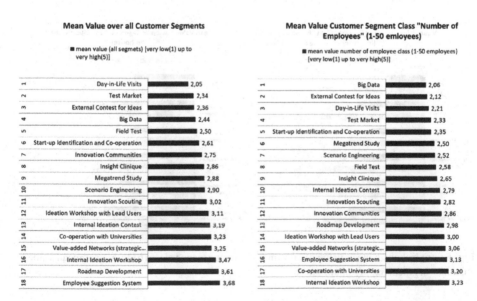

Fig. 4. (a) Mean value over all customer segments (b) Mean value of customer segment "Number of Employees' Class" (1–50 employees)

The following findings can be drawn from Fig. 4(a) and (b):

- The innovation method "Day-In-Life Visits" has by far the lowest application level (rank 1, mean value 2,05) of all innovation methods in all investigated customer segments. It becomes clear that the following three innovation methods are similarly applied concluded by their very similar mean value: "Test Market" (2,34), "External Contest for Ideas" (2,36) and "Big Data" (2,44). Obviously, the innovation methods "Employee Suggestion System" (3,68), "Roadmap Development" (3,61) and "Internal Ideation Workshop" (3,47) are most frequently used in all customer segments.
- The figures show that in the customer segment *number of employees' class 1 to 50*, the innovation method "Big Data" has the lowest application level (rank 1, mean value 2,06) of all innovation methods in this survey. The method "External Contest for Ideas" follows on rank 2 (2,12) and "Day-In-Life Visits" on rank 3 (2,21). Obviously, the innovation methods "Internal Ideation Workshop" (3,23) and "Co-operation with Universities" (3,20) are currently most frequently used in the customer segment *number of employees' class 1 to 50*.

In Sect. 3.3 the various innovation methods are represented in the innovation radars for the cooperation fields customer, supplier, and in-house. Interesting conclusions can also be drawn from a deeper quantitative analysis of the innovation radar in-house (Fig. 3). The method "Big Data" has by far the lowest application level (mean value 2,44 in all segments, in-house). The results will be presented in detail in Fig. 5 and Fig. 6 for the customer segments *revenue, supply chain, innovation type* and *number of employees' class.*

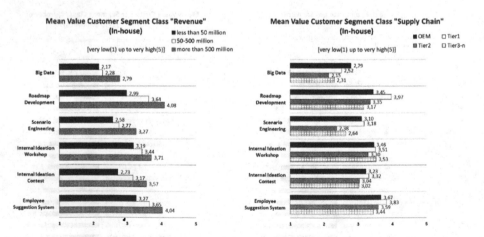

Fig. 5. (a) In-house: mean value of customer segment *revenue* class (b) In-house: mean value of customer segment *supply chain class*

The following observations can be made from Figs. 5 and 6:

- Featuring the in-house innovations methods across all customer segment classes (exception customer segment *innovation type* class *(business)* in Fig. 6(a)), the innovation method "Big Data" has by far the lowest application level (mean value). This is confirmed, for instance, in Fig. 5(b) that shows the low application level in the customer segment *supply chain class* (OEM (2,79), Tier1 (2,52), Tier2 (2,15) and Tier3-n (2,31)).

- The innovation method "Employee Suggestion System" has by far the highest application level (mean value) across all customer segments. This is confirmed, for instance, in Fig. 5(a) that shows the high application level in the customer segment *revenue* class (less than 50 million (3,27), 50–500 million (3,65) and more than 500 million (4,04).

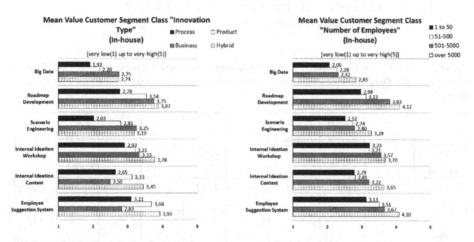

Fig. 6. (a) In-house: mean value of the customer segment innovation type class (b) In-house: mean value of the customer segment number of employees' class

The findings of this survey bring us to the conclusion that the innovation method "Big Data" is among all innovation methods valued very low across all costumer segments. Although "Big Data" is applied very low currently, the innovation method will be essential for the generation of new innovations in the future [10]. Scientific studies show that the revenue of "Big Data" solutions worldwide will increase from 2019 to 2026 about 88% [28].

3.5 Customer Segment Evaluation for Big Data

The well-known Minkowski metric can be used for the calculation of the distance measurements, when a metric structure of variables is given [10, 29]. A lower distance between the variables represents a higher similarity.

Detailed calculations can be drawn from the distance measurements between the customer segments in terms of innovation type, revenue, number of employees' class and value chain, using the Minkowski metric for the innovation method "Big Data" (see Table 3(a) for the customer segment revenue class, see Table 3(b) for the customer segment value chain class, see Table 4(a) for the customer segment innovation type class, and see Table 4(b) for the customer segment number of employees' class).

$$d_{k,l} = \left[\sum_{j=1}^{J} \left| x_{kj} - x_{lj} \right|^r \right]^{\frac{1}{r}}$$

(1)

$d_{k,l}$: distance of the objects (customer segments of various segment classes)
x_{kj}, x_{lj}: value of variable j of objects $k, l (j = 1, \ldots, J)$ here: $J = 1$
$r \geq 1$: Minkowski constant, here: $r = 2$

Table 3. (a) "Big Data" Distance Analysis Customer Segment "Revenue Class": Minkowski Metric (b) "Big Data" Distance Analysis Customer Segment "Supply Chain Class": Minkowski Metric

	< 50 million	50-500 million	> 500 million
< 50 million	0,00	0,11	0,62
50-500 million		0,00	0,51
> 500 million			0,40

	OEM	Tier1	Tier2	Tier3-n
OEM	0,00	0,27	0,64	0,48
Tier1		0,00	0,37	0,21
Tier2			0,00	0,16
Tier3-n				0,00

The Minkowski Metric shows the distance measurement of "Big Data" between the customer segment classes. A lower distance measurement represents a higher similarity between the customer segment classes. In Table 3 the following conclusions can be derived regarding the method "Big Data":

- Table 3(a): The customer segments revenue class *less than 50 million* and *more than 500 million* shows the highest distance (0,62). Referring to the mean value, they differ significantly. Calculating a high distance level (0,51), the segments revenue class *50–500 million* and *more than 500 million* vary referring to the level of usage. The lowest distance level (0,11) can be observed between the customer segments revenue class *less than 50 million* and *50–500 million*.

- Table 3(b): The highest level of distance (0,64) is obtained between the customer segments supply chain classes *OEM* and *Tier2*. Comparing the customer segment of the supply chain classes *Tier2* and *Tier3-n*, the lowest distance level (0,16) in this survey is observed.

Table 4. (a) "Big Data" Distance Analysis Customer Segment "Innovation Type Class": Minkowski Metric (b) "Big Data" Distance Analysis Customer Segment "Number of Employees' Class": Minkowski Metric

	Process	Product	Business	Hybrid
Process	0,00	0,28	0,83	0,82
Product		0,00	0,55	0,54
Business			0,00	0,01
Hybrid				0,00

	1 to 50	51- 500	501- 5000	over 5000
1 to 50	0,00	0,22	0,26	0,77
51- 500		0,00	0,04	0,55
501- 5000			0,00	0,51
over 5000				0,00

The following observations can be made concerning the method "Big Data" in Table 4:

- Table 4(a): The customer segments innovation type class *process* and *business* have the highest level of distance (0,83), followed by the segments innovation type class *process* and *hybrid* with the distance measurement (0,82). It can be observed that the lowest distance level (0,01) is given between the customer segments innovation type class *business* and *hybrid*.
- Table 4(b): The measurement with the highest distance (0,77) is calculated between the customer segments number of employees' class *1 to 50* and *over 5000*. Furthermore, the lowest distance measurement (0,04) shows the comparison of the customer segment number of employees' classes *51–500* and *501–5000*.

According to this study, most of the interviewees valued the "Big Data" innovation method very low. Nevertheless, the survey also reveals that the valuation of this innovation method differs significantly in the different customer segments (see Tables 3 and 4 Minkowski Metric). Scientific studies in Germany show that 35% of the companies use "Big Data" technologies, 24% of the companies will apply this method and 18% discuss the use in future [30]. In addition, "Big Data" will be essential for the generation of new innovations in future [10, 31]. Therefore, this method will be presented as a tool for the development of new ideas, services and products in the automotive industry.

4 Big Data Analytics as an Essential Method for Innovation Ideas Within the Automotive Industry

4.1 Fundamental Aspects of Big Data

For the automotive industry, the generation of innovations is essential to be continuously successful in the future. Besides the analyzed innovation method, especially Big Data technologies can help to offer new services and products to attract old and new customers in the very competitive automotive market [31]. Therefore, Big Data should be perused more prominently, as means for driving innovations.

Big Data is about processing large amounts of (complex) datasets using new technologies that have emerged with the growing amount of data being available [32]. The data being processed in Big Data scenarios bears the so-called "*5-Vs*" characteristics – namely: *volume* (growing size of datasets), *velocity* (high frequency data production), *variety* (disparate data formats), *veracity* (trustworthiness of data), and *value* (usage of the data) [32, 33].

As for the automotive industry, it is important to extract information and knowledge from Big Data scenarios for developing new services, getting new insights from available data sources, and for streamlining product development and operations.

4.2 General Architectural Concerns and Requirements

The usage of Big Data technology can enable the automotive industry to generate new innovations. In order to do this, the following aspects need to be taken into consideration when developing a Big Data analytics platform [based on 31–34]:

- **Scalability:** When various players and data sources are involved (e.g. connected vehicles or smart cities), the overall platform needs to be able to deal with a growing number of participants.
- **Platform resiliency:** For the aggregation and processing of data, a high degree of resilience and robustness is required in order to allow immediate and transparent processing and provisioning of data without data loses and service interruptions.
- **Real-time & batch processing:** In order to cover various use cases in the resulting platform, data processing needs to be adaptive for optimal performance and service availability.
- **Privacy preserving data sharing:** As privacy concerns become increasingly important, the resulting Big Data platform needs to protect personal data in a compliant and controllable way. Especially the management of the user's consent is important. The privacy by design approach needs to be integrated into the platform.
- **Security:** Tying into privacy aspects, also security aspects need to be proactively managed, so that the platform's availability, integrity, and confidentiality can be guaranteed in a multi-lateral way.
- **Data Interoperability:** Finally, data exchange between different entities and other platforms seems to be required to fully develop the potential of Big Data technology in automotive scenarios.

Consequently, a general platform architecture needs to fulfill all the aspects stated above, in order to allow for new innovations and innovative automotive services to arise. Technologies need to be applied that help to manage the before mentioned "5-Vs" characteristics of Datasets in Big Data [33].

4.3 Proposed Automotive Big Data Platform (ABDP) Reference Architecture

The proposed Automotive Big Data Platform (ABDP) reference architecture (see Fig. 7) should help to aggregate and analyze the collected data, in order to derive new insights from various data sources being ingested into the platform itself. To this regard, data can stem from connected vehicles and complete fleets of cars, but also from smart devices being connected to the car's infotainment system or from smart cities. The data itself is either provided as real-time data streams or as data packages, being send to the ABDP in a deferred manner (e.g. as bulk data when being connected to a local network). From a content point of view, the provided data can cover all sorts of purposes such as telemetry data of a car's engine, vehicle position data, or personalized usage data of on-board services. However, as data bandwidth for transferring the different types of data can be limited, appropriate measures need to be taken to only collect the necessary data [31, 32, 34]. Same applies to the notion of data privacy, as data collection and usage should be minimal and purposeful, as laid out by the General Data Protection Regulation (GDPR) [35]. Therefore, the collection and usage of data in the ABDP must be privacy preserving by design, taking into consideration the user's consent to use his/her personal data. Finally, the platform needs to be managed with regard to the cyber security aspect, so that potential security breaches can be mitigated in a timely manner (e.g. by using a managed security lifecycle).

Following a capability-based approach, the proposed reference architecture is segregated into several layers, which provide the necessary services and functionalities for Big Data analyses in the automotive domain. These layers are:

- **Data Ingestion Layer:** Data of various sources are (pre-) processed for being used in the ABDP. Besides the commonly used ETL processes (extract, transform, load) for standardizing data formats, data is filtered and tagged. This way data can be reduced in advance, or personal data can be identified more easily in the following analysis.
- **Data Management & Persistence Layer:** As data sources differ in the way how their data is provided to the ABDP, different technologies need to be supported for storing the data in a meaningful way. To this regard, a data lake helps to offer a common and structured interface to various technologies such as relational or NoSQL databases, file storages, or BLOBs, and the data being stored [33]. Finally, by using standardized storage schemas, an ABDP can offer an interoperable way of exchanging data with other OEMs or with smart city environments.
- **Data Processing Layer:** In order to support different types of usage scenarios, real-time and batch processing capabilities are provided for analyzing the platform's data. The platform should allow for an intelligent and flexible combination of processing methods (hybrid processing), so that a timely data and result delivery can be achieved.

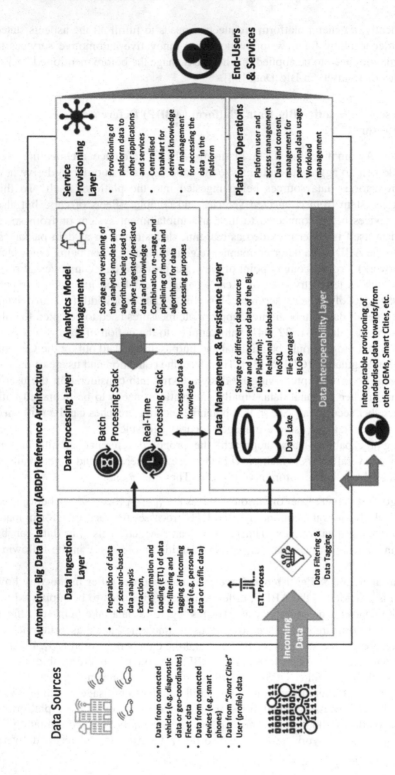

Fig. 7. Proposed Automotive Big Data Platform (ABDP) Reference Architecture.

- **Analytics Model Management:** The necessary analytics models such as individual or combinations of algorithms (pipelined models) are stored in a separate layer. This way, data scientists can develop and test new and existing models in a sandbox, before they are used on productive data of the ABDP.
- **Platform Operations:** In order to manage the platform in an efficient way, user and access management to the ABDP, privacy management, and workload management functionalities need to be provided.
- **Service Provisioning Layer:** Finally, the service provisioning layer allows for a standardized access to the data stored in the ABDP. The data itself is distributed via application interfaces (APIs) or data-marketplaces which ultimately provide it to end-users or services for consumption.

5 Summary and Outlook

According to their level of application in the automotive industry, eighteen different innovation management methods are examined in this empirical survey. The innovation methods "Employee Suggestion System", "Roadmap Development" and "Internal ideation workshop" have the highest application level overall customer segments. The innovation method "Big Data" differs in the level of application between the different customer segments, significantly. Comparing the mean value for in-house innovation methods for the customer segments value chain, revenue, innovation type and number of employees' classes, the empirical data set identifies the "Big Data" method as an essential tool for the generation of new innovations in future [10].

A proposed automotive Big Data Platform (ABDP) Reference Architecture is introduced in Sect. 4. The architecture encompasses a platform approach for ingesting, analyzing, and delivering data and knowledge for new insights and innovative services. When developing such a Big Data platform, privacy, security, and interoperability are important aspects, which need to be taken into consideration.

References

1. Strategy& 2018: The Global Innovation 1000 – What the top innovators get right (2018). https://www.strategy-business.com/media/file/sb93-What-the-Top-Innovators-Get-Right.pdf. Accessed Feb 2018
2. Oliver Wyman 2018: FAST 2030 – Future Automotive Industry Structure until 2030. https://www.oliverwyman.com/our-expertise/insights/2018/jun/fast-2030.html. Accessed Feb 2018
3. Statista 2019: Trends in der Automobilindustrie. http://de.statista.com/. Accessed Feb 2018
4. Statista 2019: Weltweite Automobilindustrie. http://de.statista.com/. Accessed Feb 2018
5. BCG 2016: What's ahead for car sharing? http://image-src.bcg.com/Images/BCG-Whats-Ahead-for-Car-Sharing-Feb-2016_tcm9-64441.pdf. Accessed Feb 2018
6. Roland Berger 2016: The CPO Agenda 2016. https://www.rolandberger.com/en/Publications/CPO-Agenda-2016.html. Accessed Feb 2018
7. Ili, S., Albers, A., Miller, S.: Open innovation in the automotive industry. In: R&D Management 4.0 (2010)

8. Chesbrough, H.: Open Innovation: The New Imperative for Creating and Profiting From Technology. Harvard Business School Publishing, Boston (2003)
9. Richter, K., Witt, N.: Introduction. In: Richter, K., Walther, J. (eds.) Supply Chain Integration Challenges in Commercial Aerospace, pp. 1–17. Springer, Cham (2017). https://doi.org/10.1007/978-3-319-46155-7
10. Lüke, K.-H., Walther, J., Wäldchen, D.: Innovation management methods in the aviation industry. In: Hodoň, M., Eichler, G., Erfurth, C., Fahrnberger, G. (eds.) I4CS 2018. CCIS, vol. 863, pp. 161–177. Springer, Cham (2018). https://doi.org/10.1007/978-3-319-93408-2_12
11. Adamczyk, S., Bullinger, A.C., Möslein, K.: Innovation contests: a review, classification and outlook. Creat. Innov. Manag. 21(4), 335–336 (2012)
12. Dahlander, L., O'Mahony, S.: A Study Shows How to Find New Ideas Inside and Outside the Company (2017). https://hbr.org/2017/07/a-study-shows-how-to-find-new-ideas-inside-and-outside-the-company. Accessed 22 Feb 2018
13. Bullinger, H-J., Warschat, J.: Innovationmanagement in Netzwerken. In: Garcia Sanz, F.-J., Semmler, K., Walther, J. (Hrsg.) Die Automobilindustrie auf dem Weg zur globalen Netzwerkkompetenz, Heidelberg, S. 109–127 (2007)
14. Fichter, K., Beucker, F.: Innovation Communities, Promotorennetzwerke als Erfolgsfaktor bei radikalen Innovationen, Stuttgart (2008). https://www.borderstep.de/wp-content/uploads/2014/07/Fichter-Beucker-Innovation_Communities_Promotorennetzwerke_als_Erfolgsfaktor_bei_radikalen_Innovationen-2008.pdf. Accessed 22 Feb 2018
15. Schmolze, R.: Unternehmen Idee, Wie kundenorientierte Produktentwicklung zum Erfolg führt, Frankfurt/New York (2011)
16. Blattberg, R., Golanty, J.: Tracker: An Early Test Market Forecasting and Diagnostic Model for New Product Planning, Perspective on Promotion and Database, pp. 177–187 (2010). https://doi.org/10.1142/9789814287067_0011. Accessed 22 Feb 2018
17. Katsikis, N., Lang, A., Debreceny, C.: Evaluation of open innovation in B2B from company culture perspective. J. Technol. Manag. Innov. 32(3), 95–100 (2016)
18. Breuer, H., Steinhoff, F., Wogatzky, M.: User Clinic Formate und ihr Beitrag zur Innovationserfolgsrechnung. In: Schmeisser, W. (Hrsg.) Technologiemanagement und Innovationserfolgsrechnung, S. 1–23 (2010)
19. Steinhoff, F.: Tools for User-driven innovation at Deutsche Telekom Laboratories. In: Arnold, H., Erner, M., Möckel, P., Schläffer, C. (eds.) Applied Technology- and Innovation Management, pp. 72–88. Springer, Heidelberg (2010). https://doi.org/10.1007/978-3-540-88827-7_8
20. Chapodos, J., Desmond, K., Schlett, Ch.: Creating a Suggestion System as part of a Continous Improvement Initiative (2014). https://toyotaproductionsystemus.wordpress.com/2014/04/18/creating-a-suggestion-system-as-part-of-a-continuous-improvement-initiative. Accessed 22 Feb 2018
21. Höber, B.: Firm Internal Innovation Contests, Work Environment Perceptions am Employees' Participation, pp. 18–59 (2017). http://springer.com/978-3-658-17491-0.2017. Accessed 22 Feb 2018
22. Barbour, M.: How to run an ideation workshop that actually leads to innovation (2016). https://ozcontent.com/blog/how-to-lead-an-ideation-workshop-that-results-in-innovation. Accessed 22 Feb 2018
23. Durance, Ph, Godet, M.: Sceanrio building: uses and abuses. Technol. Forecast. Soc. Change 77, 1488–1492 (2010)
24. Oliveira, M.G., Rozenfeld, H.: Integrating technology roadmapping and portfolio management at the front-end of new product development. Technol. Forecast. Soc. Change 77(8), 1339–1354 (2010)

25. UN Global Pulse: Big Data for Development: Challenges & Opportunities, May 2012. Accessed Feb 2018
26. Lüke, K.-H., Kapitány, D.: Business (lead) customer involvement in the innovation process. In: Arnold, H., Erner, M., Möckel, P., Schläffer, C. (eds.) Applied Technology- and Innovation Management, pp. 59–71. Springer, Heidelberg (2010). https://doi.org/10.1007/978-3-540-88827-7_7
27. Rohrbeck, R., Thom, N., Arnold, H.: IT tools for foresight: the integrated insight and response system of Deutsche Telekom Innovation Laboratories. Technol. Forecast. Soc. Change **97**, 115–126 (2015)
28. Statista 2019: Prognose zum Umsatz mit Big-Data-Lösungen weltweit von 2014 bis 2026 (in Milliarden US-Dollar). http://de.statista.com/. Accessed Feb 2019
29. Backhaus, K., et al.: Multivariate Analysemethoden. Springer, Heidelberg (2016). https://doi.org/10.1007/978-3-662-46076-4
30. Statista 2019: Inwieweit setzt Ihr Unternehmen bereits Big-Data-Lösungen ein bzw. plant oder diskutiert diese zukünftig zu nutzen? http://de.statista.com/. Accessed Feb 2019
31. Johanson, M., et al.: Big Automotive Data – Leveraging large volumes of data for knowledge-driven product development. In: 2014 IEEE International Conference on Big Data (Big Data), pp. 736–741 (2014)
32. Haroun, A., et al.: A big data architecture for automotive applications: PSA group deployment experience. In: 2017 17th IEEE/ACM International Symposium on Cluster, Cloud and Grid Computing (CCGRID), Madrid, pp. 921–928 (2017)
33. Luckow, A., et al.: Automotive big data: applications, workloads and infrastructures. In: 2015 IEEE International Conference on Big Data (Big Data), Santa Clara, CA, pp. 1201–1210 (2015)
34. Wozniak, P., et al.: Volvo single view of vehicle – building a big data service from scratch in the automotive industry. In: CHI Extended Abstracts (2015)
35. Plappert, C., et al.: A privacy-aware data access system for automotive applications. In: 15th ESCAR Embedded Security in Cars Conference, Berlin (2017)

Knowledge Management
for the Digital Transformation
of Enterprises – Literature Based
Trend Analysis

Marcus Wolf$^{(\boxtimes)}$ and Christian Erfurth

University of Applied Sciences Jena, Carl-Zeiss-Promenade 2, 07745 Jena, Germany
{marcus.wolf,christian.erfurth}@eah-jena.de

Abstract. The digital transformation of companies and society is progressing. The rapid realization of projects or the accelerated implementation of new "disruptive" technologies endanger aspects of sustainability. A sustainable aspect can be seen in the knowledge management of companies: The digital transformation, new technologies and the new production factor knowledge are putting established models for knowledge management under pressure. This paper presents the current state of research on knowledge management in relation to digital transformation. It could be worked out that knowledge management must gain more importance in companies. The way in which knowledge management is operated is changing at the same time, which makes new rules necessary. Due to the plurality of concepts and models, knowledge management is difficult to apply holistically for companies. Enterprises experience a technological upgrading which makes learning of the organization together with technology and humans possible. New forms of access to knowledge enable more target-oriented access in each situation.

Keywords: Digital transformation · Knowledge management ·
Literature research

1 Introduction

The digitization of work is continuously progressing in various societies around the world. Companies are confronted with a multitude of challenges. A special aspect in the context of a sustainable digital transformation can be seen in the knowledge management of a company. The rapid realization of projects or the accelerated implementation of "disruptive" technologies can result in the loss of knowledge. But the importance of knowledge gained in projects is increasing. Especially if you want to conduct research through project management in the future and at the same time the profession of the project manager has to constantly expand its knowledge and this is enhanced with individual experience. [1] Experience knowledge is capital for a company. For example, there is discussion

K.-H. Lüke et al. (Eds.): I4CS 2019, CCIS 1041, pp. 142–155, 2019.
https://doi.org/10.1007/978-3-030-22482-0_11

of a new production factor "knowledge". [3] The sustainability of technologies and processes that have been established in the company in the context of digital transformation, for example, could disappear with the leaving of project employees. The company cannot generate value in knowledge, which helps to quickly adapt business processes in a dynamic market environment. In view of this, established knowledge models can come under pressure and be modified or expanded.

In the research project "Healthy work in pioneer industries" (German Federal Ministry of Education and Research (BMBF), 02L14A073), case studies were conducted on the introduction of technology related to the digital transformation. Based on these case studies, the question of aspects of a sustainable digital transformation of companies was asked. One factor came into a special focus: the management of knowledge in relation to the introduction of technology or the modification of business processes as a result of digital transformation. Increasing complexity and interdependence of IT solutions, coupled with new technological possibilities, can result in new requirements for the knowledge management of companies. At this point, we want to focus on the following questions within this paper: 1. Is the topic of knowledge management to support the digital transformation of companies in the scientific domain identifiable? 2. Which methodological approaches are currently present in the research literature regarding the digital transformation of companies and knowledge management? 3. Which challenges and issues can be derived from the research literature for future work?

The consideration should not include further terms from other scientific disciplines, like system theory etc., in the analysis, because this represents a further theoretical work, which can generate an extra value from the comparison of the different approaches.

The following Sect. 2 takes a look at the state of the art. Then, various terms related to knowledge management will be set and classified in Sect. 3. As a result, queries are made in specific databases in Sect. 4. The research results will be presented afterwards in Sect. 5. In addition, Sect. 6 discusses the results on the basis of theses, where there are possibilities for further research for knowledge management in relation to digital transformation. In the last Sect. 7 a summary of the work will be given.

2   State of the Art

There is a multitude of different models for knowledge management. One of the most common models comes from Nonaka and Takeuchi [10]. It is known as SECI model. Through processes of externalisation, combination, internalisation and socialisation, knowledge is created that can be transferred from a person to a group or company. The knowledge should be made available to an organization, because an organization cannot create knowledge itself, but rather its members. Therefore, preconditions must be created to enable this in the company.

Another model for knowledge management is, for example, the model of "Building Blocks of Knowledge Management". It is a practical approach that tries to provide a practical framework for companies based on defined standards for knowledge management - compatibility, problem orientation, comprehensibility, action orientation and appropriate instruments. The blocks in the cycle model represent activities that are directly knowledge-based. An internal cycle consists of identification, acquisition, development, distribution, preservation, and use of knowledge. An external cycle still has goal-setting and measurement, which focuses on goal-oriented interventions [11]. In the model, however, the focus is strongly on management control. But teams are increasingly working independently.

In addition to models for knowledge management, the current research literature contains explanations on new technological possibilities in interaction with a better distribution of knowledge for humans and machines. For example, Rettinger et al. outlines that semantic technologies are the prerequisite for "Knowledge 4.0". Knowledge graphs can enable value creation by making unstructured content accessible to machines and people simultaneously [13]. Knowledge is important as a resource for companies. Therefore, so-called knowledge workers must be able to analyze and interpret complex phenomena and define suitable measures. Kohlegger et al. see in this and in the interaction with digital tools new possibilities for a better creation of value [6]. New technologies such as data analysis, process mining and text mining open up new possibilities for the externalisation of knowledge in companies. Experience can be shared more easily through simpler interfaces. Targeted information can be enabled by IT systems that know what an employee needs and when [9].

Research on knowledge management is conducted from different perspectives and there are a number of publications on this. With regard to digital transformation, which is understood as a process that changes the whole enterprise, it has been difficult to find generalizing treatises. However, there is a multitude of models and different concepts for knowledge management.

Technological possibilities and knowledge work, are only partial aspects in the research literature. For example, cultural factors are also at work in a globalised world, where people can work together in virtual teams. Jelavic et al. outlines the understanding about eastern and western views of knowledge can make a significant contribution to efficient knowledge transfer [5]. In this context it seems necessary to draw attention to different concepts of digital transformation: Industry 4.0 in Germany and Society 5.0 in Japan.

In addition, digitized companies are becoming more and more dependent on the software they use. Also here knowledge management is essential, as Maciel et al. explains. They see knowledge management as a major challenge, especially for software development companies, as the quality of software products depends to a large extent on it. The work referenced here has carried out a Systematic Literature Review in order to get an overview of approaches for the diagnosis of knowledge management in software companies [8].

There are different approaches, theories and models that deal with knowledge management. In view of the digital transformation of companies, there is a lack of a generalizing view of knowledge management, which combines different theories and models and takes new technologies into account. This work would like to contribute to this with its research.

3 Term Search

During an initial term search, it was observed that the topic of knowledge management is practiced in various scientific disciplines and has a special focus depending on the subject, as can be seen with some examples in Table 1.

Table 1. Examples for research disciplines and research interests

Research disciplines	Research interests
Computer Science	Improved data models and their representation in IT systems
Business Economics	Optimization of productivity of the company
Sociology	System theory

As the table shows, sciences have different focuses on knowledge management, information management or data management. This makes interdisciplinary research more difficult. This can be very important in view of the digital transformation, because knowledge management is subject to several influencing factors, which are especially technologically determined. However, this variety of focal points with regard to knowledge management is reflected in various model and concept terms and the lack of a generalizing model. This paper focuses on knowledge from the perspectives of computer science and economics: Data and information that define knowledge in enterprises for value creation.

Since the digital transformation is also changing the input and output devices for the users in companies, it may also be useful in the future to include ethnological aspects, as the handling of knowledge and the behavioral use of employees can be a special focus. This is only mentioned under the keyword human-technology interaction.

From the focus and from a first search the following terms could be identified, which can be considered for a literature search. In addition, it was possible to classify the terms independently, as can be seen in Table 2.

Due to the large number of model and concept terms relating to the topic of knowledge management, the present literature research was initially limited to this terms for the queries.

Table 2. Terms for research

Basic terms digital transformation	Concept terms digital transformation	Basic terms knowledge
Digitalisation	Industry 4.0	Data management
Digital transformation	Society 5.0	Information management
		Knowledge management

4 Data Collection

Two scientific databases were selected for the search, which provide specified search options and can deliver specialized results. The keywords identified in the term chapters are queried via the databases. As knowledge management should refer to digital transformation, the terms of knowledge are always queried in connection with the terms of digital transformation. The result is limited knowledge management, which refers to digital transformation.

4.1 IEEE Xplore

The IEEE Xplore is a research database that provides technical knowledge in the fields of electrical engineering, electronics and computer science. Publications on knowledge management were requested in relation to Digital Transformation with the following search query:

```
("digitalization" OR "digitalisation" OR "digital
   ↪ transformation") AND ("knowledge management" OR "
   ↪ data management" OR "information management")
```

A result of 71 database entries was found.[1] The emphasis of the publication focuses especially on the last years. Topics include for example innovation management, the application of big data technologies, industry 4.0 topics and other challenges.

4.2 ACM Digital Library

The ACM Digital Library is a research database primarily addressed to researchers in the field of computer science. Similar to the IEEE Xplore search query, the following search query was used for the ACM Digital Library:

```
+("digitalization" "digitalisation" "digital
   ↪ transformation") +("knowledge management" "data
   ↪ management" "information management")
```

---

[1] https://ieeexplore.ieee.org, Access on 9 march 2019.

A result of 1540 database entries was found.[2] Compared to the IEEE Xplore database, considerably more entries were found. This may be due to the fact that the ACM Digital Library also recorded data from presentations. In comparison to IEEE Xplore, more results from the 1990s are also listed. Thematically, for example, the last entries show publications on social networks, models, neural networks or challenges for organizations.

5   Evaluation

In Fig. 1 you can view all results from the two research databases. The period from 1990 to 2018 is shown here. In the period under consideration new contents on the topics of knowledge management, information management and data management were published. After 2009 and 2012 highlights were reached, the publication rate apparently decreased, in order to achieve 2018 almost again a high publication activity. Apparently, the topic of knowledge management is of great importance in the current debate.

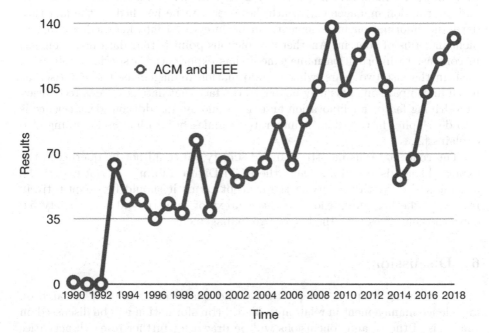

Fig. 1. Results in the research databases

In Fig. 2 the topics data management, information management and knowledge management are presented. Also here a trend can be found in the period 1990 to 2018 with all three individual topics, which allows conclusions to be

---

[2] https://dl.acm.org, Access on 9 March 2019.

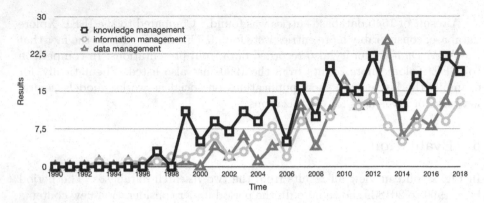

Fig. 2. Development of data management, information management and knowledge management

drawn about an increased research activity in these areas. It is also noticeable that knowledge management tends to achieve a higher publication rate than data and information management, which, however, can be justified by the fact that data and information management can be integrated into knowledge management in terms of content. Another conspicuous point is that data management, in contrast to information management, has experienced a special publication push in the last two years, whereas information management has not risen as much in comparison. This may be due to the fact that data science is recognised as a driving factor for innovation and the economy. In addition, data science is also developing fast because it integrates seamlessly into life, as Longbing Cao explains [2].

The concept terms industry 4.0 and society 5.0 could not be queried in the exported spreadsheet files because the ACM Digital Library did not export the abstracts also. With a query of the concept terms it should be quantitatively reviewed whether publications in the context of industry 4.0 and Society 5.0 concern themselves with the knowledge management.

6   Discussion

In the following chapter, the qualitative and quantitative state of research on knowledge management in relation to digital transformation will be discussed on the basis of theses and conclusions will be drawn for further research activities in this field.

In Fig. 3 the discussed theses can be seen in the overview, which influence on the knowledge management is based on the digital transformation.

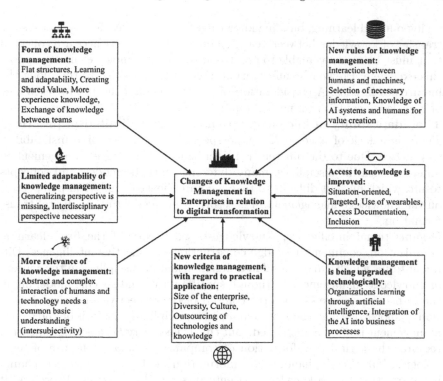

Fig. 3. Changes in knowledge management in relation to digital transformation

1. **Digital transformation has an impact on the way knowledge management is applied in enterprises.**

   Enterprises established on the market have developed structures. Through digital transformation, these established enterprises are challenged by new start-ups in competition, which with flat structures and agility can successfully attack value creation models of established enterprises faster than in the past. Therefore, many established enterprises today try to consolidate hierarchical levels and work in teams on tasks similar to start-ups [14]. But this also changes knowledge management: 1. Hierarchies make information move only slowly and filtered. In flat structures, information moves fast and there is potentially a lot of redundant information. 2. This results in adjustments to employee competencies. With hierarchical structures, management and control of the work are in the focus. With flat structures, continuous learning and the willingness to adapt as well as the ability to adapt. 3. In the hierarchical structure, much depends on individual productivity, which also results in competition among one another. In the flat structure, the focus is on creating common value, where the mutual achievement of tasks with differentiated talents and knowledge focuses. 4. Ultimately, hierarchical structures also have other knowledge focuses because here assessments must always be made on known assumptions for advance planning. In flat structures, the focus is on trying out and learning, building knowledge from mistakes. 5. One focus is the transfer of knowledge between teams. This is where experiences are collected that must be made available to other teams. New technologies must support this exchange. Previously, information in companies tended to run along the hierarchies in silos. A consideration of the vertical and horizontal exchange of knowledge could mean new results for research.

2. **The adaptability of knowledge management is limited in practice.**
There is a lack of a generalising perspective and a lack of transferability to practice. Due to the different consideration of knowledge management in different scientific disciplines, many different concepts, models and concepts result, which make it difficult to take a comprehensive analytical perspective on the knowledge management of enterprises in the light of the digital transformation.
Organizational intelligence, Knowledge-based theory of the firm, learning organization, common knowledge construction or collective intelligence. Different terms which can be found in different scientific disciplines in the context of knowledge management. Although specific terms and specific modelling in the respective science sharpen the contour of the respective analytical dimension of knowledge management, a more interdisciplinary analysis of knowledge management is often complicated. But this is necessary because digitalization requires the digital transformation of companies. Not only the use of technologies, but also the handling of information in the organization is changing in relation to the knowledge of enterprises and employees. Therefore, it is essential to take a generalizing look from different scientific disciplines, because Digital Transformation is a global issue for companies. Individual perspectives help companies with knowledge management only to a very limited extent. A comprehensive view of knowledge management in connection with the changed technological, structural and social aspects in particular is necessary.

3. **Due to the digital transformation, knowledge management in companies is becoming more important.**
As seen in Fig. 1, publication on knowledge management has increased in recent years. The digital transformation increases the share of technologies and information technology solutions in enterprises [9]. The dependencies between IT systems (system integration) and people (human-technology interaction) are becoming ever greater and the resulting relationships more complex. In addition there are new programming languages, artificial intelligence and other new technologies or processes which make more and more data and information possible in enterprises. (As seen in Fig. 2, publications on data management are increasing.) In order for this to remain controllable for employees and the management of companies, measures for understanding complex interrelationships [6] must be increased. One example is the creation of intersubjectivity, which is necessary if people are to collaborate on an abstract problem. The increase in the production of intersubjectivity will have to be done by companies through higher internal communication efforts.

4. **The transfer of previous knowledge models into companies is difficult for companies due to the size of organisations, the focus of topics and the abstract character. There are new criteria for knowledge management with regard to practical application.**
   The application of knowledge models in companies can be difficult due to the size of the company. Small and medium-sized enterprises have different information requirements than large enterprises. (analogous to the tendency of large companies to mature at an advanced stage in industry 4.0 topics [12]) In addition, aspects of diversity and internationality may be more relevant for large enterprises than for smaller, more local market participants. For example, the handling of knowledge can be viewed differently in different cultures. (as outlined in [5]) For a globally operating company, this results in special demands on the skills of employees and processes that take these cultural differences into account. Small and medium-sized enterprises also tend to rent or buy information and data services as well as specific technologies from third-party companies because of the smaller number of employees. In such a case, the small or medium-sized company also gets rid of the knowledge management for the technology. On the other hand, market observation and the company's own value-added processes, which build on the purchased or rented technologies, remain relevant. The more technologies are outsourced, the less knowledge management the company has to operate on its own in relation to the respective technology. Regardless of the size of the company, whether large or small, the models of knowledge management are to abstract from their own problems and complex in day-to-day business for a practical application that is understood by different target groups.
   Knowledge management can only be successful in collaborative networks if the employees with different talents and competencies are familiar with a minimum standard for knowledge management. If knowledge management is operated in a fragmented way and only from specific thematic aspects, there are knowledge deficits and knowledge imbalances in the organizations. Value creation that results from the knowledge of employees and management is thus sometimes not taken into account. This can be solved by general knowledge management concepts that are known to all members of an organization and are lived in everyday business. This is also a question of corporate culture, which should enable the exchange of knowledge within the organization.

5. **Knowledge management is being upgraded technologically: Organizations can learn through artificial intelligence.**
   With the SECI model, the view is that an organization can learn through its members. The model is also designed to ensure that the knowledge of its members is converted into knowledge for the organisation. There are four modes: socialisation, externalisation, combination and internalisation. (as outlined [10]) New technologies and their combination with existing technological solutions now enable a company to learn independently. Artificial intelligence, for example in the form of an API as a service [7] connected to individual or in future all business processes, can store knowledge in interaction with a company's data storage systems of employees and management and expand it

through machine learning. A company can no longer learn only through members, but also independently with artificial intelligence. Initial approaches can be seen, for example, in automatic information and consulting systems such as a chatbot or a language assistance system. It is therefore necessary to integrate artificial intelligence in companies into the various business processes and to allow them to interact with each other.

6. **Access to knowledge is improved, as it can be more situation-oriented and targeted.**

   New devices enable new forms of interaction and thus new possibilities for targeted access to knowledge [9]. This has to be considered especially in the background of collaborative forms of work - for example digital teams or virtual teams. Context-based access to information is particularly important in the area of wearable computing. Targeted information that is relevant in the respective business process can be communicated to the users. It also offers the possibility of inclusion. People who have been overburdened with certain tasks because they did not have the knowledge, experience or competence to do so can be equipped with the appropriate devices and the information and competences necessary for the business process. In interaction with new devices, knowledge can be purposefully shared in organizations. This can also increase the willingness to document, as hurdles can be compensated by new knowledge input and knowledge access. As a result, reworking can be reduced.

7. **Knowledge management with digital technologies needs new rules in organizations.**

   The potential availability of data and information in enterprises results in a potential knowledge (for example knowledge acquisition through projects [1]), which can be available for specific business processes and individual employees with different competences and talents. Ultimately, wisdom can also be formed through the interaction of human and machine. (as outlined in the DIKW pyramid in [4]) The role of knowledge management in digital transformation is: 1. To establish rules for the interaction between humans and machines, so that enterprises can focus on individual determinants, which enable the targeted exchange of knowledge, as the topic becomes more complex. 2. From the potential availability of data and information, differentiated solutions must be researched which take into account enterprises with different characteristics and different enterprise purposes as well as value creation projects, so that the further development of the enterprise and the quality of the products and services can be optimized as well as the enterprises which can access differentiated rules of knowledge management. 3. Rules must be developed on how knowledge of AI systems and humans can be generated from this data and information. This knowledge should in turn be available to different people with different requirements and enable a meaningful activity that increases the value creation of the organisation.

7   Conclusion

The paper showed that knowledge management is an essential aspect of sustainability in the digital transformation of enterprises and is becoming more and more important. At this point, the questions from the Sect. 1 will be answered.

Within the 1. question, the introduction asked, is the topic of knowledge management to support the digital transformation of companies in the scientific domain identifiable. Both qualitative sources and quantitative queries of databases have shown that knowledge management as a field of research has been actively practiced in recent years. Even in the present, the topic seems to be relevant in science, as the increasing publication entries in the databases demonstrate recently. In addition, qualitative literature research has also shown that knowledge management is a significant factor in the digital transformation of enterprises. However, there is a lack of global approaches and publications that focus on practical application in companies.

Our 2. question asked, which methodological approaches are currently present in the research literature regarding the digital transformation of companies and knowledge management. There are individual approaches, but none that view knowledge management as a global topic in the enterprise. Different results from different scientific approaches could provide new findings here. The human-technology interaction, caused by new devices, or questions about the increase in complexity in enterprises and autonomous programs, through the use of AI services, as well as the behavior of employees, such as new technologies are used with which motivation, can enable new conclusions about an optimized knowledge management in the age of digital transformation for enterprises.

Related to 3. question some challenges and issues for knowledge management in relation to digital transformation can be derived from the research literature for future work. In the Sect. 6 some theses could be made and discussed on the basis of the previous research. Thus, the way in which knowledge management is to be carried out changes in companies in relation to the digital transformation. The companies have difficulties with the application of knowledge management, because a generalizing point of view is missing, which is understandable to all members of an organization. Knowledge management is technologically upgraded and organizations can learn with artificial intelligence. New technologies provide new access to knowledge for members of companies. This in turn makes new rules for handling knowledge in companies necessary.

In order to further optimise quantitative research, it may be recommended to classify the found sources, whether the publications address models, procedures, case studies, etc. It may also be useful to include other scientific databases such as Google Scholar. Furthermore, the multitude of concept and model terms for knowledge management from different scientific disciplines can be included.

In addition to the processing of some qualitative sources, the work was also able to realize a quantitative research and to discuss these in the Sect. 6 on the basis of theses. From this it can be deduced that the models of knowledge management have to be extended or adapted. Specific requirements of the digital transformation should be considered. In this way, a basis for practice could be created. It has also been found that a generalizing view of the topic can generate new findings. Furthermore, future research activities can also empirically research practical approaches to knowledge management in companies.

References

1. Bierwolf, R., Romero, D., Pelk, H., Stettina, C.J.: On the future of project management innovation: a call for discussion towards project management 2030. In: 2017 International Conference on Engineering, Technology and Innovation (ICE/ITMC), pp. 689–698, June 2017. https://doi.org/10.1109/ICE.2017.8279952
2. Cao, L.: Data science: a comprehensive overview. ACM Comput. Surv. **50**, 43:1–43:42 (2017). https://doi.org/10.1145/3076253
3. Enachi, M.: The knowledge - as production factor. Studies and Scientific Researches - Economic Edition, 12 2009. 10.29358/sceco.v0i14.40
4. Hey, J.: The data, information, knowledge, wisdom chain: The metaphorical link. Relatório técnico, Intergovernmental Oceanographic Commission (UNESCO) (2004)
5. Jelavic, M., Ogilvie, K.: Knowledge management views in eastern and the western cultures: an integrative analysis. J. Knowl. Globalization **3**, 51–69 (2010)
6. Kohlegger, M., Ploder, C.: Data driven knowledge discovery for continuous process improvement. In: North, K., Haas, O. (eds.) Knowledge Management in Digital Change, pp. 65–81. Springer, Cham (2018). https://doi.org/10.1007/978-3-319-73546-7_4
7. Lee, K., Ha, N.: Ai platform to accelerate API economy and ecosystem. In: 2018 International Conference on Information Networking (ICOIN), pp. 848–852, January 2018. https://doi.org/10.1109/ICOIN.2018.8343242
8. Maciel, C.P.C., de Souza, E.F., de Almeia Falbo, R., Felizardo, K.R., Vijaykumar, N.L.: Knowledge management diagnostics in software development organizations: a systematic literature review. In: Proceedings of the 17th Brazilian Symposium on Software Quality, pp. 141–150. SBQS, ACM, New York (2018). https://doi.org/10.1145/3275245.3275260
9. Maier, E., Reimer, U.: Digital change-new opportunities and challenges for tapping experience and lessons learned for organisational value creation. In: North, K., Maier, R., Haas, O. (eds.) Knowledge Management in Digital Change. Springer, Cham (2018). https://doi.org/10.1007/978-3-319-73546-7_5
10. Nonaka, I., Takeuchi, H.: The Knowledge-Creating Company: How Japanese Companies Create the Dynamics of Innovation. Oxford University Press, New York (1995)
11. Probst, G., Romhardt, K.: Building blocks of knowledge management - a practical approach. Ecole des Hautes Etudes Commerciales, Universite de Geneve-, Papers, 01 1997
12. Puchan, J., Zeifang, A., Leu, J.: Industry 4.0 in practice-identification of industry 4.0 success patterns. In: 2018 IEEE International Conference on Industrial Engineering and Engineering Management (IEEM), pp. 1091–1095, December 2018. https://doi.org/10.1109/IEEM.2018.8607580

13. Rettinger, A., Zander, S., Acosta, M., Sure-Vetter, Y.: Semantic technologies: enabler for knowledge 4.0. In: North, K., Maier, R., Haas, O. (eds.) Knowledge Management in Digital Change. Springer, Cham (2018). https://doi.org/10.1007/978-3-319-73546-7_2
14. Wolf, M., Semm, A., Erfurth, C.: Digital transformation in companies - challenges and success factors. In: Hodoň, M., Eichler, G., Erfurth, C., Fahrnberger, G. (eds.) Innovations for Community Services, pp. 178–193. Springer, Cham (2018)

Data Analytics and Models

Rank-Based Similarity Index (RBSI) in a Multidimensional DataSet

Michel Herbin[✉], Amine Aït-Younes, Frédéric Blanchard, and Didier Gillard

CReSTIC, Université de Reims Champagne-Ardenne, Reims, France
{michel.herbin,amine.ait-younes,
frederic.blanchard,didier.gillard}@univ-reims.fr

Abstract. When exploring a data set, we generally use a distance to evaluate the similarity or dissimilarity between data. In a multidimensional space, usual distances combine the values of the variables. This approach has two significant drawbacks. First, the variables have neither the same unit nor the same scale. That requires standardization of variables before computing a distance. Second, some variables could be irrelevant to assess the similarity between data. This paper proposes to build a new similarity index based on data rankings. The index is called Rank-Based Similarity Index (RBSI). The goal is to use RBSI instead of the standard distances to avoid their drawbacks. The build of RBSI is based on three steps. The first step defines a similarity function for each data and each variable. Each function is based on the rankings of data. The second step computes the mean of similarity values to define two characteristics for each variable. These characteristics are called sensitivity and specificity which assess the relevance of a variable for evaluating the similarity. The third step aggregates the values of the similarity functions to define RBSI by an ordered weighted averaging (OWA) [3]. The weights of the OWA operator then integrate the relevant characteristics of the variables. Finally, we compare RBSI to the usual distances: RBSI gives better results to assess the similarity between the data.

Keywords: Dataset analysis · Similarity index ·
Multi-dimensionality · Ranking

1 Introduction

When exploring a dataset, one of the first tasks consists in comparing the data. For this purpose, we usually use a distance to evaluate the similarity or the dissimilarity between two data. In a one-dimensional space, the distance is trivially defined: when data are characterized by a single variable, they are considered instances of this variable. The distance between a pair of two data is then deviation between the two values of the variable. In other words, the distance is equal to the absolute value of the difference between the values of the variable. In a multidimensional space, computing distance becomes troublesome. The data is characterized by several variables, and there are as many deviations between

© Springer Nature Switzerland AG 2019
K.-H. Lüke et al. (Eds.): I4CS 2019, CCIS 1041, pp. 159–165, 2019.
https://doi.org/10.1007/978-3-030-22482-0_12

two data as variables in the data set and a distance should aggregate these deviations. In this context of multidimensional data space, Euclidean distance is the best-known method of aggregation. It is based on the quadratic mean of the deviations. More precisely, it is equal to the square root of the sum of the squares of the differences between the values of each variable. Beyond the choice of an aggregation method, the approaches using standard distances have two significant drawbacks: the standardization of variables [1] for aggregating the deviations, and the relevance of each variable to assess the similarity. When variables use different units, then the deviations are difficult to aggregate. So there is a need for standardization of the variables. When the deviation has no meaning regarding the data, then the variable is irrelevant for computing the similarity. For instance the deviation of an extremely noisy variable could be irrelevant to assess the similarity of the data. This paper explains how we build a similarity index to solve these difficulties. The goal is to evaluate the similarity between data with this index instead of the usual distances.

In a multidimensional space, we have several variables. Instead of standardizing the variables, we propose to assess the deviations by a similarity function for each variable. With such a function, the similarity value lies between 0 and 1 for each deviation. We obtain as many similarity values as the number of variables. The similarity index we propose is the weighted mean of the assessed deviations of each variable. The challenge is to determine the weights. When computing the similarity using classical distances, each variable has the same weight. Unfortunately, some variable could be irrelevant to evaluate the similarity between instances. For example, let us consider a variable that assess the color of objects with a red scale from vermilion red to carmine red. If two objects have a green color, this variable may no longer be relevant to evaluate their similarity. This paper proposes to assess the relevance of each variable for determining its weight. Then we can compute the similarity index.

We propose three steps to build a new similarity index. The first step describes the similarity function we define for each data and each variable. Let X and v be respectively a data and a variable. The similarity function sim_X^v associates a value $sim_X^v(Y)$ to each data Y. In this paper, the similarity between data is not symmetrical. The observation of Y seen from X is different from the observation of X seen from Y. Thus the similarity from X to Y could be different from the similarity from Y to X. The value $sim_X^v(Y)$ evaluates the similarity from X to Y using the variable v. Section 2 explains the build of these similarity functions based on the rankings of data. Section 3 is devoted to the second step of our proposal. The goal is to assess the similarity relevance of each variable when evaluating the similarities. The mean of $sim_X^v(Y)$ for all of Y permits us to assess the relevance of the variable v with respect to X. The third step aggregates the values of the similarity functions to define a similarity index. The aggregation uses ordered weighted averaging (OWA) [3]. Section 4 explains the way we use OWA operator to define the new similarity index. In Sect. 5 we compare our rank-based similarity index to the most popular distances when assessing similarity. Finally Sect. 6 proposes a conclusion and some elements of discussion.

2   Similarity Functions

Let X and Y be two data in a multidimensional space. The function sim_X^v is proposed to evaluate the similarity from X to Y for the variable v. The values $sim_X^v(Y)$ are obtained by comparing $v(X)$ and $v(Y)$. The function sim_X^v is defined by two thresholds: α and β with $0 < \alpha < \beta$. If $|v(Y) - v(X)| < \alpha$, then the deviation between X and Y is considered too small. So X and Y are similar and $sim_X^v(Y) = 1$ If $|v(Y) - v(X)| > \beta$, then the deviation between X and Y is considered too large. So X and Y are dissimilar and $sim_X^v(Y) = 0$. Between the two thresholds, the similarity lies between 0 and 1. Thus the similarity function sim_X^v is defined by:

$$sim_X^v(Y) = \begin{cases} 0 & \text{if } v(Y) < v(X) - \beta \\ \frac{v(Y)-(v(X)-\beta)}{\beta-\alpha} & \text{if } v(X) - \beta \leq v(Y) < v(X) - \alpha \\ 1 & \text{if } v(X) - \alpha \leq v(Y) < v(X) + \alpha \\ \frac{(v(X)+\beta)-v(Y)}{\beta-\alpha} & \text{if } v(X) + \alpha \leq v(Y) < v(X) + \beta \\ 0 & \text{if } v(X) + \beta \leq v(Y) \end{cases} \quad (1)$$

In this paper α and β are based on the ranks relative to the data X. Let A be the k-th nearest neighbor of X using the variable v with a small value of k. We propose $\alpha = |v(A) - v(X)|$. Let B be the k-th nearest neighbor of X using the variable v with a large value of k. We propose $\beta = |v(B) - v(X)|$. In the following a small value of k is equal to 5 and a large value of k is equal to 100. The values 5 and 100 are evaluated empirically. Then A is considered close to X and B is considered far from X. This approach allows us to define a similarity function that does not depend on the unit of the variable v. It is no longer necessary to standardize the variables.

3   Similarity Relevance of Variable

Let E be the multidimensional dataset. This section defines two characteristics of the function sim_X^v within E. The characteristics are called sensitivity and specificity of the variable v.

Let $sens_X^v$ be the mean of $sim_X^v(Y)$ when $Y \in E$:

$$sens_X^v = \frac{1}{n} \sum_{Y \in E} sim_X^v(Y) \quad (2)$$

The value $sens_X^v$ lies between 0 and 1. It assesses an average similarity from X to the whole dataset E in respect with the variable v.

If $sens_X^v$ is close to 1, then the similarities $sim_X^v(Y)$ are also rather close to 1. The data Y of E are rather similar to X. Then the value $sim_X^v(Y)$ becomes highly symptomatic of a dissimilarity with X when $sim_X^v(Y)$ becomes close to 0.

In contrast, if $sens_X^v$ is close to 0, the similarities $sim_X^v(Y)$ are also rather close to 0. Then the data Y are rather dissimilar from X. Then the value $sim_X^v(Y)$

becomes highly symptomatic of a similarity with X when $sim_X^v(Y)$ becomes close to 1.

Based on these remarks when evaluating the similarity from X, $sens_X^v$ is called sensitivity of v and $1 - sens_X^v$ is called specificity of v.

4   Ordered Weighted Averaging (OWA)

The similarity from X to Y is equal to $sim_X^v(Y)$ for each variable v. These similarity values could change with the variables. Thus we have as many evaluations of similarity as the number of variables. We aggregate these values $sim_X^v(Y)$ by a weighted mean for obtaining a similarity index from X to Y for all variables. This section explains the way we determine the weight associated with each variable v.

Let p be the dimension of the multidimensional data space. Let v_1, v_2, $v_3, ... v_p$ be the variables. The similarity index from X to Y is obtained by the weighted sum of $sim_X^{v_1}(Y)$, $sim_X^{v_2}(Y)$, $sim_X^{v_3}(Y), ... sim_X^{v_p}(Y)$. In this paper we use the Ordered Weighted Averaging (OWA) that proposed Yager [3]. The OWA operator needs for ordering the values by increasing order. We obtain $sim_X^{v_{(1)}}(Y) \le sim_X^{v_{(2)}}(Y) \le sim_X^{v_{(3)}}(Y) \le ... sim_X^{v_{(p)}}(Y)$. The OWA-based similarity index from X to Y is defined by:

$$sim(X, Y) = \sum_{1 \le j \le p} w_j \times sim_X^{v_{(j)}}(Y) \qquad (3)$$

where w_j is the weight associated with the variable $v_{(j)}$. The weights w_j are defined between 0 and 1 so that $\sum_{1 \le j \le p}(w_j) = 1$. In fact the weights are not associated with the variables but with the ordered positions of the variables. The challenge is to determine the weights.

The weight vector is $W = [w_1, w_2, w_3, ... w_p]$. If $W = [1, 0, 0, ...0]$, then OWA operator corresponds to the minimum operator. If $W = [0, 0, 0, ...1]$, then OWA operator corresponds to the maximum operator. If $W = [1/p, 1/p, 1/p, ...1/p]$, then OWA operator corresponds to arithmetic mean. The OWA operator we propose is a trade-off between the minimum operator and the maximum operator.

Pérez and Lamata [4] discusses the weights determination by means of linear functions that we use in this paper. To emphasize the minimum, we use the decreasing weights w_{min} defined by using the linear orders of de Borda [5] where :

$$w_{min}(j) = \frac{2(p + 1 - j)}{p(p + 1)} \qquad (4)$$

where $1 \le j \le p$. To emphasize the maximum, we use the increasing weights w_{max} defined by increasing linear orders with:

$$w_{max}(j) = \frac{2j}{p(p + 1)} \qquad (5)$$

where $1 \le j \le p$. Note that $w_{min}(j) + w_{max}(j) = 2/p$.

Our OWA operator is a trade-off between the operator emphasizing the minimum and the one emphasizing the maximum. The sensitivity $sens_X^v$ argues in favor of the operator minimum. The specificity $1 - sens_X^v$ argues in favor of the operator maximum. Then the weights of our OWA operator are defined by:

$$w_j = C\left((sens_X^{v_{(j)}})w_{min}(j) + (1 - sens_X^{v_{(j)}})w_{max}(j) \right) \qquad (6)$$

where C is the coefficient for obtaining $\sum_{1 \leq j \leq p}(w_j) = 1$.

Using these weights, the OWA-based similarity index $sim(X,Y)$ aggregates the similarities of all the variables. The value $sim(X,Y)$ lies between 0 and 1. If $sim(X,Y) = 1$, Y is similar from X. If $sim(X,Y) = 0$, Y is dissimilar from X. The higher $sim(X,Y)$, the higher the similarity from X to Y. In this paper, sim is called Rank-Based Similarity Index (RBSI).

5   Comparison with Classical Metrics

This section compares RBSI with the most popular metrics: Euclidean distance, Manhattan distance, Chebyshev distance, Canberra distance, Mahalanobis distance. Table 1 gives the definition of these distances.

Table 1. Definition of the most popular metrics between quantitative data defined with p variables

Popular metrics	
Euclidean	$dist(X,Y) = \sqrt{\sum_{1 \leq k \leq p} (v_k(X) - v_k(Y))^2}$
Manhattan (city block)	$dist(X,Y) = \sum_{1 \leq k \leq p} |v_k(X) - v_k(Y)|$
Chebyshev	$dist(X,Y) = \max_{1 \leq k \leq p} |v_k(X) - v_k(Y)|$
Canberra	$dist(X,Y) = \sum_{1 \leq k \leq p} \frac{|v_k(X) - v_k(Y)|}{|v_k(X)| + |v_k(Y)|}$
Mahalanobis	$dist(X,Y) = \sqrt{(X-Y)^T C^{-1}(X-Y)}$

These classical distances are dissimilarity indices that we transform into similarity indices with:

$$simil(X,Y) = 1 - \frac{dist(X,Y)}{\max\limits_{A,B \in E} dist(A,B)} \qquad (7)$$

where $dist$ is the distance, X and Y are two data in the multidimensional dataset E.

For our comparison, the similarity indices are computed using the databases from *Machine Learning Repository of UCI* [2]. We use six numerical multivariate datasets with clusters: *iris, wine, ecoli, haberman, glass* and *seeds*. Let us describe the way we use to compare the similarity indices based on distance with RBSI.

Let X and Y be two data within the dataset E. If X and Y belong to the same cluster, then an optimal similarity index from X to Y should be equal to one (i.e. X and Y are similar). On the contrary, if X and Y belong to two different clusters, then an optimal similarity index from X to Y should be equal to zero (i.e. X and Y are dissimilar). Let *simil* be a similarity index. Thus we define the intra-cluster similarity of *simil* with:

$$intra(simil) = \frac{1}{n_1} \sum_{C_X = C_Y} simil(X, Y) \tag{8}$$

where n_1 is the number of couples (X, Y) where X and Y belong to the same cluster. The inter-cluster similarity is defined with:

$$inter(simil) = \frac{1}{n_2} \sum_{C_X \neq C_Y} simil(X, Y) \tag{9}$$

where n_2 is the number of couples (X, Y) where X and Y belong to two different clusters. The similarity index *simil* is optimal for the clusters when $intra(simil) = 1$ and $inter(simil) = 0$. Therefore we define a criterion to evaluate the similarity index *simil* with:

$$crit(simil) = intra(simil) - inter(simil) \tag{10}$$

The value $crit(simil)$ lies always between 0 and 1. The higher $crit(simil)$, the more optimal *simil* with respect to the clusters.

Table 2. Comparison of similarity indices based on popular distances with the Rank-Based Similarity Index (RBSI) using classical datasets from UCI repository: best results in bold

| | Dataset | | | | | |
	iris	wine	ecoli	haber.	glass	seeds
Number of objects	150	178	336	306	214	210
Number of attributes	4	13	7	3	9	7
Number of clusters	3	3	8	2	7	3
Index of similarity						
Euclidean	0.336	0.175	0.230	0.020	0.098	0.275
Manhattan	0.331	0.176	0.210	0.026	0.097	0.272
Chebyshev	0.344	0.175	0.211	0.017	0.085	0.258
Canberra	0.422	0.222	0.142	**0.048**	**0.166**	0.238
Mahalanobis	0.113	0.047	0.078	0.027	0.064	0.080
RBSI	**0.509**	**0.279**	**0.284**	0.047	0.151	**0.452**

This criterion permits us to compare the similarity indices through multi-dimensional datasets with clusters. Table 2 displays the results we obtain. The results are discussed in conclusion.

6 Discussion and Conclusion

The rank-based similarity index we propose gives generally better results (i.e. higher criterion value) than the classical distances. Canberra distance gives only a very small improvement with the datasets "haberman" and "glass" (see Table 2). When the classes have a large overlap as for "glass" and "haberman" the criterion has a low value and it becomes less significant. In the other cases, the improvement of RBSI is significant. These results are confirmed with simulated datasets.

In a future work we propose to use this new index to analyze multidimensional datasets for applications in medical domain. We propose also to compare the results of classical algorithms of clustering when we use RBSI instead of a distance. We also propose to study RBSI to see how RBSI works for high dimensional spaces especially how it deals with a curse of the dimensionality.

References

1. Jajuga, K., Walesiak, M.: Standardisation of data set under different measurement scales. In: Decker, R., Gaul, W. (eds.) Classification and Information Processing at the Turn of the Millennium. Studies in Classification, Data Analysis, and Knowledge Organization, pp. 105–112. Springer, Heidelberg (2000). https://doi.org/10.1007/978-3-642-57280-7_11
2. Bache, K., Lichman, M.: UCI Machine learning repository. University of California, Irvine. School of Information and Computer Sciences (2013). http://archive.ics.uci.edu/ml
3. Yager, R.: On ordered weighted averaging aggregation operators in multicriteria decision making. IEEE Trans. Syst. Man Cybern. **18**(1), 183–190 (1988)
4. Perez, E.C., Lamata, M.T.: OWA weights determination by means of linear functions. Mathw. Soft Comput. **16**, 107–122 (2009)
5. de Borda J.C.: Memoire sur les elections au scrutin. Academie Royale des Sciences, Paris (1784)

A Distributed Metadata Platform
for Hybrid Radio Services

Markus Friedrich[1]([✉]), André Ebert[1], Carsten Hahn[1], Georg Schneider[1],
Liza Obermeier[1], Alexander Erk[2], and Iris Jennes[3]

[1] LMU Munich, 80539 Munich, Germany
{markus.friedrich,andre.ebert,carsten.hahn,
georg.schneider,liza.obermeier}@ifi.lmu.de
[2] Institut für Rundfunktechnik, 80939 Munich, Germany
erk@irt.de
[3] Vrije Universiteit Brussel, 1050 Brussel, Belgium
iris.jennes@vub.be

Abstract. Hybrid radio is an umbrella term for the combination of classic broadcast radio with online services enabling highly personalized and interactive content. Hybrid services heavily rely on well-maintained metadata but currently, a multitude of different data sources and models exist, each with certain aspects and different levels of quality. We propose a distributed metadata platform which harmonizes relevant metadata from a variety of data sources and makes it comfortably searchable. The distributed and open nature of the platform renders centralized aggregators obsolete and allows even smaller stations to participate in a search network which significantly increases their visibility. The capability of the platform is proven by the implementation and evaluation of a metadata-based radio station recommender system which is one of the most important hybrid radio building blocks. Finally, the platform is evaluated by a qualitative analysis which juxtaposes requirements based on pre-defined user scenarios with its technical features.

Keywords: Hybrid radio · Multimedia services ·
Distributed databases · Data models · Interoperability

1 Introduction

Hybrid radio describes the combination of broadcast-based radio with programme-accompanying internet services. It enriches traditional radio shows with personalized and interactive multimedia content and functionalities. While analogue or digital radio is leveraged and fused with specialized online services, hybrid radio is not bound to specific standards or technologies and is advanced in terms of content variety and interactivity.

Hybrid radio services have strong requirements on the quality of available metadata (station descriptions, programme information, etc.) but accessible

K.-H. Lüke et al. (Eds.): I4CS 2019, CCIS 1041, pp. 166–183, 2019.
https://doi.org/10.1007/978-3-030-22482-0_13

sources are very diverse and not always well-maintained. Furthermore, currently available radio metadata aggregation platforms are closed-source, commercial and mostly built upon a centralized architecture which makes it hard for smaller radio stations to be added or newly appearing metadata sources to be integrated. As a reaction to the status quo, one of the goals of the HRADIO project is to develop an open, extensible and distributed metadata platform for hybrid radio use cases. It should support the integration and harmonization of diverse metadata sources and provide a distributed search component which enables smaller stations to be part of a metadata search network increasing the visibility of each participant. Of further importance for hybrid radio services is a capable recommendation engine for radio stations which is also a goal of the HRADIO project.

In summary, this paper makes the following contributions: It (1) provides an overview of the constantly evolving hybrid radio metadata landscape with its technologies and standards, (2) describes a metadata platform for the harmonization, enrichment and distributed search of available metadata and (3) proposes a metadata-based station recommender system that proves the suitability of the platform for hybrid radio use cases.

2   Background and Related Work

This section provides detailed information concerning hybrid radio metadata formats and platforms. In addition, the fundamentals of knowledge discovery needed for metadata integration and station recommendations are discussed. These insights are later used for the derivation of requirements for the metadata platform in Sect. 3.

2.1   Metadata in Hybrid Radio Scenarios

The combination of highly diverse radio content requires the consideration of a multitude of different metadata formats. The following is an overview of the most important sources of station metadata relevant for this work.

RadioDNS. In order to model radio stations and their descriptive content in a standardized way, the European Telecommunications Standards Institute (ETSI) developed the RadioDNS standard [5]. It defines an XML-based model for station and programme metadata together with a structured process to distribute it in a way similar to the Domain Name System (DNS) [10]. Currently, it encompasses more than 8000[1] radio stations worldwide. The limitations of RadioDNS lie in its inability to describe content events such as songs or spoken word fragments that occur during a radio broadcast. Furthermore, each station maintains its own RadioDNS metadata records, which results in varying metadata quality.

---

[1] RadioDNS Limited (2019): https://radiodns.org/.

Accompanying Text. Radio Data System (RDS) and ETSI's Dynamic Label standard enable textual information that accompanies programmes within analogue and digital radio broadcasts [15]. For internet broadcasting, the so-called ICY tag protocol ("I can Yell"), initially developed by SHOUTCast and adapted by the Icecast[2] community project, are used to transport integrated programme information, e.g. played songs, artists, etc., within compressed audio streams [17]. Compared to the Dynamic Label standard, only unstructured data can be transferred via ICY tags, thus complex modeling is not possible. Still, the use of ICY tag-based technologies is widespread in IP-based broadcasting due to their easy integration.

Audio Metadata Databases. RadioDNS enables complex station and programme modeling while accompanying text technologies deliver programme complementing live content. Nevertheless, metadata often lacks of in-detail information related to specific programme events, like artists, release year, genre, etc., which is important for an exact characterization of radio programmes (and thus for the implementation of content-based recommender systems). Table 1 provides an overview across rich databases targeting the aforementioned use case. The Discogs service offers the by far largest song metadata database which can be accessed via an API as well as via a downloadable XML dump file. It is licensed Creative Commons, which guarantees its free usage.

Table 1. Overview of various audio metadata databases available on the market. We chose the Discogs database for our system as it provides extensive song metadata and has a liberal licensing model [16].

Database	Tracks	Releases	Artists	Licensing	Access
Discogs	151.200.000	10.000.000	5.000.000	PD/CC0	API, XML dump
Gracenote	ca. 100.000.000	ca. 8.000.000	n.a.	n.a.	API
ACRCloud	ca. 40.000.000	n.a.	n.a.	n.a.	API
MusicBrainz	25.819.528	2.098.709	1.413.302	GPL/LGPL/PD/ CC-BY-NC-SA	API, XML dump

To sum up, there are various different sources for radio metadata with varying levels of detail and quality. Therefore, their selection, gathering, and harmonization will be a key task in Sect. 3.4.

2.2 Hybrid Radio Metadata Platforms

While open standards for the description of hybrid radio metadata exist, this is not the case for radio-related processing, storage and search platforms. Existing technologies in this field are part of commercial metadata aggregator services,

---

[2] Xiph.org (2019): https://icecast.org/.

like TuneIn[3] or Radioplayer[4]. These follow a centralized client-server paradigm, are closed source and not available as on-premises software. Although public service interfaces are provided, the level of control for a single client (e.g. a radio station that registers itself to be visible for the aggregator's search functionality) over its own metadata is restricted. In addition, these platforms are not suited for the harmonization of different metadata sources but expect input that fits exactly their defined formats.

We propose a metadata platform that is open source and free to use even for commercial use cases. It follows a distributed philosophy which allows also smaller radio stations to run their own deployments while still being visible to a large group of potential listeners. Additionally, participating radio stations have full control over their own metadata and can leverage the built-in importer unit to harmonize their existing metadata landscape.

2.3   Knowledge Discovery in Databases

In order to design modular and extensible components as well as a suitable data model for the proposed metadata platform, a process chain for dividing the whole workflow of crawling, aggregation and data analysis into subtasks is necessary. Therefore, the Knowledge Discovery in Databases (KDD) paradigm introduced by Fayyad et al. is utilized [6]. It describes the advance as a not trivial process of identifying valid, new, potentially useful, and finally more understandable patterns in big data pools. The advance serves as a guideline for metadata integration and harmonization as well as for specifying a recommender system. Figure 1 provides an overview of the process steps.

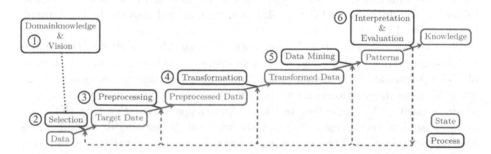

Fig. 1. The Knowledge Discovery in Databases (KDD) process model as proposed in [6] and implemented by the metadata platform. The different process steps also serve as orientation for the description of the platform concepts in Sect. 3.

Within the first task *(1) Domain knowledge and vision*, the application's final objectives and technical circumstances are identified. This is followed by

---

[3] TuneIn Incorporation (2019): https://tunein.com/.

[4] Radioplayer Worldwide Limited (2017): http://www.radioplayerworldwide.com.

a *(2) Selection* of promising and rich target data sources. *(3) Preprocessing* ensures that the target data is revised and checked for inconsistencies. Additionally, statistical noise or errors, measurement deviations and outliers, which could affect the data mining process significantly, are removed [13]. Data from external sources can be aggregated and enriched with additional information, enabling a more meaningful discovery of knowledge. The input for the *(4) Transformation* step is consistent and enriched data ready to be transformed into a readable format (e.g. feature sets, histograms, dictionaries, etc.) as needed by the *(5) Data Mining* procedure applied afterwards. For this purpose, different approaches (e.g. supervised or unsupervised learning, pattern and distance analysis, etc.) can be chosen [8]. Finally, an *(6) Interpretation and Evaluation* of the process model's outcomes is conducted which results in knowledge extracted from the underlying data.

2.4   Taxonomies of Recommender Systems

In order to design a powerful metadata platform capable of crawling, enriching, organizing and providing expressive radio metadata as needed by recommendation approaches, the different types of recommender systems need to be understood. For media items, these can be categorized into four different classes, all with its specific advantages, disadvantages and requirements.

With the publication of a data set containing more than a 100 million movie ratings from more than 480,000 users, the media-services provider Netflix invited experts and students around the world to challenge its own recommender system Cinematch, which combines *Collaborative Filtering* (CF) with a *You May Like* (YML) approach [1]. The main idea behind this recommender technique is the fusion of information about movies users watched and how they rated them (YML) with information about similar user profiles and movies the corresponding users liked (CF).

In contrast to CF and YML concepts, *Demographic Filtering* (DF) determines similarity not on basis of user preferences or their behavior, but on basis of the categorization of demographic attributes, e.g. age or language [2,12]. Thereby, recommendations can be provided by comparing profiles within a user group as well as by inspecting overlaps. *Knowledge Based Filtering* (KF) is a model based on knowledge about how the user can be satisfied by giving a specific recommendation. The needed input are the interests or necessities of a user [2,12]. An exemplary implementation of this concept would be the web interface of the search engine provided by the internet service company Google.

A recommender concept independent of user data is the *Content Based Filtering* (CBF). Here, a domain-specific measure of content similarity is used to recommend similar items. The higher the measured similarity between two items' content features is, the more similar they are.

Despite the fact that all approaches are able to offer good results, they also show specific disadvantages. One of these is the so-called *Cold Start* problem, which describes the inability of a recommender system to function properly if the amount of existing user data available for creating recommendations is small [3]. This typically occurs at an early stage by the time of a system's initial deployment and applies for CF, DF and KF approaches. Depending on the exact implementation, only CBF systems are not susceptible. Another critical point is the emergence of so-called *Filter Bubbles*, which occur mainly in CF and DF approaches. It describes the problem that on the basis of data from profiles that are always similar, also always the same items are recommended resulting in a synthetic, closed off filter bubble environment [11]. In addition, privacy concerns are relevant to CF, DF, and KF approaches as detailed information on consumer behavior is needed in order to work properly. The metadata-based station recommender system proposed in this paper is based on the CBF concept.

3   Concept

To develop a sustainable concept for a distributed metadata platform, the initial step *(1) Domain knowledge and vision* mentioned in Fig. 1 is applied to focus on the platform's goals. Its main goal is the creation of an enriched listening experience paired with enhanced usability, whereby several studies show that played songs and music genres are the most important impact factors for a satisfying radio experience [4,14]. High-quality content recommendations and descriptive metadata for making radio content discoverable in an easy and usable way, even within hybrid radio scenarios, are identified as key features. In the following, the requirements for the platform as well as its specific implementation are presented in detail.

3.1   Requirements

In order to further specify the requirements for the proposed platform, an additional study with 47 initial user scenarios clustered into 10 subject areas was carried out within the HRADIO project[5]. A key insight was that from a user's point of view, the easy discovery and accurate recommendation of new content is essential for a satisfying radio experience. Together with the basic process model described in Sect. 2.3, these insights allow the derivation of requirements for the metadata platform as stated in the following:

Metadata. In order to provide hybrid radio services and rich content to radio users, detailed metadata must be available. Since radio metadata may originate from different sources, it needs to be aggregated and harmonized. In addition, its accuracy and completeness must be ensured. Available sources need to be selected carefully based on data quality and availability. Retrieved metadata must contain station and programme descriptions, and detailed information about specific programme events, e.g. songs, genre etc.
Station Recommendations. Personalized content is important for hybrid radio services and scenarios. A station recommendation engine is crucial and must be part of the platform.

---

[5] HRADIO Deliverable *D2.1: HRADIO User Scenarios*, (2018): https://www.hradio. eu/outcome.

Searchability. For the purposeful delivery of metadata and the processing of complex search requests (e.g. range queries, spatial nearest neighbor queries, etc.), a publicly available service interface is necessary.

Scalability. Scalability with respect to the amount of stored metadata and increasing search and recommendation service load must be guaranteed.

Modularity. In order to import a variety of diverse metadata sources as required, to support an extensible data model and to enable the integration of different recommendation algorithms, the platform must have a highly modular architecture.

Availability. The architectural design should guarantee high service availability. Services should be accessible even if some platform instances fail.

Persistency. All imported metadata needs to be stored in a persistent way and in a human readable format.

Simplicity. The distributed platform has to ensure a standardized and easy-to-use deployment routine in order to enable large as well as small radio stations or privately interested users to participate in the network.

Openness. The platform itself, its usage and all aggregated metadata should be provisioned free of charge to all stakeholders. Therefore, all data sources and underlying technologies must be freely available and modifiable.

3.2   Architecture

The following architecture is based on the requirements defined in Sect. 3.1 and was built from scratch with focus on modularity and extensibility. It consists of five main building blocks (see Fig. 2 for an overview): (1) The databases module for metadata search and storage, (2) the importer unit for metadata crawling and preparation, (3) the radio station recommender engine, (4) the service layer which provides access to the platform's functionality and (5) the coordination module for distributed searches.

Databases. The platform contains two database components: The document warehouse and the Discogs database. The document warehouse persists preprocessed and transformed metadata and handles the processing of complex queries. It contains two databases, one with a relational scheme that persists the data model in all its detail and one document-oriented database that stores a flat and de-normalized representation of the data model for highly efficient and scalable query execution. The document database is filled by an indexing component that crawls the relational database (using the metadata maintenance service) in configurable intervals, transforms it to an optimized representation and creates corresponding documents.

The Discogs database contains a complete snapshot of the Discogs data set and is updated automatically with new versions. The importer unit uses it to extract programme event information based on song title and artist. The underlying storage employs a relational scheme and can be accessed via standard SQL queries.

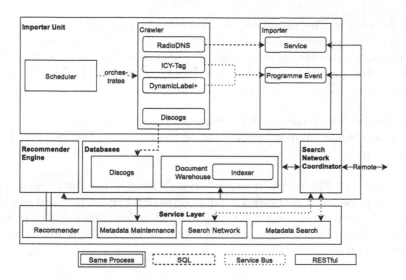

Fig. 2. Overview of the general architecture of the proposed metadata platform including all building blocks, communication routes and interfaces. The importer unit manages metadata crawling and preprocessing. Processed data is stored in the databases module and used by the recommender engine and the search network coordinator. The service layer provides public and private access to the platform's data.

Importer Unit. The importer unit is responsible for the crawling, preprocessing and transformation of service and programme event data. The scheduler located in the importer component coordinates crawler instances whereas both, the service and the programme event importer process incoming raw data and create new service or programme event items (see Sect. 3.4). For the communication between crawlers and importers, a message bus is employed which increases decoupling, extensibility (e.g. adding crawlers for new metadata sources) and scalability (with respect to number of running crawlers and update frequency). In addition, it offers a multitude of options for handling high-load phenomenons, like e.g. queue back pressure.

Service Layer. The service layer provides access to the main functionalities of the platform. All services follow the Representational State Transfer (REST) paradigm [7] and use a JSON-encoded transfer format. Some services are publicly available whereas others are restricted to be used in local networks only. All services are inherently pageable, enabling the incremental processing of large data sets.

Metadata Maintenance: The metadata maintenance service provides read and write access to the complete hierarchical data model and is available in the local network of its infrastructure. It is e.g. used by the importer unit to persist crawled metadata in the document warehouse.

Metadata Search: The metadata search service is a publicly available service for station and programme search. It forwards search requests to the search network coordinator (see next section) and responds with the search result. A comprehensive query language allows for data type-aware and arbitrarily nested queries.

Recommender: The recommender service is the public interface to the station recommender engine and retrieves a list of recommended stations based on a given station.

Search Network: The search network service manages the distributed search functionality (see next section). Its publicly available part provides read-only access to the search index and token-based search index enlisting. The privately available endpoint allows for token generation as well as for search index and description updates.

Search Network Coordinator. Essential for the platform is the distributed execution of metadata searches across a set of platform deployments (in the following referred to as search nodes). Besides forwarding the incoming query to its own document warehouse, each search node forwards query requests recursively to other search nodes selected from a locally maintained list (the search node index). Local responses are merged with those from selected remote search nodes and sent back to the requester (see Fig. 3 RESPONSE block).

The query formulation is therefore split in two separate pieces (see Fig. 3 REQUEST block): The *Top-Level Query* which defines keywords, genre and region information with which the requested search node can select a suitable set of search nodes from its search node index and the *Local Query* which is processed on the requested search node and recursively sent to selected search nodes. In addition, the requester can select the maximum depth (search hops) and breadth (number of selected search nodes per hop) of the query. The resulting query distribution graph forms a tree, with the root node being the search node that received the initial request.

The search index is stored in the document warehouse and holds descriptive properties of a search node (e.g. keywords, genres or regions) together with its URL. Search node descriptions might change over time. In order to update all local copies of a search node description (as it is stored in search node indexes), a Peer-to-Peer (P2P) approach based on the Kademlia protocol [9] was chosen. Each search node maintains its own mutable description item in the P2P network which is addressable via a search node-specific globally unique identifier. All search nodes with this particular node in their search node index are aware of this identifier and thus are notified if the contained description changes (see Fig. 3).

Entering the search network as a new search node works as follows: At first, an existing search node generates and transfers a token manually via a secured channel (e.g. encrypted email) to the new search node. With that token, the new

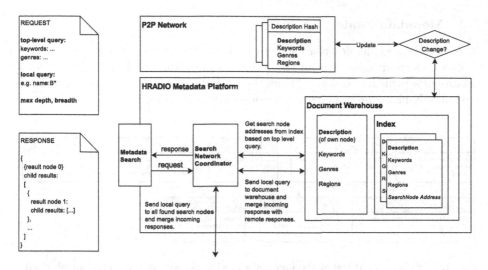

Fig. 3. The distributed search model. Each search node maintains a search index containing descriptions of other search nodes. An incoming search request contains the *Top-Level Query* for finding other suitable search nodes as well as the *Local Query* which represents the actual search expression. The search request is forwarded to other search nodes matching the *Top-Level Query* and the *Local Query* is executed on all of them (including the local search node). The combined response is sent back to the inquirer. Since search node descriptions might change over time, a P2P approach is used to keep them updated across all participants of the search network.

search node is able to manually enlist itself in the search index of the existing search node as a new node. This manual process ensures correct search node identities and is sufficient for the targeted amount of search network members. The search index of a search node is populated via different mechanisms:

- Search indexes of other search nodes can be accessed and manually added to the search index.
- Search nodes whose results constantly appear in search results are added to the search index.
- Search nodes whose empty response frequency exceeds a certain threshold are deleted from the search index.
- Search nodes whose response time constantly exceeds a certain limit are deleted from the search index.

The functionality for search network management is provided by the search network service (see Sect. 3.2).

Recommender Engine. This module is thoroughly described in Sect. 3.5.

3.3   Metadata Model

The metadata model describes structure, fields and types of the metadata that is processed and stored within the proposed platform (see Fig. 4). It follows a relational scheme and is derived from the RadioDNS standard which is extended with JSON-based programme event and genre descriptions.

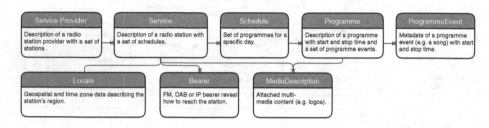

Fig. 4. High-level overview of the metadata model as used by the metadata platform. The hierarchical model is based on the RadioDNS standard with added expressiveness for genre and programme event description.

3.4   Metadata Acquisition and Aggregation

As shown in Fig. 2, the steps *(2) Selection*, *(3) Preprocessing* and *(4) Transformation* as described in Sect. 2.3 are implemented by the importer unit. For additional data enrichment, the Discogs database is used. Therefore, the scheduler of the importer unit starts and coordinates the different crawlers which collect raw metadata from different sources. After transformation and enrichment, the metadata is stored in the document warehouse which makes it available for steps *(5) Data Mining* and *(6) Interpretation and Evaluation* as well as for complex search queries.

Metadata Selection. Metadata crawling essentially maps to step *(2) Selection*. Currently, metadata crawlers for RadioDNS, Dynamic Label, ICY tags, and Discogs exist. As described in Sect. 3.2, the underlying architecture is highly modular and the integration of further metadata sources is straightforward.

Transformation and Preprocessing. The following process is aligned with steps *(3) Preprocessing* and *(4) Transformation* and its output is formatted and enriched metadata describing radio stations and their content, whereby the basic data model is based on RadioDNS.

Figure 5(a) depicts the raw metadata initially crawled from a RadioDNS source. Its structure is already capable of rendering a hierarchical model of a service provider, its specific services, their schedules, the encompassed programmes and a rough description of the current programme events. Still, a more detailed

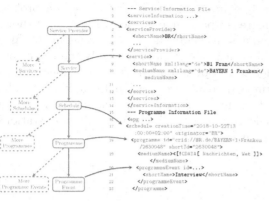

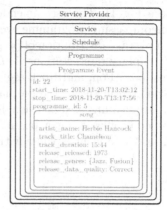

(a) Raw RadioDNS data input.

(b) Example of preprocessed and transformed metadata.

Fig. 5. The basic data structure in (a) is derived from the raw RadioDNS data model. After identifying specific programme events on basis of their ICY tags and the aggregation with additional detail information from Discogs, the final, revised and transformed metadata structure visible in (b) is created and stored in the data warehouse.

description of programme events (e.g. artists, genres, topics) is usually missing, which makes it hard to use raw RadioDNS input as a basis for expressive metadata-based recommendations.

In this context, several publications and studies state, that played music is the essential ingredient which makes users prefer a particular radio station or programme [4,14]. Thus, it is inevitable to extract further information about basic programme events in order to create a stable foundation for meaningful recommendations. To achieve this, the proposed metadata platform integrates ICY tags and Dynamic Label data simultaneously to provide further information on programme events. In this process, a filtering approach removes doublets and data not related to songs out of the byte-encoded strings leaving only title and artist information.

The extracted song data is then used to retrieve further information like release year or genre from the local Discogs database. Thereby, the most complete entry for a specific title in terms of duration, release version, genre and data quality is returned to the importer unit and integrated in the specific programme event. By associating all schedules to its parent services and all services to their service providers, it is now possible to create a deep metadata representation as depicted in Fig. 5(b).

3.5   Metadata-Based Station Recommendations

The preprocessed and transformed metadata described in Sect. 3.4 is the input for a metadata-based recommender system for radio stations which is essentially an implementation of task *(5) Data Mining* of the KDD process model (see Fig. 1). The recommender system is based on ordered histogram profiles encompassing programme event genres of particular stations. Figure 6(a) shows an average distribution of programme event genres in the daily schedule of three exemplary radio stations A, B and C. For clarity purposes, only the three genres Jazz, Pop, and Rock are depicted. In operation, the full genre spectrum as available in the metadata platform is used for recommendations which results in a much higher dimensionality of the feature space. With the genre histogram based profiles it is now possible to determine distances between different stations in order to identify those with similar content.

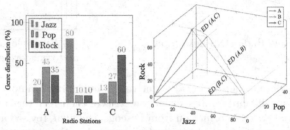

(a) Exemplary profiles (b) Profile vectors of genres
for stations by genres.   in the Euclidean space.

Fig. 6. (a) shows exemplary station profiles based on ordered histograms for three radio stations (A, B, C) selected from the evaluation data set introduced in Sect. 4.2 for genres. (b) depicts the representation of genre vectors in the Euclidean space.

As Fig. 6(b) shows, the distance of genre histograms between two different stations A, B can be determined with the Euclidean distance

$$ED(A, B) = \sqrt{\sum_{1}^{\dim(G)} (q_i - p_i)^2} \tag{1}$$

in a multi-dimensional genre vector space G, where q_i and p_i describe the average occurrence of genre i in the schedule of station A and B. The smaller the determined distance $ED(A, B)$ is, the more similar is the programme schedule of station A compared to that of station B in terms of played music genres.

4   Evaluation

The evaluation of the platform focuses on two aspects: (1) A qualitative analysis of the metadata platform and (2) a discussion of a user study conducted for the evaluation of the proposed station recommender engine.

4.1   Distributed Metadata Platform

The qualitative analysis of the proposed metadata platform should reveal to what degree the requirements defined in Sect. 3.1 are met by the platform. For this purpose, we went through the list of requirements and compared them with available platform functionalities. Table 2 depicts the results.

Table 2. Comparison of the user requirements defined in Sect. 3.1 with available platform features.

Requirement	Metadata platform feature
Metadata	Metadata is stored and processed using a comprehensive metadata model especially suitable for hybrid radio use cases (see Sect. 3.3). Metadata can be imported from various sources and is processed and enriched on its way to the storage (see Sect. 3.4)
Station recommendations	A metadata-based station recommendation engine is part of the platform (see Sect. 3.5). It is evaluated in Sect. 4.2
Searchability	With the metadata search service it is possible to search for programme and station information using complex queries. The query format is defined by the underlying search engine (Elasticsearch[a]). The proposed search network approach (Sect. 3.2) allows smaller stations to participate and gives them the opportunity to be found without any centralized aggregator instance or high use of resources
Scalability	The databases module uses technologies that are known to scale well with number of requests and amount of stored data (PostgreSQL[b] and Elasticsearch). Same goes for the employed message bus (RabbitMQ[c]). All services in the service layer are stateless and thus scale well with number of requests. However, excessive load tests are planned in order to reveal potential bottlenecks. The proposed recommender engine stores distance measures for each service to all other services which does not scale well with the number of services. Solving this problem is part of future work
Modularity	The platform consists of multiple modules (see Fig. 2) that are separated via Docker[d] containers. For inter-module communication a service bus and direct REST service calls are used. Crawler for new metadata sources are added by connecting them to the service bus. The message format is strictly defined and simple to use (Python and Java-based message APIs). A defined interface exists for adding new recommendation engines. Extending the metadata model is possible. Adding new programme event content or genre schemes comes with low effort since they are less structured (only JSON-encoded strings). Changing crucial parts of the hierarchical structure of the metadata model is costly since multiple parts have to be touched (database schemes, Java API, Python API)

Table 2. (*continued*)

Requirement	Metadata platform feature
Availability	We ran the platform for 3 consecutive months and experienced zero down-time during the user study. The databases module uses technologies that provide cluster-based fail-over mechanisms to increase availability. Platform operators can open their metadata maintenance service to others, such that metadata can be mirrored to other platform instances. Even if one instance fails, data can be accessed via other instances
Persistency	Imported metadata is stored in the databases module (see Sect. 3.2)
Simplicity	The platform is shipped with a build and deployment script for Linux distributions. It covers all necessary steps from code repository cloning to monitoring all started modules
Openness	The metadata platform itself is licensed under the MIT[e] open source license. Employed third-party software components are all free software. Used metadata sources are publicly available and free of charge

[a]Elasticsearch B.V., (2019): https://www.elastic.co/
[b]The PostgreSQL Global Development Group, (2019): https://www.postgresql.org/
[c]Pivotal Software Inc., (2019): https://www.rabbitmq.com/
[d]Docker Inc., (2019): https://www.docker.com/
[e]Opensource.org, (2019): https://opensource.org/licenses/MIT

4.2   Metadata-Based Station Recommendations

In order to evaluate the recommendation capabilities and therefore the value of the metadata provided by the proposed platform, two experiments for task *(6) Interpretation and Evaluation* of the KDD process model were conducted.

The first experiment evaluates recommendations quantitatively and compares the detected genre similarity for radio stations, which are known for having an overlapping programme schedule. Figure 7 shows the automatically detected genre occurrences encompassing 4 days of programme schedule and 5 regional stations belonging to the broadcaster Bayern 1. During this period, more than 650 programme events were detected for each station. The programme of these regional stations is nearly similar in terms of played music and programme events with slight differences in the adverts, the news and local reports. Hence, Fig. 7 traces these circumstances and indicates that the metadata provided by the proposed platform provides a solid foundation for metadata-based recommender systems.

In the second experiment, the goal was to investigate how actual users asses specific recommendations in terms of perceived versus estimated similarity. A comprehensive user study encompassing 19 participants between 25 and 59 years of age was conducted. In the first part of the study, the participants were asked for their reasons to consume audio media. 90% stated that they listen for entertainment, 60% to relax, 45% as a pastime and 45% want to stay informed. When asked how often they listen to audio media, 10% stated once monthly or once weekly, 25% several times a week, 10% daily and 55% several times daily.

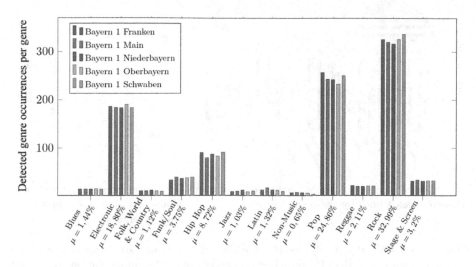

Fig. 7. Estimated similarity of regional radio stations of the same broadcaster on basis of programme event genres.

In the second part of the study, 47 radio stations were presented to the participants in a web interface. Subsequently, each participant had to choose one of the stations and the recommender responded with an ordered list of 10 most similar stations, based on programme event genres (see Sect. 3.5). The participants now had to assess the quality of the recommendations in a range from 1 to 10 on the basis of their perception and knowledge about the stations (a brief description of each station was given as a guide). 1 corresponds to a very bad recommendation, 10 to a perfect one. In addition to generated recommendations, 50% of the returned suggestions were created randomly in order to verify the quality of the recommender against the quality of random recommendations (baseline). The station selection and recommendation assessment was conducted 10 times by each participant.

Figure 8(a) depicts a selection of 22 radio stations, which were selected at least once by the study participants. When recommendations were provided by the random recommender, the participants perceived a recommendation quality of $\mu = 4.56$, while the recommender achieved a quality of $\mu = 6.67$. When only focusing on the 6 stations which were chosen by the participants at least more than 10 times, the difference in quality between both becomes even clearer visible: As Fig. 8(b) illustrates, the random recommender again achieves a comparable quality result of $\mu = 4.59$, while the recommender's quality is assessed with $\mu = 7.49$.

These results support the hypothesis that the metadata provided by the proposed platform is suitable as a basis for metadata-based recommendations. Even with a straightforward, distance-based recommendation approach it is possible to deliver meaningful recommendations with a decent level of quality.

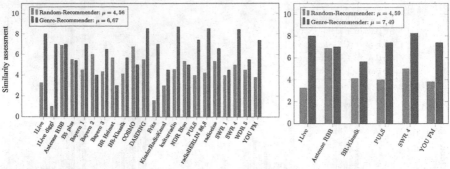

(a) Perceived recommendation quality for 22 stations chosen at least once by the participants.

(b) Corresponding perceived quality for 7 stations chosen at least 10 times.

Fig. 8. Results of subjectively perceived quality of recommendations for the proposed station recommender. Red: Proposed recommender, Blue: Recommendations generated randomly (baseline). (Color figure online)

5   Conclusion

In this paper, we proposed a distributed radio metadata platform especially designed for hybrid radio use cases. It harmonizes and enriches metadata from a multitude of sources and provides a distributed search mechanism that allows also smaller stations to be widely visible for potential listeners. By conducting a qualitative analysis, we were able to show that it meets the requirements that have been derived before from pre-defined user scenarios. As an exemplary hybrid radio use case, a metadata-based station recommendation engine was described in detail. In its evaluation we could show that it is possible to generate meaningful station recommendations based on the metadata provided by the proposed platform. For future work, we would like to investigate the platform's performance characteristics and integrate audio stream-based enrichment of metadata using techniques from spoken word and sentiment analysis.

Acknowledgements. The HRADIO project and thus this work was funded by H2020, the EU Framework Programme for Research and Innovation.

References

1. Bennett, J., Lanning, S., et al.: The netflix prize. In: Proceedings of KDD Cup and Workshop, New York, NY, USA, vol. 2007, p. 35 (2007)
2. Burke, R.: Hybrid recommender systems: survey and experiments. User Model. User Adapt. Interact. **12**(4), 331–370 (2002)
3. Chang, S., Zhou, J., Chubak, P., Hu, J., Huang, T.: A space alignment method for cold-start TV show recommendations. In: Twenty-Fourth International Joint Conference on Artificial Intelligence (2015)

4. Eichmann, R.: Journalismus. In: Kleinsteuber, H.J. (ed.) Radio: Eine Einfhrung, pp. 235–267. VS Verlag fr Sozialwissenschaften (2011)
5. Europäisches Institut für Telekommunikationsnormen (ETSI): ETSI TS 102 818 V3.1.1 (2015-01), Hybrid Digital Radio (DAB, DRM, RadioDNS); XML Specification for Service and Programme Information (SPI)
6. Fayyad, U., Piatetsky-Shapiro, G., Smyth, P.: From data mining to knowledge discovery in databases. AI Mag. **17**(3), 37 (1996)
7. Fielding, R.T.: REST: architectural styles and the design of network-based software architectures. Doctoral dissertation, University of California, Irvine (2000). http://www.ics.uci.edu/fielding/pubs/dissertation/top.htm
8. Haykin, S.S.: Neural Networks and Learning Machines, vol. 3. Pearson, Upper Saddle River (2009)
9. Maymounkov, P., Mazières, D.: Kademlia: a peer-to-peer information system based on the XOR metric. In: Druschel, P., Kaashoek, F., Rowstron, A. (eds.) IPTPS 2002. LNCS, vol. 2429, pp. 53–65. Springer, Heidelberg (2002). https://doi.org/10.1007/3-540-45748-8_5
10. Mockapetris, P., Dunlap, K.J.: Development of the domain name system. SIGCOMM Comput. Commun. Rev. **18**(4), 123–133 (1988). https://doi.org/10.1145/52325.52338, http://doi.acm.org/10.1145/52325.52338
11. Pariser, E.: The Filter Bubble: What the Internet Is Hiding from You. Penguin, New York (2011)
12. Ricci, F., Rokach, L., Shapira, B.: Introduction to recommender systems handbook. In: Ricci, F., Rokach, L., Shapira, B., Kantor, P.B. (eds.) Recommender Systems Handbook, pp. 1–35. Springer, Boston (2011). https://doi.org/10.1007/978-0-387-85820-3_1
13. Runkler, T.A.: Data Mining: Methoden und Algorithmen intelligenter Datenanalyse. Springer, Wiesbaden (2010). https://doi.org/10.1007/978-3-8348-9353-6
14. Singh, K.: Radio listening habits and preferences a study of urban population of Punjab. J. Commer. Manag. Res. **21**(1), 83–104 (2013)
15. Suchowerskyj, W., Kaesser, J., Braegas, P.: System for selecting route-relevant information when using the radio data system (RDS), 1 August 1995. US Patent 5,438,687
16. Wikipedia contributors: Wikipedia. https://en.wikipedia.org/w/index.php?title=List_of_online_music_databases&oldid=858557909
17. Xiph.Org: Icecast. http://icecast.org/

A Framework for Analyzing News Images and Building Multimedia-Based Recommender

Andreas Lommatzsch[✉], Benjamin Kille, Kevin Styp-Rekowski, Max Karl,
and Jan Pommering

Agent Technologies in Business Applications and Telecommunication,
Technische Universität Berlin, Straße des 17. Juni 135, 10623 Berlin, Germany
{andreas.lommatzsch,benjamin.kille,kevin.styp-Rekowski,max.karl,
jan.pommering}@campus.tu-berlin.de

Abstract. The number and accessibility of published news items have grown recently. Publishers have developed recommender systems supporting users in finding relevant news. Traditional news recommender systems focus on collaborative filtering and content-based strategies. Unlike texts, multimedia content has received little attention. However, images and other multimedia elements affect how users perceive the news. In this work, we present a system that aggregates text-based, image-based, and user interests-based features to foster recommender systems for news. The system monitors a live stream of news and interactions with them. It applies text analysis and automatic image labeling methods for enriching the news stream. A web application visualizes the collected data and statistics. We show that image features are valuable for developing news recommender systems. The created feature-rich dataset constitutes the basis for developing innovative news recommendation approaches.

Online news is ubiquitously available and serves as a vital information source. Readers struggle to discover exciting stories as publishers release an ever-increasing amount of news. Frequently, images accompany news articles and significantly affect their perception. Traditional content-based news recommender systems analyze the texts but largely ignore the pictures. Still, images draw the readers' attention. They could play a decisive role in understanding readers' behavior.

How do readers' actions toward headlines, texts, and images reflect their preferences? To answer this question, we have developed a system designed to collect, transform, and analyze news-related data. First, the system stores images along with statistics describing users' reading behavior. Second, Artificial Intelligence-based annotators automatically assign descriptive labels to each image. Third, a web-based user interface displays the images and highlights statistics. Finally, several multimedia-based recommender algorithms are implemented and evaluated. We discuss the challenges and experiences with multimedia-based recommendations.

© Springer Nature Switzerland AG 2019
K.-H. Lüke et al. (Eds.): I4CS 2019, CCIS 1041, pp. 184–201, 2019.
https://doi.org/10.1007/978-3-030-22482-0_14

This work contributes to state of the art in the following ways:

- We summarize approaches for analyzing and annotating images.
- We create a multimedia dataset and extend it continuously.
- We evaluate a selection of image labeling frameworks and analyze their strengths and weaknesses concerning the news recommender scenario.
- We implement a GUI revealing dataset characteristics.
- We release a dataset combining texts, images, and user preferences thus facilitating a comprehensive analysis.
- We implement and evaluate recommendation algorithms using multimedia data.
- We enable researchers to track shifting user interests and investigate multimedia-based recommendation strategies.

The paper is structured as follows: Sect. 1 describes the scenario and the problem in detail. Section 2 provides background information and discusses related work. Section 3 introduces our approach for building a corpus for a multimedia-based recommender. Section 4 discusses the properties of the created dataset. We explain baseline recommendation algorithms and discuss their precision on the newly created dataset in Sect. 5. Finally, Sect. 6 concludes and gives an outlook on future work.

1   Problem Description

In this section, we analyze the scenario. We discuss the used data sources and explain the specific challenges.

1.1   The Analyzed Scenario in Detail

Web-based news portals offer users a broad spectrum of the news. News publishers have added recommendations to their portals to help readers navigate. This has motivated introducing the NEWSREEL challenge[1].

Therein, researchers gain access to a collection of authentic recent news as well as news-user interactions. Participants must develop innovative recommendation algorithms. The *Open Recommendation Platform* (ORP) enables researchers to evaluate algorithms in a "living lab" environment. At the same time, participants obtain a collection of recorded data facilitating offline experiments.

The NewsREEL data arrive in the form of a stream of events [14]. Events' features describe the news articles as well as readers' behavior. Specifically, events refer to the title, teaser, image, and creation date of the news items. Besides, the system monitors users' reading and clicking behavior in the form of "impressions" and "clicks." The NewsREEL data stream describes events in the JSON message format. On average, the stream amounts to $\approx 5\,\mathrm{GB}$ per day. This corresponds to ≈ 800 newly published items ("item updates") and ≈ 3.5 million impressions. We observe a high variance regarding the frequency of messages over the day.

---

[1] http://www.newsreelchallenge.org/.

1.2   The Challenges

Processing the data stream entails several challenges. The data reveal merely a limited view of user preferences. Thus, researchers must define models suitable for computing high-quality recommendations. Traditional recommender approaches apply Collaborative Filtering (CF) relying on the user-item interactions but ignoring the item content. Due to the cold start problem of Collaborative Recommender algorithms [4] these approaches are ill-suited for news streams. For freshly published items, sufficient feedback remains unavailable. Content-based recommenders represent an alternative to CF. These approaches usually focus on the item descriptions. They tend to ignore accompanying images. As the images have a substantial impact on the perception of the item, researchers should consider them when computing the items' relevance. Diversity as well as ambiguous meanings impede establishing images as the source of information for recommender systems.

Scalability represents another challenge. Participants must deal with variations in request frequency while maintaining a maximum response time limit. During especially demanding hours, systems can receive hundreds of requests per second. Each request expects a reply within 100 ms. Recommendation algorithms which use image features experience additional requirements. They must process the images promptly such that they can include recommendations of newly added articles quickly.

1.3   Discussion

Existing news recommender systems predominantly consider textual representation and similarities concerning preferences among readers. At the same time, most news recommender systems appear to ignore the images displayed alongside articles. On the other hand, the images draw the attention of readers. Thus, analyzing how images, user preferences, and texts correlate becomes an interesting research question. Thus far, this topic failed to gain attraction and remains an open question. We want to change this and introduce a system capable of collecting, analyzing, and presenting information regarding news and news recommender systems. This work shall foster research on this topic by combining advanced image analysis and recommendation algorithms. The new dataset can be used to evaluate new ideas and benchmark existing work.

2   Background Information

This section discusses related work and existing components related to our scenario. We focus on image annotation frameworks, models for annotating images, and existing systems.

Systems and Scenarios. The automated analysis of images has become a research topic relevant to an increasing number of domains. Well-known applications include annotating photos on FACEBOOK or FLICKR [20]. Several research initiatives and conferences try to foster the research in this domain such as ACM MULTIMEDIA[2], IMAGECLEF[3], and MEDIAEVAL[4]. Relevant topics range from traffic analysis [12] to MR brain image classification [10] to interestingness prediction [2,6] and to knowledge extraction from satellite images [3].

Similar Systems. Several recent research prototypes have emerged in the scope of automatic labeling and data mining from images:

(1) Nogueira et al. [15] present a system that crawls pictures from social media portals. They use the collected data to train Convolutional Neural Networks to discover flood events in pictures or texts. The evaluation shows that combining image-based and textual data achieves the highest precision. Their findings encourage us to analyze how textual and image-based features combine in different domains.

(2) Kumaresan et al. [13] combine textual and visual features to detect spam e-mails. The conducted experiments show that incorporating visual features improves classification accuracy: Image-based features complement the text-based features. Incorporating visual features remains a rather young research direction; a stronger focus on this topic could improve the results in different domains.

(3) Corsini et al. [6] have developed a system that investigates the idea, that the thumbnail provides the most valuable selection criterion for choosing a news article. The system classifies an image as "interesting" or "not interesting" based on whether or not it detects human faces. The results indicate that the analysis of images represents a promising approach for computing the relevance of news items. A more comprehensive analysis appears as a promising research topic.

Overall, the analysis shows that combining textual and visual features improves the prediction accuracy in several domains. The methods for incorporating visual information are rather new—thus different approaches and methods should be considered in order to define a high-quality solution.

Image Annotation Frameworks. Annotating images represents a complex task. The system has to convert images to an informative representation in the form of features. Subsequently, the system has to generate a meaningful classification model. In recent years, artificial neural networks have become the most popular tool for this task in the domain of image classification. Designing the network

---

[2] http://www.acmmm.org/.
[3] http://www.imageclef.org/.
[4] http://www.multimediaeval.org/.

topology represents a difficult challenge. Finally, the system has to infer the optimal parameters for the model such that the system can automatically annotate unknown images. Various frameworks simplify developing image annotating systems. The most popular frameworks are THEANO/KERAS and TENSORFLOW.

Theano and Keras. KERAS is a deep learning library for Python usable on top of THEANO. THEANO is a Python library tailored for solving computationally-intense mathematical problems. Both libraries are open-source and well maintained by an active community. KERAS enables researchers to start quickly with neural networks thanks to predefined models. Pre-trained models for several domains, including image annotation, are available for download. These features render the THEANO/KERAS library well-suited for our scenario.

Tensorflow. TENSORFLOW is an open-source machine learning library which makes use of data flow graphs for numerical computations. Image and speech processing represent the main application scopes. TENSORFLOW can be used with `Python` or `C++`. Pre-trained data models and a large number of extensions are available thanks to an active community.

Models. At their core, image annotation frameworks rely on pre-trained models. The most frequently used models (when working with KERAS and TENSORFLOW) are trained on the IMAGENET datasets [7]. IMAGENET collects pictures for different words or labels fetched from the WordNet dataset[5]. These pre-trained models classify images into up to 1000 different labels which have been chosen from a subset of the WordNet dataset. These labels originate from various areas and include different animals as well as sports and other topics. Strikingly, the 1000 labels cannot tell whether images showed humans or not.

KERAS is able to use the `VGG-16`, the `VGG-19`, as well as the `ResNet50` model, while TENSORFLOW is able to use the `VGG-16`, the `VGG-19`, and the `Inception-v3` model. The main difference between these neural network models lays in the number of layers, the number of neurons as well as how they combine. Details concerning these neural networks have been described in the literature [11]. Training these models on a large dataset needs much computational power and therefore time. With limited resources, this work strongly necessitates using pre-trained models.

Discussion. The analyzed image annotation frameworks and models have shown considerable precision in the majority of the application scenarios. This promises adding value to image annotation tasks in different domains. Both analyzed frameworks have strengths and weaknesses. We have decided to integrate both frameworks in order to ensure comprehensive annotations.

---

[5] http://www.image-net.org/.

3 Building a Corpus for Multimedia-Based Recommender Systems

In this section, we introduce our approach to building a corpus for learning and evaluating multimedia-based recommender. We explain the system architecture and discuss the implemented components in detail.

3.1 System Architecture

Processing the NewsREEL data stream and building a reusable corpus represent our main objective. The corpus should keep the raw data enriched with meta-information describing the texts and images. In addition, we develop a web application allowing users to explore the corpus visually. The web application enables users to search, examine, and filter by labels and terms. The application computes summarizing statistics.

Figure 1 visualizes our system's architecture. A database stores the data received from the NewsREEL data stream. Periodically, the system computes item statistics—e.g., the item popularity—and stores this information in the database. In addition to the popularity statistics, the system analyzes the item texts and stores the results as features in the database. Concurrently, the system collects the image meta-data and downloads the images for the next processing steps. Selected automatic image annotators assign labels to the stored images. Simultaneously, the system extracts labels from the texts and stores raw features of text and images. A web application visualizes the collected data, providing detailed statistics and different types of diagrams.

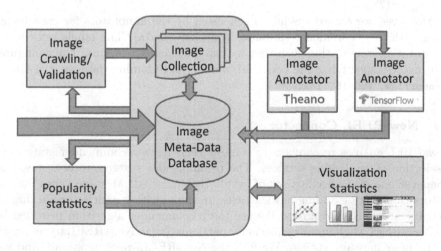

Fig. 1. The architecture of the system.

3.2   Database and Data Management

We have decided to use `MySQL` as database to store images' meta-data.

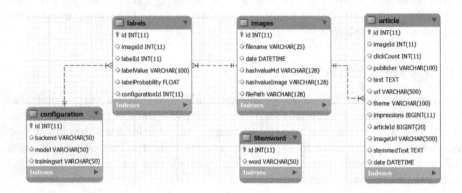

Fig. 2. The database schema.

Figure 2 illustrates the database scheme. We store the meta-data for the news item (relation `article`) including the item title, the teaser, publication date, publisher, and the total number of clicks and impressions. Computing a stemmed version of the items' teaser text simplifies later analysis. The system stores image data in a separate table (relation `images`). We compute two hashes for each image: The hash `value-Md` corresponds to the files MD5 hash and facilitates identifying duplicates. The hash `value-Image` allows us to detect resized or cropped versions of images [17].

Moreover, we record the labels generated by the annotators for each image along with their confidence estimates (relation `labels`). The labels refer to an annotator's configuration such that we can trace labels' origins. The configuration involves specifying the back-end, model, and training data—e.g. a triplet (`Tensorflow, VGG-16, ImageNet`).

3.3   NewsREEL Connector

NewsREEL enables researchers to connect their news recommender systems to a selection of publishing services. The recommender systems receive messages whenever one of a specified set of events has occurred. Message types include editors changing or adding news articles, readers visiting articles or clicking on recommendations, and errors. We use the recommender algorithm provided by the NewsREEL challenge organizers for participating in NewsREEL to get access to the news message stream. We fork the NewsREEL message stream and use it as input for our image analysis system.

3.4   Text-Processing Component

Textual item descriptions represent one of our system's key aspects. For detailed text analysis, we preprocess the textual data. First, we remove symbol characters, such as periods, exclamation points, or question marks. Second, we tokenize the text obtaining a list of words. Third, we remove frequently occurring terms. Finally, a stemmer reduces the remaining terms to their word stems—using a German Snowball stemmer. The system stores the preprocessed text in addition to the original text in the database.

3.5   Image Tagging Components

A modularly implemented component computes the image annotations. The component supports several different annotation frameworks and configurations. Additional annotators can be easily integrated.

The system establishes a preprocessing pipeline for images. It crops images to a fixed 224 by 224 pixels. Subsequently, the system decodes each pixel's RGB-values to obtain a 224 by 224 by 3 tensor. Next, we normalize the tensor by subtracting each color's mean value and change the ordering to BGR. The annotators get this representation as input. We have implemented the annotation components as artificial neural networks. The networks consist of multiple layers including convolutional, pooling, and fully connected layers. We use four pre-trained models: (VGG-16, VGG-19, INCEPTIONV3, RESNET50). In case of the VGG-19 model with TENSORFLOW, we push a NUMPY array representation of the fourth pooling layer to the database. The arrays enable us to include a compact representation of images as part of the dataset. The frameworks return a list of the top ten possible labels selected by the annotators' confidence score.

3.6   The Visualization Web Application

We have wrapped the database and image collection in a web application allowing users to browse the dataset. Users get access to statistics and graphs.

We have used FLASK[6] for that purpose. FLASK is a python framework for building websites implementing the Model-View-Controller (MVC) pattern. The backend passes the data to a JINJA[7] template engine. Through FLASK, we can query our database as well as to generate statistics about the latest data. Besides, the app facilitates visiting articles or images.

The GUI is predicated on a Bootstrap SB-Admin template[8], jQuery, and JavaScript libraries. The platform's main page shows a list of all articles, their impressions, related images, image labels, dates, and annotation configuration (Fig. 3). Users can sort the list by each attribute. In addition, the GUI offers three filter options. The first option eliminates all but the·most likely label for each

---

[6] https://flask.pocoo.org/.

[7] https://jinja.pocoo.org/.

[8] https://startbootstrap.com/template-overviews/sb-admin/.

image. The second option presents a multi-select dropdown menu. Users may filter by image name, label, annotator configuration, or date. The third option shows an input field with auto-completion. Users may search for particular labels.

The GUI includes a statistics overview (Fig. 4): Users can compare images showing persons with images without persons. Another dynamic figure tracks the frequency of labels occurring against their probabilities. The third chart contrasts labels from news texts and their probabilities. Users may filter the statistics by filtering with the auto-completion input field.

Workflows. The GUI supports three use cases:

(1) A user finds a specific image in the image collection. The search is based on the most fitting labels. The web application allows the user to filter on the top-left buttons to select desired images. Subsequently, they can sort the labels by their confidence scores.
(2) A user has a specific "concept" in mind. The user searches for the most related articles or images. For this scenario, the auto-completion field at the top allows selecting the potentially relevant search terms. When the user starts typing, the database lists possible labels. After the label selection, a threshold can be set to avoid the platform from showing irrelevant results.
(3) A user can get an overview of the results provided by the different models; the user can use the various graphs shown on the statistic pages which provide a general overview of the generated data.

Overall, the web application gives users quick access to the created dataset. Users can search for specific images or labels as well as explore the dataset statistics. The web application is open for additional extensions.

3.7   Technical Aspects - Implementation Details

We have implemented the system in PYTHON3. The selected framework and components enabled us to rapidly prototype and efficiently integrate the image annotators. Further, we employ python scripts to aggregate user-item interactions and to crawl images.

The web UI has been implemented using FLASK; we use a MYSQL database server included in the standard Ubuntu Linux distribution. The python database connector and SQL query optimizer has been implemented using SQLALCHEMY[9].

The integrated image analysis libraries support GPUs to speed up the annotation. In our virtualized runtime environment, GPU support has been unavailable. Thus, image annotation typically needs several hours. Still, the system performs well overall. We have not observed significant issues with a large amount of data in our scenario. The pre-trained models help to restrict computational efforts as learning them would bind considerable resources.

We have measured the time needed by TENSORFLOW and KERAS to label the images. Keras and Tensorflow annotators used the VGG16 and VGG19 models.

---

[9] https://www.sqlalchemy.org/.

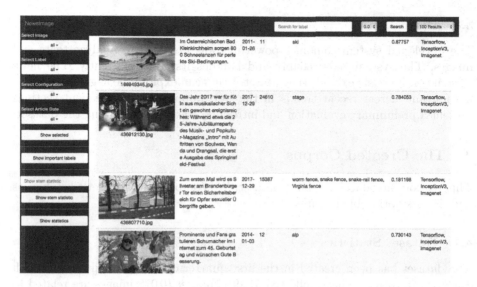

Fig. 3. The main window shows the images and the key meta-features. Users can define search criteria and filter as well as sort matching images.

Using the VGG16 model the Keras annotator has spent an average time of 1.18 s to label one image. With the VGG19 model, the Keras annotator has spent an average time of 1.37 s for a single image. For the Tensorflow annotator, we have observed 0.55 s on average with the VGG16 model, and 1.00 s with the VGG19 model. Platform and frameworks represent separate entities. Thereby, annotators and platform run independently whereby errors cannot affect the other entity.

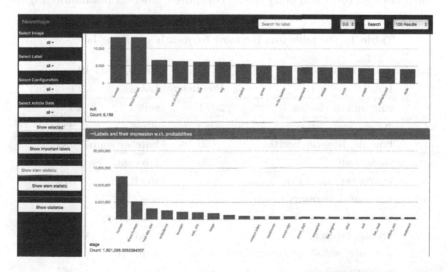

Fig. 4. The figure show the visualization of the statistics for a selected set of images.

3.8   Discussion

The developed system combines powerful tools designed to analyze texts and images. The system runs reliably and handles its tasks efficiently. The news stream continuously extends the dataset. Users can explore the aggregated information and detect recent trends in the web application. Subsequent sections present a preliminary evaluation and introduce statistics describing the dataset.

4   The Created Corpus

This section introduces the built dataset. We compute the dataset's key figures and discuss noticeable features.

4.1   Dataset Statistics

The dataset has been created in the first quarter of 2018–January 1 to March 31, 2018. In total, we have collected 51 291 images: 10 078 images are related to recent news items; 41 213 images belong to images released in 2010–2017. The system collects around 800 new images per day. Thereby, the image collection grows by about 80 MB.

Seven configurations produced image annotations: four use TENSORFLOW, three are based on THEANO. Each configuration has provided ≈ 10 k annotation. We consider a maximum of ten labels for each image by a configuration. Table 1 shows the most frequently assigned labels by the VGG-19 model. Therein, we have considered merely the labels with the highest confidence for each image.

We analyze the best label's confidence. Figure 5 shows that for a large number of images, the maximal confidence score ranges between 0.1 and 0.5. Despite the low confidence scores, the quality of the computed labels is reasonably high.

Table 1. The table lists the most frequently occurring labels.

Rank	TensorFlow/VGG-19		Keras/VGG-19	
	Label	Frequency	Label	Frequency
1	suit, suit of clothes	2471	suit	2590
2	stage	955	stage	957
3	bow tie, bow-tie, bowtie	750	butcher shop	699
4	rugby ball	706	lab coat	679
5	sports car, sport car	624	torch	570
6	lab coat, laboratory coat	587	wig	522
7	wig	515	hair spray	511
8	groom, bridgeroom	505	groom	508
9	web site, website, internet site	485	fountain	497
10	military uniform	484	racer	467

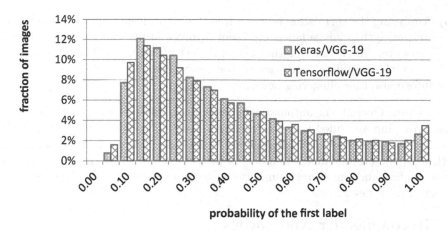

probability of the first label

Fig. 5. The figure shows the distribution of the confidence scores for the labels with the highest probability.

4.2 Qualitative Analysis

Working on the system and analyzing the computed annotation, we have encountered the following issues.

(1) Our news dataset is strongly biased towards sports news. We observe this bias both in the texts and the labels assigned to images. Frequently occurring labels, such as a suit of clothes, ball, and wig, suggest that many images show athletes. The particular sports remain hard to detect. The classifiers tend to confuse European sports with American ones. This indicates that the used training set is only partially suitable for our scenario. In addition, we have noticed, that for several images a label has been recognized without the key object in the picture. For instance, annotators labeled images as 'basketball,' despite no basketball being shown in the image. The labeling seems to rely on features, not directly apparent for humans.
   Manually checking the images, we found even human experts struggle to predict the kind of sport.
(2) Stage represents another frequent label signaling the presence of a celebrity. In addition, we found images showing the blue lights of emergency service cars. The blue lights may be perceived as similar to the situation in concerts.
(3) The labeling components often derive labels from one single image element. For instance, they focus on a person's coat such as military uniforms or trench coats. This seems to indicate that the complexity for different "concepts" varies. Thus, the annotators focus on the elements easiest to use for deriving a label.
(4) Our image collection contains images for which the annotators failed to assign a reliable label. This means that the probability for the best label falls below 10%. Such situations indicate that the underlying model lacks certain concepts. These cases require additional training to improve the classifier.

(5) Analyzing the correlation between items' text and the derived image labels, we notice that image labels represent appropriate keywords. Typically, the computed labels describe the central aspect of the news. The labels do not cover the complete semantics of the news item but could provide useful information for clustering news.

Discussion. Overall, the automatically computed labels provide useful information providing an added value to the textual data. Models trained on domain-specific data will allow computing more precise and more reliable labels. Nevertheless, the current image annotators provide valuable information and help us to understand the correlation between texts and images as well as the user preferences in news items.

5   Recommender Approaches

We have implemented several baseline recommendation algorithms to study the problem of news recommendation. We have evaluated these algorithms on a subset of the created dataset.

5.1   Dataset for the Recommender Evaluation

Based on the crawled items, we define a dataset that covers four selected publishers. The dataset consists of the first thirteen weeks in 2018, starting on January 1st, 2018. As user feedback information, we observe for the news items a total of about 153 million impressions, 397 million recommendations, and 1.1 million clicks. We partition the dataset into a training set and a test set. The test set comprises the weeks 4, 10, 11, and 12.

The dataset includes the following features for each item:

- item data (ID, URL, image URL, timestamp of publication).
- text features (headline, snippet; in German).
- image features (up to ten labels per image and a weighting, activation weights of a standard deep learning network encoding the image). The images have been annotated by means of different frameworks (*Keras* [5], *TensorFlow* [1] and existing, pre-trained models (VGG16, VGG19 [18]) (see Sect. 3).
- items' popularity data (numbers of visits, clicks, recommendations). The image popularity data cover only the training weeks.

As we are interested in computing baseline recommender algorithms, we refrain from computing additional features. Adding informative features remains for users of the dataset to do.

5.2   Baselines

NewsREEL Multimedia tasks the participants to find the news items which users will read most frequently. The participating teams must predict the number of impressions for each item listed in the test weeks.

We introduce three baseline strategies for predicting the number of impressions: random, document-based, and feature-based.

5.3 Random

The *random* baseline assigns each item a random non-negative integer as number of impressions. This random guessing should be the lower bound for all prediction strategies.

5.4 Document-Based Approach

The *document-based* approach centers on the notion of document similarity. The algorithm employs the basic concept of the k nearest neighbor classifier [8]. First, we represent each news items as a bag of words. We obtain the words either from the articles' texts or image annotations. Next, we determine the ten most similar news items employing cosine distances amid their term vectors. The computation exhibits linear complexity in the number of news items. With the NewsREEL Multimedia dataset, the computation took several minutes. Finally, we estimate the number of impressions as the sum of the ten neighbors' impressions.

5.5 Feature-Based Approach

The *feature-based* approach considers features rather than documents. We derive features as terms occurring in the news article as well as labels assigned to images. For each term and label, we compute the average number of impressions of all articles related to them. We estimate the number of impression for a given article by averaging the expected impressions of all its features.

The NewsREEL Multimedia dataset contains further information facilitating variations of this approach. Image labels carry a reference to their annotator's configuration. Thus, the baseline can focus on particular annotators' input or combinations thereof. In addition, each label entails a confidence score. The score indicates how confident the annotator is that the label applies to the image. We can modify the baseline to consider these scores as weights.

5.6 Recommender Evaluation

We have evaluated the implemented algorithms paying attention to the configurations used to annotate the images. In the evaluation, we only report the results for the three publishers with the highest number of news items. Table 2 shows that the results differ sharply between the publishers.

The random baseline performs at $\approx 10\%$ for all publishers. In contrast, the text-based method achieves 34.7% for publisher 13554, 19.2% for publisher 17614, and 22.5% for publisher 39234. The image-based method exhibits noticeable differences as well. While it scores 19.0% for publisher 13554 with configuration 7, it barely exceeds the random baseline for publisher 17614 and 39234. The relatively good performance of image-based recommenders for domain 13554 ("cars") compared with the other domains ("world and local news") could be explained by the fact, that articles on 13554 have a longer lifecycle and are less influenced by breaking news.

Comparing the text-based predictors with the image-based predictors, we find that text feature-based methods on average show a better performance. The approach focusing on selected text features performs significantly better than the terms-based document similarity method. The document similarity method which uses images obtains similar results to the image-based feature methods. For publisher 13554, they score 23.2% with configuration 7, whereas they remain on the random baseline level for the remaining publishers. Specific terms appear to affect items' popularity more than assigned images do. A suitable weighting scheme is of significant importance. Comparing word features with image features, the results indicate that the words are more suitable for forecasting the popularity of items than the computed images labels. An analysis of the correlation between image labels and text terms should be conducted. The use of different languages—English for image labels and German for news texts—introduces an additional difficulty.

We analyze the differences between the feature-based and the document-based approaches. On average, the feature-based methods outperform the document-based approaches. This could be explained by considering more robust data (when using features) instead of merely considering the documents most similar to the current news item. Top text terms in domain 13554 (domain cars) are *middle-class*, *unique*, *mar* and *grand*; the top image labels are *snake* (referring to cables), *roof*, and *folding chair*.

Comparing the influence of the image annotator configuration, we find that the annotator 4 based on the INCEPTIONV3 [19] performs worse than the predictors using the VGG [9] component. Analyzing the labels computed by the algorithms, we found, that the annotators typically describe selected objects in the image, but are not optimized for interestingness prediction. The example "stock" images introduce further challenges. Publishers use these for news articles which currently lack photos.

Overall, the evaluation results show specific differences between the configurations and domains. The underlying rules should be researched in detail to improve the prediction algorithms and to optimize the parameter configurations.

5.7 Recommender Evaluation Discussion

In this section, we have evaluated several baseline algorithms developed to predict the popularity of news items based on multimedia data. The results suggest that performance strongly depends on the individual publisher. We have observed that text-based features perform better than image-based features. This could be due to terms being more closely linked to the events reported by the articles.

While text-based methods have outperformed the random baseline consistently, image-based approaches merely overcome the random baseline for some publishers. This indicates that news articles' popularity may be disconnected from images for some publishers. Furthermore, we have seen that the quality of image-based recommendations depends on the annotator used to create the labels.

Table 2. Prec@top-10% for the baseline algorithms

Recommender name	Labeler configuration	Domain (publisher)		
		13554	17614	39234
doc. similarity using images	(2) Tensorflow - VGG16	0.207	0.103	0.110
doc. similarity using images	(3) Tensorflow - VGG19	0.223	0.109	0.104
doc. similarity using images	(4) Tensorflow - InceptionV3	0.200	0.114	0.104
doc. similarity using images	(5) Keras - VGG16	0.224	0.112	0.104
doc. similarity using images	(6) Keras - VGG19	0.227	0.109	0.121
doc. similarity using images	(7) Keras - ResNet50	0.232	0.109	0.091
doc. similarity using text	(–) [none]	0.186	0.100	0.137
image feature-based	(2) Tensorflow - VGG16	0.159	0.097	0.123
image feature-based	(3) Tensorflow - VGG19	0.137	0.099	0.127
image feature-based	(4) Tensorflow - InceptionV3	0.091	0.108	0.113
image feature-based	(5) Keras - VGG16	0.108	0.104	0.110
image feature-based	(6) Keras - VGG19	0.129	0.109	0.110
image feature-based	(7) Keras - ResNet50	0.124	0.106	0.096
text feature-based	(–) [none]	0.347	0.192	0.225
random	–	0.101	0.102	0.102

The implemented recommender algorithms are an initial baseline for the multimedia recommender scenario. For improving the recommender algorithms, we see several ways to extend the recommender algorithms:

(1) Our work has focused exclusively on "high-level" features such as image labels. Low-level features deserve further attention.
(2) In our experiments, we have analyzed annotators' configurations and the token-based methods separately. A weighted combination of both might yield a performance boost for some publishers. A recommender should consider the context in which a user engages with an item.
(3) Our feature-based approach linearly combines features. More sophisticated methods—such as neural networks or SVMs—should be tested. They could capture the underlying distributions more accurately.

6   Conclusion

Analyzing images as part of news recommendations has emerged as a new but exciting challenge. We have introduced a system designed to create multimedia datasets featuring news articles, images, and readers' actions. Users may obtain the initial data from the NewsREEL challenge. The system iterates a log file and collects multimedia data as well as statistics. Besides, we have developed a web application visualizing the data and showing the most relevant statistics.

The system has run reliably without inconsistencies. We have designed the application in a modular fashion facilitating the integration of new components. For instance, developers may explore additional image annotation libraries.

The user interface facilitates grasping the most important characteristics of the data. Researchers can use the dataset as a valuable resource as it combines different types of data. The system will continue to add data over time. Thus, we will be able to provide data for big data research projects.

As an initial application, we have presented the computation of news recommendations based on multimedia data. We have presented several algorithms and have shown that the analysis of image data can help to predict the interest of news. In this paper, we have discussed rather simple algorithms still offering room for further improvements and the evaluation of new recommender approaches.

Future Work. Currently, we run our system to grow the dataset. In the future, we plan to develop more sophisticated news recommendation algorithms using image data. We expect to gain performance because images draw the attention of readers noticeably. Also, we plan to use a variety of machine learning algorithms to discover hidden regularities in the data. Modeling how attractive a particular item is to users represents a vivid research direction. In addition, we plan to incorporate the image processing pipeline into our search engine framework as well as our automatic press review dashboard [16]. Furthermore, we plan to evaluate the image-based news recommender online based on the live news stream.

References

1. Abadi, M., et al.: Tensorflow: a system for large-scale machine learning. In: Proceedings of the 12th USENIX Conference on Operating Systems Design and Implementation. OSDI 2016, pp. 265–283. USENIX Association, Berkeley (2016). http://dl.acm.org/citation.cfm?id=3026877.3026899
2. Acar, E., Hopfgartner, F., Albayrak, S.: A comprehensive study on mid-levelrepresentation and ensemble learning for emotional analysis of videomaterial. Multimedia Tools Appl. **76**(9), 11809–11837 (2016). https://doi.org/10.1007/s11042-016-3618-5
3. Arenas, H., Islam, M.B., Mothe, J.: Overview of ImageCLEF 2017 population estimation (remote) task. In: WN for CLEF 2017 Conference, Dublin, Ireland, 11–14 September 2017 (2017)
4. Bobadilla, J., Ortega, F., Hernando, A., Bernal, J.: A collaborative filtering approach to mitigate the new user cold start problem. Knowl.-Based Syst. **26**, 225–238 (2012). https://doi.org/10.1016/j.knosys.2011.07.021
5. Chollet, F., et al.: Keras (2015). https://keras.io
6. Corsini, F., Larson, M.: CLEF NewsREEL 2016: image based recommendation. In: WN of CLEF 2016, Évora, Portugal, 5–8 September 2016, pp. 618–827 (2016)
7. Deng, J., Dong, W., Socher, R., Li, L.J., Li, K., Fei-Fei, L.: Imagenet: A large-scale hierarchical image database. In: 2009 IEEE Conference on Computer Vision and Pattern Recognition, pp. 248–255, June 2009. https://doi.org/10.1109/CVPR.2009.5206848

8. Duda, R.O., Hart, P.E., Stork, D.G., et al.: Pattern Classification, 2nd edn, p. 55. Wiley, New York (2001)

9. Dutta, A., Gupta, A., Zissermann, A.: VGG image annotator (VIA) (2016). http://www.robots.ox.ac.uk/vgg/software/via/

10. Fang, L., et al.: Brain image labeling using multi-atlas guided 3D fully convolutional networks. In: Wu, G., Munsell, B.C., Zhan, Y., Bai, W., Sanroma, G., Coupé, P. (eds.) Patch-Based Techniques in Medical Imaging, pp. 12–19. Springer Intl. Publishing, Cham (2017)

11. Filonenko, A., Kurnianggoro, L., Jo, K.H.: Comparative study of modern convolutional neural networks for smoke detection on image data. In: 2017 10th International Conference on Human System Interactions (HSI), pp. 64–68, July 2017. https://doi.org/10.1109/HSI.2017.8004998

12. Jin, Y., Li, J., Ma, D., Guo, X., Yu, H.: A semi-automatic annotation technology for traffic scene image labeling based on deep learning preprocessing. In: 2017 IEEE International Conference on Computational Science and Engineering (CSE) and IEEE International Conference on Embedded and Ubiquitous Computing (EUC), vol. 01, pp. 315–320 (2017)

13. Kumaresan, T., Saravanakumar, S., Balamurugan, R.: Visual and textual features based email spam classification using s-cuckoo search and hybrid kernel support vector machine. Cluster Comput. (2017). https://doi.org/10.1007/s10586-017-1615-8

14. Lommatzsch, A., et al.: CLEF 2017 NewsREEL overview: a stream-based recommender task for evaluation and education. In: Jones, G.J.F., et al. (eds.) CLEF 2017. LNCS, vol. 10456, pp. 239–254. Springer, Cham (2017). https://doi.org/10.1007/978-3-319-65813-1_23

15. Nogueira, K., et al.: Data-driven flood detection using neural networks. In: Proceedings of the MediaEval 2017 WS co-located CLEF 2017, Dublin, Ireland, 13–15 September 2017 (2017)

16. Ploch, D., Lommatzsch, A., Schultze, F.: An advanced press review system combining deep news analysis and machine learning algorithms. In: Proceedings of the 54th Annual Meeting of the ACL, Berlin, Germany. ACL 2016, pp. 109–114. Association for Computational Linguistics, Stroudsburg (2016)

17. Python Software Foundation: Imagehash 4.0 - a image hashing library written in python. https://pypi.python.org/pypi/ImageHash. Accessed 25 Feb 2018

18. Simonyan, K., Zisserman, A.: Very deep convolutional networks for large-scale image recognition. CoRR abs/1409.1556 (2014)

19. Szegedy, C., Vanhoucke, V., Ioffe, S., Shlens, J., Wojna, Z.: Rethinking the inception architecture for computer vision. CoRR abs/1512.00567 (2015). http://arxiv.org/abs/1512.00567

20. Villegas, M., Paredes, R.: Overview of the ImageCLEF 2012 scalable web image annotation task. In: WN for CLEF 2012 Conference, Rome, Italy, September 17–20 (2012). http://ceur-ws.org/Vol-1178/CLEF2012wn-ImageCLEF-ThomeeEt2012.pdf

Community and Quality

Towards a Metrics-Based Software Quality Rating for a Microservice Architecture
Case Study for a Measurement and Processing Infrastructure

Sebastian Apel[(✉)] [iD], Florian Hertrampf, and Steffen Späthe

Friedrich Schiller University Jena, 07743 Jena, Germany
{sebastian.apel,florian.hertrampf,steffen.spaethe}@uni-jena.de

Abstract. Microservice architectures should be based on isolated, independent and resilient services. In practice, however, that means that different concepts must be taken into account when designing, developing, and operating services. The WINNER research project is developing an application, based on such a microservice architecture in the context of Smart Home, Smart Grid and electromobility in tenant households, as a measurement and processing infrastructure. About this WINNER software, system metrics are calculated and collected, and the potential for rating software quality in the sense of ISO 25010 is examined. For analysis, a microservice architecture describing model will be designed witches describes correlations and links in the service network. Its instance in the context of WINNER, as well as source code and process analyses, are used to perform the final quality considerations.

Keywords: Microservice architecture · Software quality rating · Architectural metrics

1 Introduction

Microservices take the approach of high cohesion, or the concept of single responsibility principle, to independent, isolated, autonomous, scalable, replaceable and resilient services [10, P. 2–3]. In practice, however, this means that different concepts must be taken into account when designing and developing such services. The consideration of discovery services for finding other services, configuration services for central management, gateways for accessing service functionalities outside the network, as well as monitoring, logging and alert management, to name a few, is of central importance. Around these concepts, topics for the design of development processes in the context of DevOps, continuous integration and deployment approaches as well as concepts from the areas of containerization of services for packaging applications and isolated operation are essential.

Services are developed and maintained by efficient small teams. Therefore, positive development status of the services themselves is ensured in theory.

© Springer Nature Switzerland AG 2019
K.-H. Lüke et al. (Eds.): I4CS 2019, CCIS 1041, pp. 205–220, 2019.
https://doi.org/10.1007/978-3-030-22482-0_15

Projects, with usually more than one team, that implement their application solution in a microservice architecture, however, face the challenge of adequately evaluating the achieved qualities of the services, the deployments, or the entire system from a macro perspective. The question of whether each service meets the requirements of a microservice is usually quite complex without detailed knowledge. Furthermore, the question includes the ability for automated analysis and continuous evaluation based on meaningful metrics.

The "Wohnungswirtschaftlich integrierte netzneutrale Elektromobilität in Quartier und Region" (WINNER) [5] research project is developing a central application based such a microservice architecture, our so-called WINNER Data-Lab (WDL). In the context of Smart Home, Smart Grid and electromobility in tenant households, a measurement and processing infrastructure is realised and growing. This infrastructure integrates a heterogeneous system setup and its endpoints, enables data processing, allows the forecasting of data series, and thus supports the optimised control of our local Smart Grid. This community-focused system allows not only optimised control but also the direct involvement of residents using information accesses. Electric vehicles are offered to the community via a car sharing approach. Users can inquire about the operational readiness of the vehicles via digital house boards, make their vehicle bookings when vehicles are charged, and users can decide on the current charge status whether an ad-hoc usage is possible.

This paper examines the question of how a software quality assessment based on the characteristics of ISO/IEC 25010:2011 [9] can be implemented in the context of microservice architectures, DevOps, CI/CD and containerization. For this purpose, an application case study based on the microservices in the WDL will be presented in the following. The aim is to examine feasible metrics in the context of microservices and to assess their suitability for the use of quality ratings. These considerations can be realised at various levels: the actual services, the deployments, which include the service and its direct dependencies, as well as the overall system level. In this consideration, we focus in particular on the service level.

The paper proceeds with an insight into metrics from different software areas in Sect. 2. Afterwards, in Sect. 3, the architectural concept will be taken, reviewing structures, defining levels for quality rating, and deriving relevant quality characteristics. The following Sect. 4 deals with these quality characteristics and derives possible metrics. Finally, Sect. 6 refers to the application case WDL and measures the current state of development. The results are discussed in Sect. 7.

2   Related Work

Metric-based analyses find their usability in various aspects and viewpoints to rate software qualities. The basis of most reflections and studies is the ISO/IEC 25010 [9] as standardisation for software qualities, or its predecessor ISO 9126 [1]. These standards describe the essential characteristics for software qualities which include the central categories portability, maintainability, performance efficiency, functional suitability, reliability, and usability as well as the two new main categories compatibility, and security in ISO 25010. Metrics in this scope can be found in object-oriented design, testing, operations or project management.

Regarding object-oriented design metrics, an important publication is related to "a metrics suite for object oriented design" [6]. This publication develops and validates a set of metrics for use in object-oriented design. Further, there are models, like MOOD [2] and QMOOD [4], which map object-oriented metrics on software qualities. As an example, QMOOD [4] uses the software qualities from ISO 9126 as attributes, which have to be evaluated, derives influencing properties and develops the suitability for evaluation of these metrics. As a result, the created formalised attributes enable a metric-based quality assessment. Metrics in this context include for example method or attribute hiding and inheritance factors as well as factors regarding polymorphism, cohesion and coupling. An overview of object-oriented metrics is provided in [12]. This report goes into metrics based on MOOD and QMOOD in this context and gives an example. An evaluation of MOOD is provided in [8], which uses multiple commercial samples and metrics to prove their qualities. As outlined, if "information hiding, inheritance, coupling, and dynamic binding are concerned", then "MOOD metrics can be [...] valid measures within the context of this theoretical framework" [8]. In addition to using metrics to evaluate qualities, [7] shows how they can be used to identify starting points for the development of software patterns.

Another field of interest, related to evaluations of architectures, are microservice validations. One example in this context is [11], which studies the difficulty of validating correctness in the context of growing infrastructures. The ucheck tool is used for this purpose, "which specif[ies] the set of messages a microservice can send, and how its local state changes in response to receiving a message" [11]. Another publication in this context is [14], which describes their "model of validation of microservice systems and its implementation as a prototype". Further, in [13], one more "validation methodology and a software support for microservice testing" is presented. While the approaches do not directly focus on the evaluation of software qualities, in all three cases software is available for automated analysis and must be taken into account.

In summary, it can be stated that, as far as we know, no models are currently available for quality assessment. In addition, there is a multitude of work that automatically examines the evaluation of software and realises an assessment of quality by means of the measured values obtained. We use the existing findings as a starting point to carry out our subsequent investigation.

3 Qualitites in Microservice Architectures

In the first step, we want to deal with the object to be valued – microservices. This service architecture considered here can be understood as a specific approach for service-oriented architecture (SOA) [10, P. 9]. As outlined, "the differences between microservices and [...] service-oriented computing do not concern the architectural style [...], but its concrete realization" [16]. Microservices

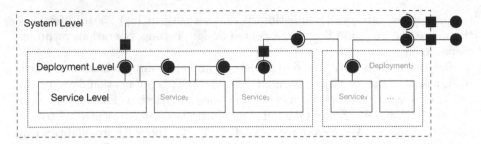

Fig. 1. Abstract example of services and deployments within a system setup, including consumed and provided ports on each level. Software quality might be rated for each level. We assume at this point that each level requires its own rating criteria using a suitable set of metrics.

target on autonomy, scalability, resilience, technology heterogeneity, ease of deployment, composability, and easy replaceability as well as a suitable over-all size of the service itself [10]. While the question of size is not defined directly but much more by limiting factors, e.g., team sizes, transactions, consistency, overhead and avoidance of modularization, as well as theories regarding domain driven design and conway's law [15, P. 34]; as a result, services emerge that are small, but bring with them infrastructure requirements that need to be considered. As we already outlined in [3], to realise a microservice architecture like this in our infrastructure, requires to take various aspects into account. These aspects cover the management of configuration, discovery of other services, external access to endpoints through gateways and message middlewares, as well as monitoring, logging and alert management. In addition, the need remains that the service undergoes a clearly defined build process, and the appropriate information (e.g., where to find the configuration, the discovery service, and where to place logs) has to be provided for the execution of artefacts.

Service, dependencies, and infrastructure components leads to three possible levels of consideration when implementing and operating services of this kind: the *Service Level* (1), *Deployment Level* (2), *system level* (3). This levels of consideration are visualised as an abstract example in Fig. 1. As shown, the *service level* is characterised as a single executable artefact and may act with required other services or provide endpoints. The *Deployment Level* is characterised as a group of services, including the service itself as well as other services required to run this deployment. This deployment may provide a subset of endpoints from services for the whole system. Finally, the *System Level* is characterised as the set of all deployments and finally provide the subset of endpoints provided by the *Deployment Level* for external usage. In this context, it is important that qualities can be and has to be assessed at all levels. In this paper, we want to focus mainly on the service level and the evaluation of its qualities.

The ISO 25010 describes software qualities which include the main categories portability, maintainability, performance efficiency, functional suitability, reliability, usability, compatibility, and security. As a (backend-) service is not

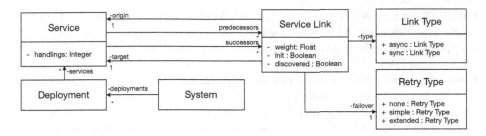

Fig. 2. Metamodel for the description of service contexts in a microservice architecture: Its deployments using the services describe the system architecture. Each service has links to other services (communication protocols are not included in this abstraction), and each link has properties related to synchronicity, failover handling, weighting, required for initialisation, and linkage via discovery service.

directly user related, and portability already covers adaptabilities, we decided to not rate usability. Related to this microservice context, the following aspects have to be rated:

- **Portability:** This is defined as how well a service can be installed in general cloud-like infrastructure, how easily it can be replaced and its adaptability to the specific situation.
- **Maintainability:** The focus here is on how well a service can be modified, its testability (or test coverage), its general analyzability (does the service provides information about its current state), or its reusability. Modularity is not considered here, as it is undesirable in the context of microservices beyond the limits of the service and the scope within the service is usually too small, as if a modularisation consideration is worthwhile.
- **Performance Efficiency:** The main focus here is on overheads, artefact sizes, and initialization times, as well as runtime information.
- **Functional Suitability:** What is the scope of the microservice, especially in terms of size and the criteria mentioned?
- **Reliability:** What happens if runtime dependencies are missing, how stable is the service and how does the availability look like?
- **Compatibility:** This one is related to interoperability and coexistence.
- **Security:** How is access to the information provided structured? Are there any security mechanisms?

In the following, the aim is to evaluate whether the qualities portability, maintainability, performance efficiency, functional suitability, reliability, compatibility, and security can be rated using metrics.

4   Metrics in Microservice Architectures

Measure an implemented service, which for example uses Java as primary programming language, Spring as framework, Docker as container format, Docker-Compose for configuring instances, Eureka as discovery service, Zuul as gateway,

Gitlab-CI for the building process, Spring Cloud Config for decentralized config-uration management, ELK Stack for logging, monitoring and alert management, is application specific and difficult to generalize for an automated task. Following MOOD and QMOOD, the use of an abstracted representation, which reflects the connections and enables the measuring, appears helpful. Within this abstracted representation, we need to differentiate between our already mentioned levels: the service level (1), the deployment level (2), and the system level (3). The resulting metamodel is visualised in Fig. 2. The model includes the described setup with services, deployments, and the system. In addition, the model describes the links (with entity type *Service Link*) between them. Properties are assigned to each link, whether and in which complexity it has error handling (with association *failover* and enumeration *Retry Type*), and whether it is asynchronous or syn-chronous communication (with association *type* and enumeration *Link Type*), as well as weighting and whether it is only necessary for the initialization phase.

The following are lists of possible metrics in the context of the metamodel and the implemented services. These serve as a collection of measurable aspects of a service. These were, e.g., derived from MOOD and QMOOD by counting links, communication chains and the number of failover handlings in combination with own considerations. Based on this, we can start with metrics to measure a service regarding communication:

- **Number of Produced Endpoints [NPE]** describes the communication endpoints provided by this service.
- **Number of Consumed Endpoints [NCE]** describes the communication endpoints used by this service.
- **Number of Synchronous Service Dependencies [NSSD]** is the number of connections to other services that follow a synchronous approach.
- **Number of Asynchronous Service Dependencies [NASD]** is the num-ber of connections to other services that follow an asynchronous approach.
- **Number of Service Dependencies in Initialisation [NSDI]** is the num-ber of connections to other services that are only used within the initialisation phase.
- **Max Length of Affected Service Chain per Handling [MLASCH]** is the length of the communication chain, starting from the current service, to process a request, initialization dependencies are not considered.
- **Max Affected Services per Handling [MASH]** is the amount of services needed for the treatment (in the deep).
- **Number of Dependencies with Simple Failover [NHSF]** includes con-nections that include simple strategies for handling communication errors. Simple refers, for example, to repeated trying.
- **Number of Dependencies with Complex Failover [NHCF]** includes connections that include complex strategies for handling communication errors. Complex refers, for example, to buffering and caching to compensate for failing services.
- **Part of Communication Cycle [PCC]** checks whether the service is in a cyclic communication path.

- **Number of Communication Handlings [NCH]** covers the number of handlings for events in the context of produced and consumed endpoints.
- **Number of Discovered Endpoints [NDE]** describes the number of connections explored via a discovery service.

In addition to the communication-related metrics, implementation-related metrics can also be used. Measured values of this type can be collected by code analysis.

- **Functional Lines of Code [FLC]** describes the number of source code lines that deals with the realisation of the actual functional task. Excludes comments and blank lines.
- **Project Lines of Code [PLC]** includes all source code in a project. Excludes comments and blank lines.
- **Percentage of Test Coverage [PTC]** describes the amount of source code checked by the execution of the tests.
- **Number of Tools [NT]** is the amount of tools used to realise the service.
- **Number of Languages [NL]** is the amount of configuration and programming languages required to realize the service.
- **Rating of Complexity [RC]** results from the sum of complexities per tool. For each tool its complexity is described by a factor times the sum of the complexities of necessary programming languages; programming languages used can be evaluated with a complexity factor as well.
- **Number of Implementation Dependencies [NID]** describes dependencies that arise in the deep.
- **Number of Loaded Configurations [NLC]** describes the amount of configurations that are obtained from service at runtime.
- **Number of Instantiation Configurations [NIC]** describes the number of configurations required for initialization.

Finally, metrics that relate to building, deploying, and operating. Measured values in this group can be obtained from the deployment and process descriptions as well as the resulting artefacts.

- **Size of Container artefact [SCA]** describes the size of the baked container.
- **Number of Deployment Targets [NDT]** describes how many target platforms the service is deployed, e.g. development, staging and production.
- **Number of Required Services for Development [NRSD]** covers the amount of services necessary to work on a local setup.
- **Number of Local Runnable Services for Development [NLRSD]** includes the number of services that can be operated locally.
- **Usage of CI/CD [UCID]** results from the process description, in particular, whether construction, baking, deployment and report steps are included.
- **Memory Usage [MU]** at runtime for this service.

This list of metrics related to communication, implementation, building, publishing, and operation serves as a collection of measurement criteria. In the following, this collection will be used for our example, the WDL, and then discussed, which metrics are suitable for an evaluation of the qualities described in Sect. 3.

5   The WINNER DataLab

For the case study in the context of the WDL, the involved services are presented in the following. This section is intended to provide an introduction of the current state of the implemented microservice architecture, to illustrate service links, and most of all to instantiate the model described in Sect. 4. Figure 3 shows all related and currently running services within this architecture and uses its own notation for this purpose. The flow direction visualises client-server dependencies, the line the type of communication and the start point indicates the type of failover handling. Services within one deployment are marked with a grey background. Otherwise, each service is its own deployment. This representation is divided into five areas to increase readability (from left to right): Databases and tools, management services, adapter services, message middleware and external services.

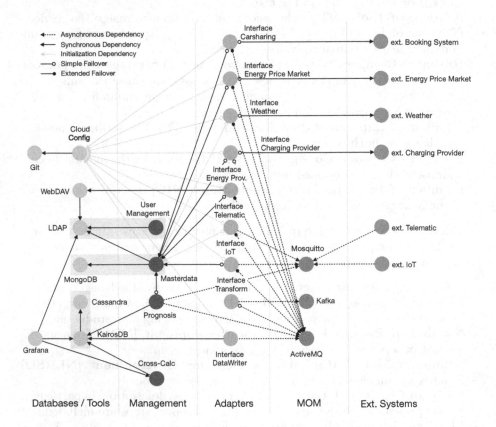

Fig. 3. Microservice network, the flow direction visualises client-server dependencies, the line the type of communication and the start point indicates the type of failover handling. Groups with a grey background describe joint deployments. Everything else is deployed as a single service and therefore its own deployment.

The first area describes services with general tasks that were not realised by us. These are for example databases like KairosDB and Cassandra (for time series), MongoDB and LDAP. Furthermore, the Cloud Config is a central configuration service (which gets configurations from a Git repository), Grafana is a web platform for the visualisation of data and WebDAV for file-based interfaces. The services are based on open source components and have been instantiated in the context of the WDL by their own deployment description. This complements a process description to deploy the service on the necessary systems (e.g. staging and production).

The second area describes management related services, like our Masterdata, which is a configurable management system for documents to store context information related to installed measuring equipment in WINNER and resulting time series descriptions. Other services use this Masterdata to ask for information about how to transform external information for further internal usage. The user management is a tool to organise users and groups, based on an LDAP database. Services like the Cross-Calc and Prognosis are examples for active components, which persists data streams, calculates dynamic metrics (based on other) or create forecasts on specific metrics. The services are implemented within the framework of the WDL. Classic tool stacks are used, for example, NodeJS applications with Angular (or Vue), Express and Mongoose. Each service manages dependencies with NPM, can be baked into a container, has its deployment description and a process to run baking and deployment.

The third area is related to adapters. Their task is to know the external systems, their data formats, and protocols as well as to transfer the resulting data streams to a format defined by the event data channel. Usually, the Masterdata is used to support the transformation through captured knowledge. One special service is the Interface Transformer, which works as a linkage and transformation between two different messaging middlewares. Another special one is the Interface DataWriter, which reacts to events and pushes them into the time series database for persistence. The services are realised with Spring, a Java framework for efficient development, and Apache Camel, Java framework for data stream handling. Each service manages dependencies with Maven, can be baked into a container, and has its deployment description. Building, baking and deployment is described in individual pipelines. An exception is the Interface Charging Provider, which is realised with Node-RED, a graphical programming language to access a webpage like an endpoint. Another exception is the Interface Transformer, which is realised with Apache Flink.

The fourth area is related to our used messaging middlewares. For asynchronous communication with external systems, a dedicated MQTT-based message middleware, the Mosquitto, is available. An ActiveMQ was used for internal communication. For ongoing analyses on the data streams, an Apache Kafka setup was also provided on an outsourced system, which is used for evaluating events to generate more complex information, for example with complex event processing strategies. While the division into ActiveMQ and Apache Kafka would not be necessary, this setup currently offers stability during operation, since test setups and prototype analyses are based on the external messaging system. Further, some analysis tools can only be used easily with Apache Kafka. In the future, it would be conceivable to consolidate here. Like the first area, they are based on open source components. Thus, a deployment descriptors as well as a process description to deploy the service on the necessary systems (e.g. staging and production).

The remaining fifth area is related to external services. As they are blackboxes, we can not go deeper into internal service networks. This is the reason, why the model described in Sect. 4 contains a weight on service links. No development related work to create, build or deploy is necessary here.

This example, based on our WDL is the instantiated metamodel from Sect. 4 and provides a visualisation that supports understanding the entire system, deployments, and services. While partial aspects of the metamodel could also be described with tools from the UML, we have decided to use our visualisation of that model to transport the type of communication and information regarding failover in the representation. As an alternative a component diagram could have been used, and stereotypes and properties may provide detailed information.

In the following, this instance will be used for the measurements. While this is a wide setup of different services, the following analysis requires some limitations. For the detailed measurement hereinafter, we will focus on the following services in this setup: Interface Weather, Interface Charging Provider, Interface Transform, Masterdata, Cloud Config, ActiveMQ, and KairosDB.

6 Measure the WINNER DataLab

Table 1 shows the communication-related, implementation-related, and building-/runtime-related metrics. The services Interface Weather, Interface Charging Provider, Interface Transform, Masterdata, ActiveMQ, Cloud Config, and KairosDB were evaluated. These selections currently provide a representative sample in which various technology stacks are used. While some measured values were collected directly from the service network, a simple script was created for the source code and artefact evaluation of the individual service projects. Runtime information was taken from the recorded information in the infrastructure. In addition to metrics listed in Sect. 4, the table lists ratios and deviations to make the various tools comparable, especially for absolute measurement values. Deviation of mean values is calculated by dividing this measurement by the aggregation of all other services.

The first observations refer to communication-related metrics. The analysis of the measured values shows three basic types of services. The first one, adapters, take data and push them somewhere else and do not provide any endpoint. The second one, endpoint provider, provide something and do not consume anything else. The third one, proxies, help to access information from endpoint providers and provide them for someone else. Endpoint providers support the infrastructure to decouple certain services. However, be careful with databases which are not suitable for decoupling in microservice architectures. Primarily because of

Table 1. Measured metrics for Interface Weather, Interface Charging Provider, Interface Transform, Masterdata, ActiveMQ, Cloud Config, and KairosDB.

		Weather	Charging Prov.	Transformer	KairosDB	ActiveMQ	Cloud Config	Masterdata
Communication (Sync. / Async.)								
Number of Produced Endpoints	NPE	0	0	0	1	1	1	1
Number of Consumed Endpoints	NCE	4	4	2	1	0	1	3
Number of Synchronous Service Dep.	NSSD	1	2	0	1	0	1	2
Number of Asynchronous Service Dep.	NASD	1	1	2	0	0	0	0
Number of Service Dep. in Initialization	NSDi	2	1	0	0	0	0	1
Max Length of Affected Service Chain / Handling	MLASCH	1	3	1	1	0	1	1
Max Affected Services per Handling	MASH	2	5	2	1	0	1	2
Number of Dependencies with Simple Failover	NHSF	1	2	1	1	0	1	2
Number of Dependencies with Complex Failover	NHCF	3	2	0	0	0	0	0
Part of Communication Cycle	PCC	No	No	No	No	No	No	No
Ration between Handlings and Failover	RHF	100 %	100 %	50 %	100 %	0 %	100 %	67 %
Number of Communication Handlings	NCH	1	2	1	-	-	1	33
Number of Discovered Endpoints	NDE	0 %	0 %	0 %	0 %	0 %	0 %	0 %
Implementation								
Stateless Handling	SH	Yes	Yes	Yes	Yes	Yes	Yes	Yes
Internal Development	ID	Yes	Yes	Yes	No	No	No	Yes
Project Lines of Code	FLC	1365	3376	840	215	64	156	10736
Functional Lines of Code	PLC	449	3045	183	0	0	8	9574
Ratio between Functional and Project	RFP	32,89 %	90,20 %	21,79 %	0,00 %	0,00 %	5,13 %	89,18 %
Percentage of Test Coverage	PTC	0,00 %	0,00 %	0,00 %	0,00 %	0,00 %	0,00 %	82,60 %
Number of Tools	NT	10	5	7	4	2	6	7
Number of Languages	NL	8	7	7	3	2	6	8
Rating of Complexity	RC	9,875	3,5	6	1	0,75	5,125	5,375
Deviation of Mean Complexity	DMC	177 %	56 %	100 %	15 %	11 %	84 %	89 %
Number of Implementation Dependencies	NID	121	355	111	0	0	53	1590
Deviation of Mean Implementation Dep.	DMID	40 %	129 %	37 %	0 %	0 %	17 %	1155 %
Number of Loaded Configurations	NLC	20	7	0	0	0	0	10
Number of Instanciation Configurations	NIC	7	2	7	1	0	3	6
Ration between Loaded and Instance Config.	RLIC	286 %	350 %	0 %	0 %	-	0 %	167 %
Building, Deploying, Operating								
Size of Container Artifact	SCA	197 MB	712 MB	146 MB	207 MB	212 MB	159 MB	119 MB
Deviation of Mean Container Artifact Size	DCAS	84 %	398 %	60 %	88 %	91 %	66 %	49 %
Number of Deployment Targets	NDT	3	3	2	3	3	3	3
Number of Required Services for Development	NRSD	9	10	4	1	0	1	2
Number of Local Runnable Services for Dev.	NLSD	8	9	4	1	0	0	2
Ratio btw. Local and Required Services for Dev.	RLSD	88,89 %	90,00 %	100,00 %	100,00 %	100,00 %	0,00 %	100,00 %
Usage of CI/CD	UCID	100 %	75 %	100 %	50 %	25 %	75 %	100 %
Memory Usage	MU	476 MB	107 MB	219 MB	575 MB	188 MB	388 MB	167 MB
Deviation of Mean Memory Usage	DMU	172 %	34 %	72 %	216 %	61 %	135 %	54 %

the decoupling, the communication chains in the infrastructure are short. Only in a few cases, due to the regular inclusion of external services in treatments, do numbers increase due to downstream database queries. This can be compensated by treating the services with failover strategies. The use of failover can be a powerful indicator, as microservices must be as resilient as possible. For adapters, e.g., simple strategies are suitable which periodically retries. However, central services, like our Masterdata, should usually be cached.

The following observations refer to implementation-related metrics. First of all, the FLC and PLC measurement values indicate small ratios between them.

This applies in particular to adapters. These usually perform specific, isolated tasks, but require the complete stack of technologies to guarantee their independent development and operation. This ratio is better for applications such as the Masterdata, with an equally focused task (administration of documents). However, measurements via FLC and PLC do not help in the case of individual tool stacks, as with the charging provider, since the numbers are blurred here. The Node-RED graphical tool is persisted with a JSON-based configuration file, which itself allows only a little information about the functional complexity. An interesting observation is achieved regarding languages, tools and complexity in our measurements. While the exact parameterisation can be decided individually for each application, it shows trends for a for project related analysis and comparisons. For the syntaxes used, a differentiation was made between programming language, rated 1, and markup/configuration language, rated 0.25. Afterwards, for each tool used, it was determined which languages are necessary to use them. For example, Apache Camel requires the use of Java, as well as configurations via XML. Alternatively, using Angular requires knowledge of TypeScript, HTML, CSS, and JSON configurations. The complexity of a single tool result from the sum of the language ratings multiplied by an additional factor that reflects the inner complexity of the tool (also freely selectable). The total complexity then results from the sum of the tool complexities used. It can be seen here that the quite simple adapters on Apache Camel and Spring basis (in relation to the FLC) have a higher complexity compared to more complex services. In general, it can be said that many tools are necessary and a multitude of hardly avoidable languages are necessary to achieve the goals of independent, isolated, autonomous, scalable, replaceable and resilient services. Besides the complexity, the vulnerabilities due to external changes show the extent of dependencies. NodeJS-based services such as Masterdata and Interface Charging Providers are usually ahead. These dependencies are smaller and have been included in the dependency tree in different versions. Maven, on the other hand, is more concerned with selecting a specific dependency version, and Java dependencies also tend to provide more functionality in one library. Concerning configuration, it is noticeable that not all services can be administered decentrally at runtime, e.g., by using a cloud configuration service. The services are particularly difficult to integrate when relying on finished services. Here, the use of configurations during instantiation is recommended. Usually, it is not possible to do this without instantiation configuration, since minimum information on access to central configuration services must be disclosed.

Finally, the third observation refers to building-/runtime-related metrics. Viewing all services, the sizes of the generated artefacts vary only slightly – an exception here the artefact of the service which was realised with graphical tools. If one compares the significant artefact size with the small memory footprint at runtime, unused resources seem to be dragged along, which could be a potential hazard for security gaps. It is exciting for the development that all necessary service dependencies can be reproduced for isolated test environments. For the considerations, therefore, at least the directly consumed endpoint dependencies are necessary, plus services that might be required for testing the functionality beyond, e.g., message infrastructures. For example, for adapters, this means that the messaging middleware, the Masterdata, as well as the data writer and the time series database are helpful for a complete running stack. This means, however, that if you look at the memory usages, a not insignificant overhead has to be provided locally for development. Regarding processes, it is positive to see that all services have at least one, if not multiple, deployment targets. Besides, there are positive signals when construction processes and reports can be found again. Memory usage generally appears to be typically distributed, databases tend to need more, Java-based applications have at least the VM requirement, and NodeJS applications scale with their load until the maximum is reached. Finally, other indicators enable simple checks: there are no cyclical correlations. Currently, there is a lack of test coverage, discovery is not realised via own services and in certain situations there is no possibility to work with failovers. Concerning discovery, however, it can be stated that this was realised and thus compensated for by the name resolution in the cloud infrastructure.

7 Rating Software Qualities

Finally, based on the metrics used and the measured WDL, the question remains as to how far software qualities can be rated from the corresponding metrics. For the consideration of the microservice architecture portability, maintainability, performance efficiency, functional suitability, reliability, and security were in focus here.

Our first quality, portability, refers to its easiness for replacement, installability in different environments, and adaptability to the specific situation. Using metrics about deployment targets, the ratio between FLC and PLC, loaded and instance configurations indicate good portability. In particular, high FLCs indicate that replaceability is at risk and missing configurations indicate bad adaptability.

The second quality, maintainability, refers to how well a service can be modified, as well as testability, analyzability and reusability. Good testability can be guaranteed with high test coverages, as well as the availability of development setup and maximization of locally providable services. Modifiability is ensured if the service is developed by itself or if necessary degrees of freedom exist. Reusability, on the other hand, is ensured if the service provides its functionalities via standard interfaces or connects other services via standard interfaces. Analyzability is currently under-represented in the metrics. As an indicator, the availability of reports as well as logging and application performance measurement tools can be used. However, high complexities might indicate less good maintainability or modifiability.

Performance efficiency, the next quality, refers to runtime and artefact information. A good quality rating is achieved if the artefact sizes do not deviate significantly and the resource use (e.g., storage) is not outside the average. Another indicator usable to rate this quality is the MASH as well as MLASCH. High values generate error risks in case of handlings.

Table 2. Software quality ratings based on metrics.

	NPE	NCE	MASH	RHF	NDE	ID	RFP	PTC	DMC	DMID	NLC	NIC	DCAS	NDT	NRSD	RLSD	UCID	DMU
Portability							↑				↑	↑	↑					
Maintainability	↑	↑				↑	↑	↓							↑	↑	↑	
Performance Efficiency			↓										↓					↓
Functional Suitablity							↑			↓								
Reliability		↓		↑	↑													
Compatibility	↑	↑											↑	↑		↑		
Security																		

Functional suitability is related to the scope of the microservice, as well as domain focus and size aspects. Currently, the use of the ratio between FLC and PLC, as well as the evaluation of used service dependencies, is suitable for this quality evaluation. Providing information from external services to internal resources might indicate good functional suitability. It may be necessary to take further measurements here. However, the information is provided by the model.

The fifth quality, reliability, focus on failover handling. Our set of metrics contains metrics of the endpoints used, both asynchronous and synchronous, as well as information about their failover handling. This quality can be assessed, for example, by means of the ratio between failover handled and overall used endpoints.

Compatibility, the sixth quality, focus on interoperability and coexistence. If services can be used via an automated process and via configurations for a specific scenario, then their interoperability is not at risk. In general, microservices should only communicate via provided or consumed endpoints, the use of the respective metrics for endpoint provisioning can be used here as an indicator. The isolation, identifiable by metrics concerning building processes, artefact availability and at least one deployment target, indicate the characteristic coexistence and thus the ability of the software to exist next to another.

Finally, the last quality, security, focus on access to information and mechanisms to secure this access. No security-related metrics are currently recorded. It would be conceivable to capture the links in the model with information indicating which communication protocol is used and whether credentials are required.

The relationships between qualities and metrics discussed above are presented and summarised in Table 2. Arrows pointing upwards indicate a positive effect on quality as the measured value increases, arrows pointing downwards indicate a positive effect as the measured value decreases in the particular metric. However, this choice as to which metrics could have an influence and which type of influence, positive or negative, is currently the result of qualitative data evaluation and the previous discussion.

8   Conclusion

The aim of the paper was the exemplary consideration of the WDL using metrics to evaluate achieved software qualities. For this, no relation to object-oriented design, as in the MOOD or QMOOD model, was used. Our focus was, on the one hand, the analysis of source code and artefacts, and on the other hand a network model, which contains information about links between services and allows evaluations. For the evaluation, we have limited ourselves to some services in the network since for example the measurements of the Apache Camel/Spring adapters are very similar, and/or services, which are based on finished components likewise comparable measurements with the same field of application produce. The measured values could then be used to discuss the influences on certain qualities. Currently, some indicators are available for portability, maintainability and compatibility. Indicators are available for the qualities performance efficiency, functional suitability and reliability, but from our point of view, further indicators could be useful to make a stable evaluation. For security quality, no metrics were collected. It is interesting to see how far communication between services has to be secured, primarily if they work in internal networks. If necessary, an evaluation at the following levels of consideration may be appropriate. In the future, the analysis of the already mentioned following levels of consideration in architecture is crucial, as well as the final formulation of a quality rating model for microservice architectures as well as the evaluation of architectures other than the WDL is necessary.

Acknowledgements. We would like to take this opportunity to thank the partners of the research project. The research project WINNER is funded by the Federal Ministry for Economic Affairs and Energy of Germany under project number 01ME16002D.

References

1. Software engineering - product quality, ISO/IEC 9126–1. Technical report. International Organization for Standardization (2001)
2. e Abreu, F.B., Carapuça, R.: Object-oriented software engineering: measuring and controlling the development process. In: Proceedings of 4th International Conference on Software Quality, Virginia, USA, vol. 186, pp. 1–8 (1994)
3. Apel, S., Hertrampf, F., Späthe, S.: Microservice architecture within in-house infrastructures for enterprise integration and measurement: an experience report. In: Hodoň, M., Eichler, G., Erfurth, C., Fahrnberger, G. (eds.) I4CS 2018. CCIS, vol. 863, pp. 3–17. Springer, Cham (2018). https://doi.org/10.1007/978-3-319-93408-2_1
4. Bansiya, J., Davis, C.G.: A hierarchical model for object-oriented design quality assessment. IEEE Trans. Softw. Eng. **28**(1), 4–17 (2002). https://doi.org/10.1109/32.979986
5. Chemnitzer Siedlungsgemeinschaft eG: WINNER-Projekt (2017). http://www.winner-projekt.de. 01 February 2018
6. Chidamber, S.R., Kemerer, C.F.: A metrics suite for object oriented design. IEEE Trans. Softw. Eng. **20**(6), 476–493 (1994). https://doi.org/10.1109/32.295895
7. Derezińska, A.: Metrics in software development and evolution with design patterns. In: Silhavy, R. (ed.) CSOC2018 2018. AISC, vol. 763, pp. 356–366. Springer, Cham (2019). https://doi.org/10.1007/978-3-319-91186-1_37
8. Harrison, R., Counsell, S.J., Nithi, R.V.: An evaluation of the mood set of object-oriented software metrics. IEEE Trans. Softw. Eng. **24**(6), 491–496 (1998). https://doi.org/10.1109/32.689404

9. ISO/IEC: ISO/IEC 25010 - Systems and software engineering - Systems and software Quality Requirements and Evaluation (SQuaRE) - System and software quality models. Technical report (2010)
10. Newman, S.: Building Microservices. O'Reilly Media, Sebastopol (2015)
11. Panda, A., Sagiv, M., Shenker, S.: Verification in the age of microservices. In: Proceedings of the 16th Workshop on Hot Topics in Operating Systems, HotOS 2017, pp. 30–36. ACM, New York (2017). https://doi.org/10.1145/3102980.3102986, http://doi.acm.org/10.1145/3102980.3102986
12. Rodriguez, D., Harrison, R.: An overview of object-oriented design metrics. Technical report RUCS/2001/TR/A, Computer Science Department, University of Reading (2001)
13. Savchenko, D.I., Radchenko, G.I., Taipale, O.: Microservices validation: Mjolnirr platform case study. In: 2015 38th International Convention on Information and Communication Technology, Electronics and Microelectronics (MIPRO), pp. 235–240, May 2015. https://doi.org/10.1109/MIPRO.2015.7160271
14. Savchenko, D., Radchenko, G.: Microservices validation: methodology and implementation. In: 1st Ural Workshop on Parallel, Distributed, and Cloud Computing for Young Scientists, pp. 21–28 (2015)
15. Wolff, E.: Microservices: Flexible Software Architectures. Addison-Wesley, Boston (2016)
16. Zimmermann, O.: Microservices tenets. Comput. Sci. Res. Dev. **32**(3), 301–310 (2017). https://doi.org/10.1007/s00450-016-0337-0

Managing Smart Home Appliances with Proof of Authority and Blockchain

Pranav Kumar Singh[1,2($\boxtimes$)], Roshan Singh[2], Sunit Kumar Nandi[1,3],
and Sukumar Nandi[1]

[1] Department of CSE, Indian Institute of Technology Guwahati,
Guwahati 781039, India
sunitnandi834@gmail.com, sukumar@iitg.ac.in
[2] Department of CSE, Central Institute of Technology Kokrajhar,
Kokrajhar 783370, Assam, India
snghpranav@gmail.com, roshansingh3000@gmail.com
[3] Department of CSE, National Institute of Technology, Arunachal Pradesh,
Papum Pare 791112, India

Abstract. With the advance in technology and growth in standard of
living, smart homes have become a reality. Smart homes consist of home
appliances and devices that communicate with each other to address the
needs of the residents. These appliances generate, share and consume
lots of data which are private and sometimes safety critical to the residents. Managing them is a challenging task. The current frameworks for
managing home appliances are centralized in nature. Such frameworks
force smart home residents to trust the service providers or a third party.
These frameworks are also prone to hacking, compromise of data and a
single point of failure. Availability of services can also never be guaranteed with such frameworks. Technologies such as blockchain and smart
contracts can help to manage these appliances. In this paper, we study
the scope of blockchain technology in smart homes. We propose, implement and evaluate a blockchain based approach using Proof-of-Authority
as the consensus mechanism for managing appliances in smart homes. In
addition, we compare the performance of our system with the traditional
Proof-of-Work based system.

1 Introduction

Smart home, a popular use case of Internet-of-Things (IoT) [7] consists of a range
of home appliances of various applications and heterogeneous electronic devices
enabled with computing and communication technologies. These appliances and
devices aim to automate domestic works by harnessing their sensing and computational capabilities, utilizing the resources efficiently by sharing information
with others. A smart home can incorporate appliances such as smartphones,
smart television, smart AC, smart cooker, smart water purifier and other IoT-
enabled devices such as motion sensors, thermal sensors, humidity sensors to
name a few. A combination of these appliances and devices to a particular home

© Springer Nature Switzerland AG 2019
K.-H. Lüke et al. (Eds.): I4CS 2019, CCIS 1041, pp. 221–232, 2019.
https://doi.org/10.1007/978-3-030-22482-0_16

use case help bringing out smart services such as the smart kitchen. With the advancement in information and communication technologies, home appliances are becoming more smarter. However, these smart devices have always been an attractive target for the hackers since the data involved in smart homes are mostly personal such as health and personal interests accessing which a hacker can obtain crucial information of the residents [8].

Assuring the authenticity and validity of the data exchanged among these appliances or devices is also a challenge. Moreover, current smart homes depend upon certain third parties for providing the services. The home data is stored, processed and managed by the third party cloud which is always prone to a single point of failure [2,14]. Such architecture for smart homes not only make the residents dependent upon third parties but also force to believe them. The home resident has no control over their own data in such architectures.

There exist services and security frameworks for providing fast services and protecting smart home devices; however, they are highly centralized and have scalability issues. Decentralized technologies such as blockchain and smart contracts turn out to be strong contenders for addressing such issues. In this work we propose, implement and evaluate a blockchain based approach for managing home appliances and devices in smart homes. Our main contribution in this paper is threefold.

- We study existing works in the domain and the scope of blockchain technology in Smart Homes.
- We briefly discuss the Proof of Work and Proof of Authority Consensus mechanism.
- And, at last, we propose, implement and analyze our proposed Proof-of-Authority (PoA) blockchain based system with the traditional Proof-of-Work (PoW) mechanism.

2   Related Work

The biggest concerns related to the IoT-based solutions for smart homes are security, privacy, access control, authorization, and management. In [13], the authors argued that smart homes appliances are vulnerable to various attacks even from users' smartphones. In [10], the authors hacked into a variety of IoT-enabled smart home devices such as a switch, light bulb, and smoke alarm. They demonstrated how these IoT devices are vulnerable to attacks and lack basic security features. In the past, numerous centralized solutions have been proposed from academia and industry to address security and other associated concerns mentioned above. Most of the solutions from industry deploy their proprietary solutions and serve as a centralized trusted third party. For example, the EU projects Connect All IP-Based Smart Objects (CALIPSO) [1], which provides solutions for IoT devices to adopt a centralized mechanism.

The major challenges associated with the centralized solutions are heavy communication and processing overheads on centralized server [3], transparency, trust and privacy-related issues, access control and single point of failure. Thus, various researchers [5,6,11,12,17] have turned-out the attention towards distributed framework and proposed popular blockchain based solutions for various IoT use cases. Our work mainly emphasizes on smart-home related issues, and we demonstrate how blockchain can manage home appliances in a distributed manner. We test the system on an Ethereum private blockchain and show how smart contracts help better management of home appliances and devices. It not only makes the smart home secure but also prevents the non-repudiation of devices. To the best of our knowledge, our work is the first to implement a PoA based consensus mechanism for blockchain integration in smart homes and to give a comparative analysis with traditional PoW based systems.

3   Background

In this section, we give an overview of the technologies such as blockchain, smart contracts, the Ethereum platform, Proof-of-Work (PoW) and Proof-of-Authority (PoA) the consensus mechanism used in our system.

3.1   Blockchain

Bitcoin [9] was the first application of blockchain technology. The blockchain is a distributed and decentralized technology where data is stored in blocks in the form of transactions and each block is chained with its previous one. The chaining of the blocks is achieved with hashing. A blockchain is maintained by a number of nodes. Each node maintains a copy of the blockchain which consists of blocks starting from the beginning of the blockchain to the present. These nodes form a peer to peer network for sharing of information and forwarding or receiving the blocks. Each node exchange information with its peer nodes and the peer nodes further propagate the information with its peers the process continues until each node in the network has obtained the information. A node bundles incoming transactions in the form of a block and broadcasts it to the network. Other nodes receiving the block check for its validity and append it to their local copy of the blockchain if it is found to be valid.

The serial ordering of the blocks on the chain is achieved with a consensus mechanism. The forks in the blockchain where a single blockchain splits into two separate chains are resolved with the longest chain rule. A blockchain with the longest chain or having the maximum number of valid blocks is considered to be the main blockchain and the others are discarded. Blockchain relies on Public Key Infrastructure (PKI) for signing and verification of transactions. Blocks on the blockchain can only be added on top of the latest block in the chain. This property makes the blockchain tamper resistant. If a malicious node tampers any one of the blocks starting from the genesis block the hash of the block will change and the change will be cascaded further thus making the entire blockchain invalid. Any peer node receiving the tampered block from the malicious node will reject the block. Blockchain-based systems provide high availability and security.

3.2 Smart Contracts

Smart Contracts [15] are lines of code deployed on the blockchain specifying a set of rules for an application. A smart contract maintains an application state. Each valid transaction on the blockchain corresponding to the smart contract updates the state of the smart contract. As a smart contract is deployed on a blockchain, it provides transparency in the proceedings of the contract. Smart contracts are immutable in nature that means once deployed the rules in the contract cannot be changed. This ensures non-repudiation from a malicious party involved in the contract.

3.3 Proof of Work

Proof of Work (PoW) is a consensus mechanism used for reaching a consensus in public and permissionless blockchain. PoW is based on a challenge-response system, where the nodes maintaining the blockchain need to compete with each other by solving certain resource-intensive complex cryptographic problems to place their proposed block onto the blockchain. These nodes are also known as the miner nodes. The difficulty of the problem is adjusted by analyzing the numbers of block added over a certain period. PoW provides true decentralization by allowing any node to participate in the network without any permission. A node can join and leave the system anytime. Bitcoin blockchain uses PoW as the consensus mechanism.

3.4 Proof of Authority

Proof of Authority [4] (PoA) is a Byzantine Fault Tolerant (BFT) consensus algorithm for permission and private blockchains. The algorithm relies on a set of trusted entities known as validators (i.e., authorities). The validators are responsible for collecting the transactions from the clients, creating and adding the blocks onto the chain. The algorithm run in rounds where in each round a validator is allowed to propose a block. A validator proposes a block in its respective round. The other validators verify the proposed block and add the block to their local copy of the blockchain if it is found to be valid. Once a block is added a global consensus is reached. However, if a validator proposes an invalid block or proposes more than one block in a round the other validators in the network calls for voting. And if a majority votes against the validator. Then the validator is considered to be malicious and is removed from the system; thus, it is no longer authorized for proposing any more blocks. PoA is an ideal consensus algorithm for private and permission blockchains where the participants are authenticated and are limited in numbers. It is often considered as a compromise between truly decentralized and efficient centralized systems. Unlike, PoW algorithm, PoA is not resourced intensive. It is lightweight and has higher throughput; hence, an ideal consensus mechanism for localized IoT blockchain implementation such as smart homes where power consumption is critical and devices have bounds on their computational and storage capacity.

3.5   Ethereum Platform

Ethereum [16] is yet another blockchain platform. It is turing complete and allows users to deploy and test their decentralized applications. It supports languages such as Solidity and Serpent. The platform provides two kinds of accounts external accounts and contract accounts. Contract account is an account which denotes the address of a deployed contract whereas external account is a user account using which a user perform transactions on the blockchain. Ethereum's working principle is based on the state transition model. Each node in the ethereum network executes each transaction in the block in the same order. Currently, ethereum provides main-net blockchain for real user applications and test-nets with different consensus mechanisms for testing purposes. However, it also provides the flexibility to deploy one's private permission instance of ethereum blockchain.

4   System Architecture

An overview of our proposed system is shown in Fig. 1. The system consists of home appliances such as smart TV, smart lights and IoT devices such as thermal sensors and motion sensors. These are the fundamental components of our system. Majority of the home appliances are generally power constrained embedded devices with limited computational and storage capability meant for dedicated applications. These home appliances are connected to a processing unit. The processing unit is a small networking device with sufficient computational power and storage capacity. The processing units are responsible for the processing of requests and management of the appliances. The blockchain is maintained by the validator nodes. Validator nodes are responsible for sealing the blocks

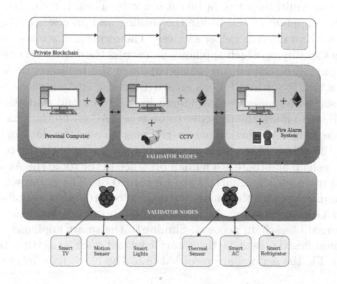

Fig. 1. Proposed system model

and adding it to the blockchain. These nodes maintain an entire copy of the blockchain and are required to be up most of the time.

It is suggested for the validator nodes to have sufficient storage capacity. We consider processing units as well as certain home appliances such as PC, computerized CCTV and alarm systems to be the validator nodes in our system. These nodes are connected via peer to peer connections. The homeowner deploys a smart contract containing a set of policies on the private blockchain specifying how she wants her appliances to operate. Each processing unit is responsible for managing a number of appliances, and each appliance is associated with an account on the blockchain. These accounts are maintained at the processing units. The processing unit constantly polls the smart contract. Depending upon the data present in the smart contract it instructs the appliances to perform certain actions. Similarly, the appliances write values onto the blockchain via the processing unit. A write operation by appliance results in a transaction denoting a state change and is recorded on the blockchain. However, reading data from the blockchain does not result in any transaction as the smart contract state is not modified.

5   Implementation

The homeowner adds a home appliance to the system by creating an external account for the appliance and deploys a smart contract onto the blockchain for managing the appliance. She needs to interface the appliance with the processing unit for enabling its control via the smart contract. The appliance communicates and shares information with each other through smart contracts. An appliance may request the processing unit to check the status or the data in the smart contract of other appliance and can obtain the results allowing it to take appropriate actions. Such information obtained from smart contracts of various appliances helps to achieve multi-sensor data fusion securely. Thus, a dedicated appliance having limited capabilities can utilize the sensing and processing capabilities of other appliances for offering better services. The owner can set access rights for the appliances specifying which appliance can access the data of other appliances.

For instance, the temperature sensor updates the temperature value in its smart contract (TP sc) to 40 °C as sensed from the environment. Similarly, a thermal sensor sense presence of a human in the room and updates the smart contract (THsc) to mark the presence to be true. (ACsc) be the smart contract managing the smart AC having access rights to access the data of TPsc and THsc reads the values of temperature and human presence. If the temperature is above a threshold and there is a human presence in the room the ACsc updates its state and instructs the smart AC to be turned on. The homeowner and the residents can interact with the smart contract for controlling the appliances using a web-based GUI application. As like the appliances each resident is assigned with an external blockchain account. Similar to the smart appliances each time a resident modifies the data in the smart contract such as setting the volume of the smart TV the actions are recorded onto the blockchain in the form of a transaction.

6   Experimental Setup

We demonstrate the feasibility of our system with a prototype implementation using the Ethereum blockchain platform. We use Geth (Go Ethereum) client for running private and permissioned instance of the blockchain. We perform experiments with both consensus mechanisms separately. We select Clique (a Proof-of-Authority consensus engine provided by ethereum) and Ethash (Ethereum Proof-of-Work consensus engine) consensus mechanism using ethereum's private network manager. The proposed system consists of three entities (PC, Raspberry Pi 3 and nodeMCU). We run a blockchain instance of two nodes on the PC. Figure 2 illustrates the setup. We use Raspberry Pi as the processing unit. The PC and the Raspberry Pi 3 is considered to be the home appliances having sufficient computational and storage capacity. The nodeMCU is used as a home IoT device which relies on the data present on the blockchain. This IoT device only reads data from the blockchain and does not perform any write operation. The nodes running on the PC are designated as the validators. A block is proposed every 2 s by one of the validators. A validator proposes its block in its respective round. We model our smart home scenario with the help of 2 LEDs and an infrared(IR) sensor. These devices can be considered as home appliances where one senses precepts from the environment and the other performs an action based upon the sensed precepts of another. We interface the IR sensor with the processing unit and the LEDs with the nodeMCU. We used D-Link WiFi for connecting the PC, processing unit maintaining the blockchain and the IoT device. For writing the smart contract, we use Solidity (a programming language for writing contracts on Ethereum blockchain). We use the Remix integrated development environment (IDE), a browser-based IDE for compiling and testing the smart contract. We write python scripts for processing the data taken from the IR sensor. Table 1 lists the devices used and their corresponding roles in our setup.

Table 1. Devices and their role

Device name	No. of device	Geth version	Role
Dell-Vostro (8 GB RAM, i7-7700 CPU, 1 TB HDD)	1	v1.8.17-stable release	Validator
Raspberry Pi 3	1	geth 1.8.18 ARMv7	Validator (Processing Unit)
IR Sensor	1		Home IoT device
LED	2		Home appliance
nodeMCU	1		Home IoT device

We perform experiments on our setup blockchain network where the IR sensor checks for the presence of an obstacle and writes the data onto the blockchain updating the state of the smart contract for the sensor if an obstacle is detected.

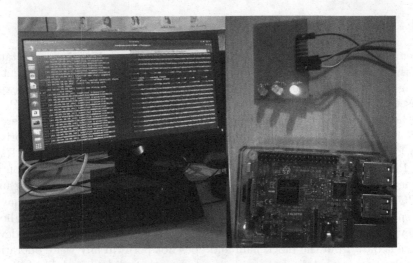

Fig. 2. Validator nodes and processing unit setup

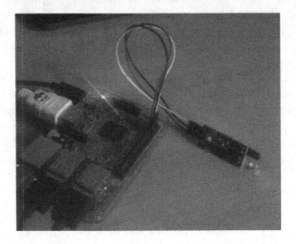

Fig. 3. IR sensor interfaced with processing unit

The IoT device continuously polls the data in the smart contract of IR sensor (Fig. 3). We authorized the nodeMCU to read data from the IR sensor smart contract. If the status of the IR sensor in its smart contract is *not detected* a red led glows continuously. As soon as the status of the smart contract changes to be *detected* the red led turns off and the green led turns on. We also developed a simple web-based GUI application as shown in Fig. 4 for managing the LEDs. The GUI facilitates the home residents to customize the way the LEDs glow (They can make the settings allowing the green led to glowing when no object is detected and glow the red led when an obstacle is detected, or they can make the led blink when an obstacle is detected instead of glowing continuously). For accessing the GUI application by the home residents, we use a display screen

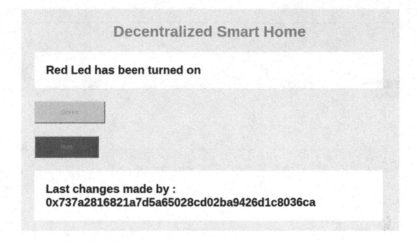

Fig. 4. Our developed smart home application

which is connected to the Raspberry Pi 3 acting as the processing unit. The GUI communicates with the Ethereum blockchain using web3.js API.

7   Evaluation

We evaluate our proposed blockchain based approach by analyzing CPU utilization as the performance parameter. For obtaining the performance plots we executed a set of 10,000 transactions from the Raspberry Pi 3 processing unit. All the transactions were of the same type and were executed at a go.

Figures 5, 6 and 7 show the performance of our proposed system under normal condition, and for consensus mechanisms with PoW and PoA, respectively. It can be observed from these figures that the CPU is utilized at its maximum when PoW is used as the consensus mechanism. This demonstrates the resource-intensive characteristic of the mechanism. Whereas, the CPU utilization is

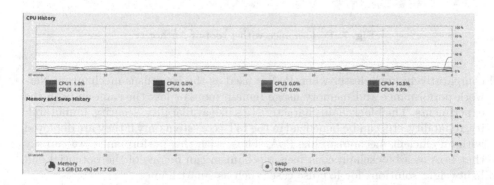

Fig. 5. Normal system performance with no nodes running

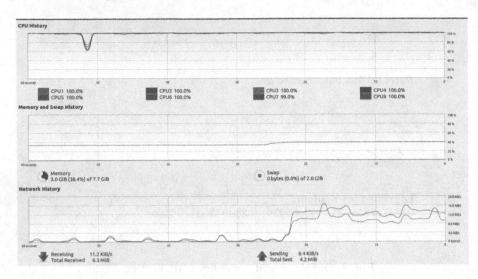

Fig. 6. Performance with Proof-of-Work

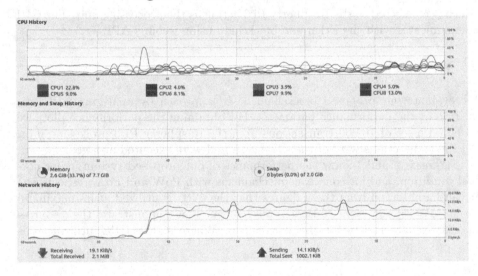

Fig. 7. Performance with Proof-of-Authority

comparatively much lesser when PoA is used as the consensus mechanism. Network performance and memory usage remain more or less the same in both the experiments. The blockchain characteristics like availability, security, immutability, reliability, etc. can be beneficial in the IoT ecosystem only if they are deployed with an efficient mechanism like PoA. Thus, with this performance, we can say that PoA as a blockchain consensus mechanism can be one of the potential and lightweight solutions for IoT use cases such as smart homes.

8   Conclusion

In this paper, we proposed a blockchain approach for managing home appliances in smart homes. We implemented our proposed system on an Ethereum private blockchain network. The evaluation result demonstrates the feasibility of our system. Besides, providing better and reliable services to the residents the system also provide an efficient way of monitoring and auditing the happenings in the home. Smart contracts help better management of home appliances and devices. With the introduction of a blockchain in the system, we make the smart home secure from cyber attacks and prevent non-repudiation of devices. Compromised and malfunctioning devices can easily be traced out and removed from the system. Our approach eliminates the overhead of third-party cloud as in the traditional architectures. The selection of a PoA consensus mechanism not only increase the performance of the system but has also reduced the power consumption level times lower than the traditional PoW based mechanisms. First-time PoA based consensus mechanism has been tested for blockchain integration in smart homes and also compared with traditional PoW based systems. Security and privacy are the major concerns which are blocking the deployment of IoT based solutions. Thus, how such decentralized solutions like blockchain can be efficiently applied to the IoT ecosystem to solve these issues is one of the future research directions.

References

1. Connect All IP-Based Smart Objects (CALIPSO) FP7 EU Project. http://www.ictcalipso.eu/. Accessed 05 Mar 2019
2. Botta, A., De Donato, W., Persico, V., Pescapé, A.: On the integration of cloud computing and internet of things. In: 2014 International Conference on Future Internet of Things and Cloud, pp. 23–30. IEEE (2014)
3. Cirani, S., Picone, M., Gonizzi, P., Veltri, L., Ferrari, G.: IoT-OAS: an OAuth-based authorization service architecture for secure services in IoT scenarios. IEEE Sens. J. 15(2), 1224–1234 (2015)
4. De Angelis, S., Aniello, L., Baldoni, R., Lombardi, F., Margheri, A., Sassone, V.: PBFT vs proof-of-authority: applying the CAP theorem to permissioned blockchain (2018)
5. Dorri, A., Kanhere, S.S., Jurdak, R.: Towards an optimized blockchain for IoT. In: Proceedings of the Second International Conference on Internet-of-Things Design and Implementation, pp. 173–178. ACM (2017)
6. Dorri, A., Kanhere, S.S., Jurdak, R., Gauravaram, P.: Blockchain for IoT security and privacy: the case study of a smart home. In: 2017 IEEE International Conference on Pervasive Computing and Communications Workshops (PerCom Workshops), pp. 618–623. IEEE (2017)
7. Gubbi, J., Buyya, R., Marusic, S., Palaniswami, M.: Internet of Things (IoT): a vision, architectural elements, and future directions. Futur. Gener. Comput. Syst. 29(7), 1645–1660 (2013)
8. Mosenia, A., Jha, N.K.: A comprehensive study of security of internet-of-things. IEEE Trans. Emerg. Top. Comput. 5(4), 586–602 (2017)

9. Nakamoto, S.: Bitcoin: a peer-to-peer electronic cash system (2008)
10. Notra, S., Siddiqi, M., Gharakheili, H.H., Sivaraman, V., Boreli, R.: An experimental study of security and privacy risks with emerging household appliances. In: 2014 IEEE Conference on Communications and Network Security, pp. 79–84. IEEE (2014)
11. Ouaddah, A., Abou Elkalam, A., Ait Ouahman, A.: Fairaccess: a new blockchain-based access control framework for the internet of things. Secur. Commun. Netw. **9**(18), 5943–5964 (2016)
12. Pan, J., Wang, J., Hester, A., AlQerm, I., Liu, Y., Zhao, Y.: EdgeChain: an edge-IoT framework and prototype based on blockchain and smart contracts. IEEE Internet Things J. (2018)
13. Sivaraman, V., Chan, D., Earl, D., Boreli, R.: Smart-phones attacking smart-homes. In: Proceedings of the 9th ACM Conference on Security & Privacy in Wireless and Mobile Networks, pp. 195–200. ACM (2016)
14. Stojkoska, B.L.R., Trivodaliev, K.V.: A review of internet of things for smart home: challenges and solutions. J. Clean. Prod. **140**, 1454–1464 (2017)
15. Szabo, N.: Formalizing and securing relationships on public networks. First Monday **2**(9) (1997)
16. Wood, G.: Ethereum: a secure decentralised generalised transaction ledger. Ethereum Proj. Yellow Pap. **151**, 1–32 (2014)
17. Zhang, Y., Kasahara, S., Shen, Y., Jiang, X., Wan, J.: Smart contract-based access control for the internet of things. IEEE Internet Things J. (2018)

Author Index

Printed in the United States
By Bookmasters